VEDA VIHANGAM

Samarpan is a Hindu monk, teacher and writer of several books, articles, memoirs, etc. His articles, under his monastic name, have appeared in different journals. His talks on scriptures are available online. He teaches ancient and modern scriptures at the deemed university of the organization to which he belongs.

Also by the Author

SPIRITUAL FICTION

Tiya: A Parrot's Journey Home

Param

Junglezen Sheru

Kratu

PHILOSOPHY

Carving a Sky

RELIGION AND SPIRITUALITY

Living Hinduism

The World of Religions

The Hindu Way

YOUTUBE

https://www.youtube.com/c/Samarpanananda

VEDA VIHANGAM

The Essential Veda

SAMARPAN

PAN

This edition first published in India 2023 by Pan
an imprint of Pan Macmillan Publishing India Private Limited,
707 Kailash Building
26 K. G. Marg, New Delhi 110001
www.panmacmillan.co.in

Pan Macmillan, The Smithson, 6 Briset Street, Farringdon, London EC1M 5 NR
Associated companies throughout the world
www.panmacmillan.com

PB ISBN 978-93-95624-66-4
HB ISBN: 978-81-19300-01-3

3 5 7 9 8 6 4 2

Typeset by Manmohan Kumar
Printed in India by Gopsons Papers Pvt. Ltd., Sivakasi

असतो मा सद्गमय ।
तमसो मा ज्योतिर्गमय ।
मृत्योर्मामृतं गमय ॥

Lead us from the unreal to the real
Lead us from ignorance to knowledge
Lead us from the mortal to immortality

BṚHADĀRAṆYAKA UPANIṢAD

◆

A humble offering to
the sages of India
who by their unselfish contribution
made freedom from the senses possible
and this world liveable

CONTENTS

PREFACE

The most sacred books of the Hindus, the Veda – *Ṛk, Sāma, Yajuḥ* and *Atharva* – are the oldest scriptures of the world, which have come down to us exactly the way they were composed thousands of years ago by the great sages of the prehistoric Indian subcontinent.

Over the millennia, the Veda have shaped Indian religious, social and cultural life, while their footprints are visible in practically every aspect of the Indian way of life. The chant of Gāyatrī, sacred symbol *Oṃ*, rituals related to birth, death, life and marriage, the growth of geometry, founding of algebra, invention of zero in mathematics, prosody in poetry, languages, dance, music, drama – all this and many more, with which a Hindu feels inextricably connected, are directly related to the Veda. Consciously or unconsciously every Indian breathes in the Veda and when his life-breath leaves the body, his onward journey too is facilitated by the Veda.

In spite of this timeless connection to their source, very few Hindus ever read, or even chance to see the Veda. One occasionally hears a chant, a mantra or a quote here and there, and that is the end of it. Talking about the dwindling interest in the Veda in Bengal, which applies equally to the whole of India, Swami Vivekananda had lamented, 'The study of the Veda has almost disappeared from Bengal. How I wish that day will soon come when in every home the Veda will be worshipped together with Shalagrama, the household deity, when the young, the old and the women will inaugurate the worship of the Veda! (CW: III.457).'

The chief reasons for this indifference are: the belief that these are meant for the priests, the truly voluminous size of the four Vedas (collectively these contain tens of thousands of verses), their archaic language, the missing context of the content, and a popular misconception that these texts are only about rituals and prehistoric ceremonies, which rarely give results in the modern-day world. In short, the Veda are believed to be abstruse, distant and irrelevant.

The problem got compounded from the time Western scholars started interpreting the Veda. These scholars, including Max Muller, failed to understand and appreciate the essence of the Veda, which is '*paramārtha lābha*' – God realization. Since the time of these scholars, the Veda are studied for various aspects like their historical, geographical and astronomical data, scientific conclusions, poetry, etc., but rarely for what they actually stand for – spirituality in all its aspects. Unfortunately for India, nearly every study on the Veda in the present times is based on works by Western scholars. Consequently, the purport of these sacred books gets terribly distorted and at times these most ancient of works even get lampooned by the vulgar.

The Veda are about *dharma* in their entirety. Dharma is the essence of any being, and also the way to reach perfection, which, for the living being, means to attain God by staying true to one's way of life. The entire corpus of the Veda talks only about this through the fourfold purpose of life – *dharma, artha, kāma* and *mokṣa,* popularly known as four *puruṣārtha*. Thus, from the perspective of the Veda, all the possible goals of humankind are valid, and part of a continuous spectrum of growth towards the ultimate reawakening of its original divine nature.

The Veda being the fountainhead of the Indian way of life, every Hindu must have at least some knowledge of it. As will be seen later, the Veda embodies soul-stirring love for God, along with the highest flights of philosophy, and a complete view of life for all. Depending on one's needs and attitudes, one can make use of these as tools for growth in life through spiritual realization, meditation, prayers or as mantras for pouring oblations in the fire of *yajña*.

In the present times, Sri Ramakrishna and Swami Vivekananda's life and words are like real-time commentaries to understand the Veda. So, incidents from their life and their words have been used in abundance to show how the Veda are not archaic pieces of poetry but a real and living source of spiritual knowledge.

This work, *Veda Vihangam* – signifying the Veda as a free flying bird in the sky of the infinite, and also as a bird's eye view of the Veda – presents the majesty, uniqueness and vastness of the Veda with the help of select mantras and hymns in their proper context and with appropriate explanation.

Every prayer and hymn in this selection addresses one or the other of the fourfold purpose of life. We hope this work is pleasing and easy to read for all. However, as the reader studies the coming chapters of the book, they may find certain sections to be attractive, indeed fascinating, while others perhaps less so. It will be of value to the reader to observe their own reactions and perhaps even take note of which chapters/ sections were attractive and which not. This could present the reader with a new compass that points to their natural inclinations in life, whether it be towards *dharma, artha, kāma, mokṣa* or any combination of these!

But can a selection be a true representation of the Veda? The answer is yes, for the Veda are like the proverbial mountain of sugar from which one will get only sugar whether one uses an excavator, a spade or a spoon. The raison d'etre of these sacred books is to help a person evolve from wherever they are. If that can be done with one *mantra*, so much the better but if one requires volumes, then so be it.

The intent of this work is to dispel the widespread notion of obsolescence of the Veda, and also to establish the currency, the immediate relevance of Vedic thought and philosophy to core aspects of contemporary life. In the process, it also narrates the mighty spiritual traditions and heritage of India. It is hoped that this work will arouse the interest of the readers to learn more about the Veda and spirituality, which is the gift of India to the world.

This work is also the culmination of my personal journey into the Veda, which began when I was a child, and continued throughout my life in various forms. It reached a crescendo when I was allowed to have sannyasa, after which a monk gives up even the *Gāyatrī*, which marks the beginning of a new outlook of life. However, when I asked my *Guru* whether or not I should stop doing *Gāyatrī jāpam* as is the norm, he sternly asked me if I had attained the *siddhi* of the *mantra*, meaning if I had realized the spiritual content of the mantra. That was the moment when I woke up to the reality that these mantras, and indeed the whole of the Veda, are not mere words, but a spiritual reality that must be realized here and now.

In this work, I have drawn heavily from the commentary on the Veda by the great Sāyaṇācārya (thirteenth CE) to align it with the Indian spiritual thought process. I take this opportunity to offer my most humble *praṇāms* to this great soul who made the Veda alive for the masses by writing such an elaborate commentary on them. If not for him, we would have miserably failed to understand the essence of the Veda.

Help has also been taken from various commentaries and translations of the Veda and other related books, some of which have been mentioned in the acknowledgements section. Works by some European scholars is indeed commendable. And even those, whose translations are not perfect, have done a great service by at least making people aware of this great treasure. I express my deepest gratitude to all these masters and scholars for making the journey of this work possible by their contribution.

With all humility, I present this work as an offering to the greatest of sages belonging to a now-forgotten era, who made the Hindu way of life possible by revealing to us the deeper layers of existence.

I also offer my deep obeisance at the holy feet of my Thakur, Sri Ramakrishna, every moment of whose presence on this earth was a living, breathing expression of the Veda.

TRANSLITERATION AND ITALICS

The International Alphabet of Sanskrit Transliteration (IAST) system has been used in this work, the table for which is given below. The words that are now in common use, like Gita, Ganga and other such, have not been transliterated. Italics for proper nouns and common names, as also the repetitive use of italics for most words have been avoided.

The rules of *Sandhi* (conjunction) and their breaking being quite complicated in Sanskrit, we have used the words as broken in the *pada pāṭha* (an arrangement of Vedic text in which each word is written and pronounced in its original form and independently of phonetic changes) of the four Vedas. Thus, words ending with 'ṃ' have been uniformly changed to 'm' while explaining the meaning. However, in the main transliterated mantra, 'ṃ' is retained as it should be.

It may please be noted that the pronunciation of some of the Vedic words are quite refined, making it difficult to write them in a work like this. So, a little less complicated form of such words has been used.

Extreme care has been taken to ensure the correctness of every Sanskrit word and its meaning; nevertheless, the possibility of some mistake creeping in exists. We apologize for that.

TABLE FOR IAST

अ	a A	क	k K	त	t T
आ	ā Ā	ख	kh Kh	थ	th Th
इ	i I	ग	g G	द	d D
ई	ī Ī	घ	gh Gh	ध	dh Dh
उ	u U	ङ	ṅ Ṅ	न	n N
ऊ	ū Ū	च	c C	प	p P
ऋ	ṛ Ṛ	छ	ch Ch	फ	ph Ph
ॠ	ṝ Ṝ	ज	j J	ब	b B
ऌ	ḷ Ḷ	झ	jh Jh	भ	bh Bh
ॡ	ḹ Ḹ	ञ	ñ Ñ	म	m M
ळ	ḻ	ट	ṭ Ṭ	य	y Y
ए	e E	ठ	ṭh Ṭh	र	r R
ऐ	ai Ai	ड	ḍ Ḍ	ल	l L
ओ	o O	ढ	ḍh Ḍh	व	v V
औ	au Au	ण	ṇ Ṇ	श	ś Ś
ं	ṃ Ṃ			ष	ṣ Ṣ
ः	ḥ Ḥ			स	s S
ँ	~			ह	h H
ऽ	‘				

ABBREVIATIONS

AV	Atharvaveda
BG	Bhagavad Gītā
CW	Complete Works of Swami Vivekananda
K.Up	Kaṭhopaniṣad
KYV	Kṛṣṇa Yajurveda
RV	Ṛgveda
SV	Sāmaveda
SYV	Śukla Yajurveda
YV	Yajurveda (Śukla)

I

FROM VEDA TO THE VEDAS

The story of humankind – its past, present and future – can be put in four simple words: one is born, lives, progenates and dies. Beyond this, the presence or absence of anyone in the history of the species has hardly any significance at the individual or societal level.

Once in a while, this chain of monotony gets broken when someone starts exploring the external or internal world by outgrowing the limits set upon them by the nature. In the case of external explorations, the body trails the mind to reach wherever it reaches, while in the case of internal explorations, the body goes dead-still to let the mind probe the silence of reality. Away from the insipid story of humankind, these are the ones who become the makers of history.

The achievements of those who explored the external world in the past, as also the world of science and philosophy, are more or less documented. However, the records of those who explored the inner world of spirituality, are scanty. One does come across the stories and teachings of prophets and saints in lore and sacred books but these are too meagre compared to the vastness of the worlds that they mapped.

The Veda constitute the greatest records of the spiritual world as experienced by the sages thousands of years ago. It is the narration of those experiences when ideas descended into the minds of the sages, frolicked and then danced away merrily to enchant the masses of the Indian subcontinent, the way Ganga came down from the heavens into the matted hair of Lord Shiva, who then released the stream for the welfare of all.

Thousands of years ago, there lived a people on the north-western part of the Indian subcontinent (now in Pakistan), whose primary roots appear to be on the banks of the Indus, while their secondary roots extended up to the borders of Iran in the west and to the Gangetic plain in the east. These people were highly skilled in various aspects of life; they mastered cultivation and animal husbandry, fought wars with the help of advanced weaponry, had fun gambling and drinking, loved kinship, and wished to have a pleasurable life after death.

As their cultivated tastes developed and evolved, they came to be known as Āryans, meaning noble or of high culture. The word 'Ārya' is denotive of a set of human qualities, and not a reference to any genetic or racial line, as is often imputed in modern discourse, particularly among the Western scholars.

Away from the grind and pleasures of a mundane existence, some of the more noble ones turned their gaze inward to contemplate and meditate on the inner nature, instead of chasing the external. These were the spiritual ones. Such individuals exist in every culture and country, but usually people let go of such impulses due to an obsession with the material world.

Spirituality is the ability of a person to move away from the snares of sense pleasures towards the freedom of the Spirit (pure consciousness, also known as God or Ātman). To be able to do so, one has to be meditative, which is the art of silencing the turbulence arising in the mind due to sense inputs, imagination, delusion, dreams and memories. Deep meditation manifests a still mind that can grasp the inaccessible secrets of existence and be one with the Divine.

According to Tantra–Yoga traditions, growth in spirituality is effected by the arousal of *kuṇḍalinī*, the psychic power that resides dormant in every person. With spiritual practices, it rises through different centres (there are seven of these) within the subtle nerve (known as *suṣumnā*) along the spine. This awakening is marked by varying spiritual experiences and a complete overhaul of the personality. The seven centres of the kuṇḍalinī are known as '*Sapta bhūmi*' (seven planes of consciousness) in the Vedic tradition.

The kuṇḍalinī usually stays in the lower three centres that makes it possible for one to enjoy the pleasures of the senses. When the kuṇḍalinī is awakened, it leaves its usual place of stay and reaches the heart centre. It is then that one feels for the first time the awakening of Divine Consciousness, characterized by visions of light, divine forms and hearing of divine sounds like Oṃ. A person attaining this state becomes saintly and a powerhouse of creativity.

The fifth centre lies behind the throat. When the kuṇḍalinī reaches here, one goes beyond the worldly desires and likes to be with God and talk of Him only. Those who attain this stage are venerated as sages. When the kuṇḍalinī reaches the sixth centre, located between the eyebrows, one sees the form(s) of God, but without becoming one with Him. This state can be achieved only by the greatest of sages and prophets.

The last stage, known as *sahasrāra,* has been described by Sri Ramakrishna in *Gospel of Sri Ramakrishna* as, 'When the *kuṇḍalinī* rises to the *sahasrāra* and the mind goes into *samādhi,* the aspirant loses all consciousness of the outer world. He can no longer retain his physical body. But the *Īśvara kotis,* such as the Incarnations of God, can come down from this state of *samādhi.* They can descend from this exalted (state) ... Their minds move between the sixth and the seventh planes. They run a boat-race back and forth, as it were, between these two planes.' The words of such masters become scriptures.

Without exception, the inner journey of a spiritual aspirant of every religion has to traverse through these stages. This also explains how devotional songs, divine words and scriptures do not come from a thinking mind but from an elevated state of consciousness, marked by the awakening of kuṇḍalinī.

One can imagine how sages must have broken out in joy at the spiritual sights that they had and the consequent knowledge that they acquired when their kuṇḍalinī was awakened. For example, one of them famously exclaimed, '*vedāhametaṃ Puruṣaṃ mahāntam ādityavarṇaṃ tamasaḥ parastāt, tameva viditvā atimṛtyumeti nānyaḥ panthā vidyate ayanāya* – I know the great *Puruṣa* (God), who is effulgent, like the sun and beyond darkness. Only by knowing Him does one cross over death; there is no other way to the Supreme Goal.'

The masters of every religion have emphasized on the reality of the Spirit as superior to that of the world. On being asked if he had seen God, Sri Ramakrishna had answered Narendranath (later Swami Vivekananda): 'Yes, I see Him just as I see you here, only in a much intenser sense.' There is no reason for us to doubt this conversation for the simple reason that every master from different lands and different ages possessed this kind of knowledge. It is rejecting such testimonies, beyond count, that is irrational and unscientific.

As a corollary to this fact about the Spirit, one has to accept that existence has finer layers and dimensions. After all, it cannot be that here we are on this earth and there is God (*Brahman*, *nirvāṇa* or any other such term), with nothing in between the two of us! It simply does not stand to reason and definitely does not agree with the experiences of the spiritual masters.

The inner experiences of an aspirant, brought about by the awakening of the kuṇḍalinī is actually about experiencing the various spheres of existence, which, according to Indian traditions, has four layers – the physical universe (*sthūla jagat*) experienced through the senses; the subtle world (*sūkṣma jagat*) experienced through a meditative mind; the causal world (*kāraṇa jagat*) experienced by the great sages and prophets; and the non-dual state of existence (*mahākāraṇa*), which is not really a state of existence, but pure existence with which one can become one, but cannot know it, since it is the state of no-mind, as the term 'mind' means.

The experience of the different spheres becomes possible due to the concentration of the mind that makes it capable of grasping the finer things. The mind is like a net – the more focused the mind becomes it resembles a net with finer weaving, and thus capable of sensing and retaining subtler perceptions.

The kind of experience that one has when the mind goes beyond the physical world is described by an event from Swami Vivekananda's life, when he was touched by Sri Ramakrishna, as described in the *Life of Swami Vivekananda*, 'The touch at once gave rise to a novel experience within me. With my eyes open I saw that the walls, and everything in the room, whirled rapidly and vanished into naught, and the whole universe together with my individuality was about to merge in an all-encompassing mysterious void! I was terribly frightened and thought that I was facing death, for the loss of individuality meant nothing short of that. Unable to control myself I cried out, "What is it that you are doing to me! I have my parents at home!" He laughed aloud at this and stroking my chest said, "All right, let it rest now. Everything will come in time!"'

Later, Swami Vivekananda was to master the four spheres of existence, as his Guru had done earlier. His words and speeches are all about those spheres.

Spiritual visions of the gods, goddesses and certain aspects of God's reality belong to the subtle world, the knowledge of which can be attained by yogis, sages and saints. Realizations concerning the relative oneness of existence, as also realization of God comes in the causal world, which can be attained only by the prophets and the greatest of sages even while living. The experience of the final one can be attained only by becoming one with it by dissolving all sense of illusory separation from it, as described when the Kuṇḍalinī rises to the sahasrāra. All the spoken languages dealing as they are with the duality of subject and object, are inadequate to describe this state, which is the One without a second (*a-dvaita*). Even the Veda only point the seeker in the right direction for this attainment, but do not attempt to describe the Indescribable.

Since these spheres can be perceived only through meditation, it is impossible to prove or disprove their existence through arguments. For example, we are all normally very clear about the external opposed to the internal, since the physical world provides objective evidence that seem to be corroborated by others and thus is considered real, whereas, internal experiences like dreams and spiritual visions are not considered real, since others cannot testify to the validity of that experience.

This work is not about such arguments. Suffice it to say, denying the existence of these spheres is tantamount to repudiating every scripture of the world, and the inspired utterances of every sage since the dawn of human existence.

Any knowledge restricted to merely one or two of these planes of existence is hopelessly inadequate to explain the world and human existence. To be complete, a system of knowledge must teach all the four states of existence and explain everything in accordance with them. Science and materialists tell us about the physical world; the scriptures of different religions describe mostly the subtle and the causal worlds.

The Veda, on the other hand, talk about all the three states, and also about the fourth, along with how to master those. They talk about oneness with God and prayers to the Supreme God, implying kāraṇa and *mahākāraṇa*; there are prayers in them for mental purity for a better life in the next world, implying sūkṣma jagat; and there are also prayers for worldly prosperity in the sthūla jagat in the form of prayers and yajña for gaining wealth, making money, gaining the affection of the loved one, being victorious in battles etc.

In short, the Veda cover the entire gamut of dharma.

Etymologically, 'Dharma' means that which sustains an object or is its way of life – living or inanimate. Thus, the dharma of fire is to burn, the dharma of water is wetness, and the dharma of man is to attain the highest. Dharma is thus both the essence, and the way of life to be taken up by an individual so as to grow to become one with one's true nature.

The Veda offer two paths of dharma – the one characterized by action and the other characterized by renunciation. The first of these paths is for those who live in the world and hence are expected to pursue one of the three goals in life –

artha, kāma or dharma. Of these, artha or wealth, helps one get free from the physical wants; kāma or enjoyment, releases one from emotional needs; and dharma frees one from rebirth in lower species. The second path of renunciation leads one to *mokṣa,* liberation, which is freedom from the cycle of birth and death. The Veda teach all these goals and the way to attain them.

The third goal, dharma, must be pursued strictly according to proper means, which, again, is dharma. Thus, the Veda show the path to dharma through dharma itself. In the process, these show the way to perfection through spiritual evolution across the four spheres of existence – sthūla, sūkṣma, kāraṇa and mahākāraṇa.

Ancient Indians, on the banks of the Indus, had a long tradition of great sages and saints dedicated to spirituality, who came face to face with the higher nature of reality, and so came to be addressed as *āpta* (lit. one who has arrived at the truth), *draṣṭā* and *ṛṣi* (lit. one who has seen the truth).

We do not know what their way of life was or how they performed *sādhanā* (spiritual practices), but those familiar with spirituality would know that the kind of wisdom that these ṛṣis have left for us, could have been attained only through the fiercest of austerities. Sri Ramakrishna, who himself had performed that kind of sādhanā, described the life of the ṛṣis beautifully, 'How hard the rishis laboured! Early in the morning they would go away from the hermitage, and would spend the whole day in solitude, meditating on Brahman. At night they would return to the hermitage and eat a little fruit or roots. They kept their minds aloof from the objects of sight, hearing, touch and other things of a worldly nature. Only thus did they realise Brahman as their own inner consciousness.' One can smell the fragrance of freshness from these words from the present that bring alive the greatness of the ancient!

The words, wisdom and prayers based on the realizations of the ṛṣis came to be known collectively as the Veda, meaning knowledge.

Since this knowledge is not attained through the usual dualistic, subject-object working of the mind, it is known as *apauruṣeyā*, meaning not created by the human mind. Also, Hindus believe that when God creates, He first lets out the Veda, which are the truths and principles of existence; the sages only discovered these truths, the way Newton discovered the law of gravitation. Since all such knowledge come from God, the Veda are apauruṣeyā – divine. Either way, the Veda are not a thought-created composition.

Two episodes, one each from the life of Sri Ramakrishna and Swami Vivekananda, are narrated here to give a feel of the divine nature of the Veda.

Sri Ramakrishna's life, words and sādhanā are well documented. By the time he was twenty, he had started taking the first steps into the inner world of spirituality from where he went meandering at times, and at other times exploring the realms of divine existence. Being barely literate, Sri Ramakrishna's knowledge of the rich Indian spiritual heritage was limited to what he had heard from the elders, so his spiritual visions and realizations are a unique testimony about the truth of the spiritual world.

After the completion of his sādhanā, Sri Ramakrishna started meeting famous people to compare his realizations with their ideas about the spiritual world. In those days, Debendranath Tagore, father of Rabindranath Tagore, had acquired fame as a sage. Sri Ramakrishna went to meet him and asked him to narrate something from the Veda. The *Gospel of Sri Ramakrishna* describes what happened next:

> He recited some texts from the Veda. He said, 'This universe is like a chandelier and each living being is a light in it.' Once, meditating in the Panchavati, I too, had had a vision like that. I found his words agreed with my vision, and I thought he must be a very great man. I asked him to explain his words. He said: 'God has created men to manifest His own glory; otherwise, who could know this universe? Everything becomes dark without the lights in the chandelier. One cannot even see the chandelier itself.'

The experience of Sri Ramakrishna and the expression by Tagore show the nature of the Veda – these are not some sublime musings, but are spiritual truths belonging to the spiritual world, distilled from the direct experience of seers at the dawn of humankind. Not only can they be experienced by anyone who makes an effort to go beyond the sensate world, even their regular reading can make the life of a person blessed.

In a different kind of experience, Swami Vivekananda, when he was travelling through Punjab during his itinerant days towards the end of the nineteenth century, had a vision of an old man standing on the banks of the Indus chanting

Vedic hymns, using intonations that were distinctly different from those used in modern times. Reminiscing, Swamiji was to say later:

> I saw an old man seated on the bank of the great river. Wave upon wave of darkness was rolling in upon him, and he was chanting from the *Ṛgveda*. Then I awoke and went on chanting. They were the tones that we used long ago ... *Śaṅkarācārya* had caught the rhythm of the Veda, the national cadence. Indeed I always imagine that he had some vision such as mine when he was young, and recovered the ancient music that way. Anyway, his whole life's work is nothing but that, the throbbing of the beauty of the Veda and Upanishads. (CW: Vol. IX)

These two incidents also show how the spiritual truths described in the Veda are not person-specific, but can be realized by anyone, anywhere, anytime, making it truly apauruṣeyā – the impersonal; and these are also the rhythm of the Indian way of life. No wonder that the Veda have been preserved without the slightest corruption for thousands of years.

As in science, contributions were made in the corpus of Vedic knowledge by hundreds of *ṛṣi* and *ṛṣikā,* the female sages, whose names abound in the Veda. For example, Ṛgveda has contributions from 329 male *ṝṣi* and 27 *ṝṣikā.* It is due to their sacrifice of the worldly life for the meditative that we have mantras like, *'bhūrbhuvaḥ svaḥ tatsavitur vareṇyaṃ bhargo devasya dhīmahi dhiyo yo naḥ pracodayāt* – We meditate on the glory of that Being who has produced this universe; may He/ She enlighten our minds,' which is chanted and meditated upon by crores of Hindus every day. It is also due to them that India's national approach towards religious tolerance comes from truths like '*ekaṃ sat viprā bahudhā vadanti* – Truth (God) is one but sages call it by various names.'

The Veda have come down to us mostly in the form of poetic metres. When of a single line, they are known as *mantra*, while each complete prayer is known as *Sūkta* (hymn). Also, the mantra of each of the Vedas has a special name, which will be mentioned later.

The word *veda* is derived from the root *vid*, which means knowledge. It was implied that the Veda contain every form of knowledge that one needed for both worldly and spiritual life. The joke was that if a person lost his cow, then he could go and search for it in the Veda!

To maintain their sanctity, the Veda were maintained by Brahmin families who were dedicated entirely to learning. Elaborate mechanisms were adopted to save the sacred from any kind of corruption.

We do not know for sure when exactly the composition of the Veda began, nor does this matter for the study of the Veda. Suffice it to say that these are the treasures of the Indian people handed down to us from the most ancient times through an unbroken chain of *guru-śiṣya-paramparā* (preceptor-learner-tradition). Just to note, the antiquity of these texts far exceeds the three-and-a-half millennia usually ascribed by western scholars; this is borne out by a wealth of archaeological, astronomical, genetic and geological evidence unearthed by contemporary research. This, however, is not the subject of this writing.

With time, the Vedic corpus grew to unmanageable proportions due to a continuous pouring into it. This gave rise to the fear of losing all of the knowledge in case a family died out. So, when Vyāsa (date unknown) appeared on the Indian scene, he collected the available Vedic literature and organized them into four books – *Ṛgveda, Sāmaveda, Yajurveda* and *Atharvaveda*. Thus, were born the four Vedas from the Veda.

Of these, *Ṛgveda* is the collection of all the *ṛk* mantras (its plural is *ṛcā),* which are a particular kind of chant, *Sāmaveda* is mostly a collection of mantras from the *Ṛgveda* that can also be sung, *Yajurveda* is composed of *yajus* (prose mantras), and *Atharvaveda* contains a particular type of metre known as *chanda.* Each of these Vedas has a particular role during the performance of *yajña.*

Ṛgveda is organized in ten *maṇḍalas* with 1028 *sūktas* (hymns) containing 10,462 *ṛca* (plural of *ṛk,* verse). Considered extremely sacred, it is a huge treasure house of spiritual wisdom, philosophical insights and information about the culture of the ancient Hindus.

Sāmaveda has 1,875 verses, most of which are from the *Ṛgveda; Yajurveda* has 1,975 verses, organized in forty chapters; *Atharvaveda* has 5,987 mantras collected in twenty *kāṇḍas* and 731 hymns. All these are collectively known as *Saṃhitā /Mantra.*

Appended to each of these *Saṃhitā,* are three more sections – *Brāhmaṇa, Āraṇyaka* and *Upaniṣads.*

Just as the higher ideas of the sciences often get used as a tool for technology and practical application, the philosophical truths and realizations of the sages were put into practical use by the Brahmins, who, by the meaning of the word, are supposed to be absorbed in the highest state of contemplation on the Divine, but most of them failed to reach that high state and instead ended up being scholars and priests. So, they focused more on using the Veda for *yajña*. This is not something unusual – since even in the present times one sees people performing Gita *yajña* and *Caṇḍī yajña*, although these two books are deeply philosophical.

Soon the Veda, as the book for *yajña*, became popular all over the country, with *yajña* of every kind and every occasion finding prominence. Even today, the marriage ceremony, *śrāddha, upanayana*, etc. are performed as Vedic *yajña* only. A good picture of this emerges from the great sacred book, *Rāmāyaṇa* by Valmiki, which belongs to the Vedic period. In that book, one finds the popularity of *yajña* everywhere. Even Sri Ramachandra was born of *Putreṣṭi yajña*, performed by *Ṛṣyaśṛṅga*, a renowned sage.

It was believed that for a *yajña* to bear results, the rituals must be performed perfectly, the mantras pronounced correctly and the priest to be of immaculate purity. During the performance of a *yajña*, Ṛgveda was used for prayers, Yajurveda for pouring oblations and Sāmaveda for chants and singing. Due to this, the term *trayī* was coined to signify these three Vedas. The Brahmin representing *Atharvaveda* superintended the *yajña*; he had to be a knower of all four Vedas.

To perform the *yajña*, there was a need for detail of various kinds, which was recorded in the *Brāhmaṇa* (not to be confused with Brahmin, the *varṇa*). In addition, these also contain tales, legends and narratives to explain or provide rational foundation for the then religious practices, the duties of men professing different occupations, popular customs, cosmogony, historical details, praise of ancient heroes and other such subjects.

As appendices to nearly all the *Brāhmaṇa,* there are *Āraṇyakas* (lit. forest texts). The main content of these texts are the mysticism and symbolism of sacrifice and philosophy, which find fullest expression in the *Upaniṣads*, which talk about the oneness of the individual with the universal through famous statements like 'I am Brahman' and 'Brahman is all'.

To study the Veda, one also needs to master six additional subjects, known as the *Vedāṇgas* (lit. limbs of the Veda): *Śīkṣā* (phonetics), *Vyākaraṇa* (grammar), *Chanda* (prosody), *Nirukta* (etymology), *Jyotiṣa* (astronomy), *Kalpa* (codes of rituals and conducts).

With time, scholarly sages came up with schools of thoughts (philosophy) based on the Veda. These are six in number and are known as *ṣaḍ darśana*: Sāṃkhya, Yoga, Nyāya, Vaiśeṣika, Mimāṃsa and Vedānta.

With the stage set for the preservation of the four Vedas, Vyasa gave the responsibility of maintaining each of these to four of his great disciples: Ṛgveda to Paila, Sāmaveda to Jaiminī, Yajurveda to Vaiśampāyāna and Atharvaveda to Sumanta.

Later, there was a quarrel between Vaiśampāyna and his prodigious disciple Yājñavalkya, following which Yājñavalkya left his guru and gave up all that he had learnt from him and went to perform *tapasyā* to Sun God to get the Veda without the intervention of any human guru. *Sūrya*, the Sun God, obliged. Thus, there was a new version of *Yajurveda,* known as *Śukla Yajurveda* to compete with the original, which came to be known as *Kṛṣṇa Yajurveda*. There is very little difference in their content, but their arrangement and tradition differ, and hence these are quoted independent of each other.

The four Vedas are respectfully addressed as *śruti* – that which is learnt through hearing. It also signifies the superiority of the Veda over other sacred books and texts, which are generically known as *Smriti*.

To understand the import of the Veda, Mimāṃsā philosophy worked out an elaborate discipline of hermeneutic or how to understand the scriptures. One important point discussed therein is that the Veda are for all, and hence these contain a lot of *arthavāda*, eulogies, as incentive to do good work and refrain from bad ones. For example, the statements related to heaven and hell mostly belong to *arthavāda*. So if a Vedic statement says that 'he who eats alone, goes to hell,' here the true import is to encourage a person to share food with others.

Another characteristic of the Veda is that they contain a lot of *nāmadheya*, categorizing and listing gods, antigods, people and others. Such lists are not to be taken as authority, but as a casual mention to drive home a spiritual point.

The Veda also have a lot of *stuti*, praise of priests, gifts, etc. These are meant to bring people out of their narrow and selfish way of life and to become more inclusive; they have no other purpose.

In a word, the Veda are about becoming spiritual and taking others along on that path; everything else that comes in these texts, are secondary.

The Veda are not hidebound; they are not absolute as in other religions, but are more like pointers and guideposts to spirituality, which can be used by any spiritual traveller. These are thus sacred in the way that any knowledge is sacred, and yet which everyone has to acquire personally. Indeed, the true relevance of the Veda lies only in personal realization of spiritual truths. Sri Ramakrishna used to say, 'The experiences of this place (meaning himself) has transcended Veda and Vedanta', implying that every seeker has to take help of the Veda, then transcend them through a personal realization, which will always be unique and yet in conformity with the Veda. There are verses in the Upaniṣads and Gita where a spiritual aspirant is advised to transcend the Veda.

Also, the Veda contain universal truths from the spiritual world, and not some one-off realization. It means that, as with reverse engineering, anyone can realize these mantras as spiritual truths through sadhana. As will be seen, many of their ideas and prayers are so universal that these can be used by followers of other religions too.

The Veda, in connection with Hindu religion, are treated as *pramāṇa* – the valid source of knowledge in spiritual matters, the way our senses are for the physical world. Consequently, every school of Indian philosophy finds the proof of its statements in the Veda, and every spiritual realization has to be in conformity with the Veda.

The corpus of the available Vedic mantras (only the *Saṃhitā)* has around 20,400 hymns in about 90,000 *pādas* (lines). This does not include the other three sections. In spite of this huge volume, the four Vedas, along with their sections are still maintained orally even though they are now available in the print form.

The Vedic language is a pitch accent language in which the same alphabet was used in three different ways – *svarita, udātta, anudātta;* the higher on scale, the normal, and the lower. The meaning of a word changed due to these accents. According to a popular story (*Taittirīya Saṃhitā, 2.4.12*): *Tvaṣṭā*, a divine being, wanted to take a revenge on Indra, and hence conducted a *yajña* to beget a son who would destroy Indra. When he chanted the mantra, '*Indraśatruḥ varddhasva ...*', he went wrong in intonation. Had *Tvaṣṭā* pronounced correctly, it would have meant 'May Tvaṣṭā's son grow to be the slayer of Indra'. Unfortunately, because of the wrong intonation, the mantra now meant, 'May Indra grow to be killer of this son (of mine).' Consequently, Tvaṣṭā*'s* son was killed by Indra!

Later sages took extraordinary precautions to preserve from loss or corruption the sacred text, including the three distinct pronunciations. Thus, was introduced the system of *pada pātha, saṃhitā pātha* and others that are used even today as technical tools to save the Veda from corruption.

When Max Muller compiled the Veda in the nineteenth century for its first printing, the world was amazed to see that there was not a single alphabet's discrepancy between the manuscripts of any two families, though they lived separated by thousands of miles and had maintained them orally! In his book, *What India can Teach Us,* he says, 'This may sound startling, but – what will sound still more startling, and yet is a fact that can easily be ascertained by anybody who doubts it – at the present moment, if every MS of the Rig-Veda were lost, we should be able to recover the whole of it – from the memory of the Shrotriyas in India. These native students learn the Veda by heart, and they learn it from the mouth of their Guru, never from a MS (that is, manuscript), still less from my printed edition – and after a time they teach it again to their pupils.

I have had such students in my room at Oxford, who not only could repeat these hymns, but who repeated them with the proper accents (for the Vedic Sanskrit has accents like Greek), nay, who, when looking through my printed edition of the Rig-Veda, could point out a misprint without the slightest hesitation.' Amazing!

The kind of Sanskrit used in the Vedas became obsolete long ago. It is due to the contributions of the great scholar Yāska (c.700 BCE) who explained a lot of Vedic grammar, etymology and semantics; and *Sāyaṇācārya* (thirteenth CE) who wrote his famous commentaries on the Ṛgveda that we are able to understand whatever we understand of the Veda. There are some other commentaries too.

Looking Ahead

This was a short description of the flow of knowledge descending in the silent minds of the sages and then gaining in volume through the contribution of thousands of years to nourish and give shape to the Hindu way of life.

To understand the true relevance and significance of the Veda, one only has to look at the riddle of why the Hindu civilization dedicated one whole *varṇa*, the Brahmins, solely to maintain the texts over thousands of years by giving up all enjoyments of life and even every possible way of livelihood! They had to live mostly on charity, basking in the glory of learning fuelled by the hunger of the belly.

The answer lies in the simple fact that the Veda are the most important knowledge bank ever discovered by the human race, and hence that knowledge had to be and has to be maintained at all costs, even if that meant voluntary poverty for an entire section of society. It is through the mastery of this knowledge and a complete dedication to the realization of that knowledge that a person can get out of the miseries of life imposed on him by the wants of the body and emotions.

The Veda are not about putting the fear of God in a helpless mind, nor are they about loving a God who is far removed from us, the Veda are what the name implies, the spiritual knowledge bank that lets its reservoir flow through innumerable channels to provide life-giving nectar to the parched. These books show what lies beyond the mere physical universe and how to become blessed by awakening to that magnificent Reality here and now. The Veda further declare this knowledge to be the heritage of every human, with the sole proviso that the individual lead a life of dharma.

This is how India, the mere land mass that it used to be earlier, became the land of spirituality because of the Veda, and will continue to be so, as long as the four Vedas are treated like the living scriptures that they are, and not like a mere piece of engraved antique consigned to the museum.

II

PRAYERS FOR ALL

It was described in the previous chapter how Indian sages contributed to the storehouse of knowledge for thousands of years through their spiritual attainment, which came to be known as the Veda. This knowledge can be put to use through meditation, *yajña* or prayer. Of these, *yajña* is a sacred act in which oblations are poured into fire with the chanting of mantras from the Veda.

With time, the art, science and technique of *yajña* were mastered by the priestly Brahmins, which gave birth to the famous Indian philosophical system, *Mīmāṃsā* which set the parameters for every aspect of Veda – its definition, usage, speciality, etc., and thus made India a highly ritualistic society.

This work does not discuss any aspect of *yajña*. Instead, the mantras and the hymns of the Veda have been explained as these should be – for contemplation and as prayers.

Prayers are the verbal connect of an individual or a group with the Divine, with or without rituals, in anticipation of getting some favour from God that cannot be achieved through the available means of the world. Prayers must be accompanied by related effort towards the result, without which prayers became hollow words. In their highest form, prayers are offered silently while meditating on its meaning, and in their lower forms they can be chanted aloud.

The prayers can be for worldly well-being, such as getting out of some crisis, or gaining wealth. They can also be offered for peace, purity and self-growth – traits that are signs of inner blooming of character.

One may wonder why pray at all if something is coming from within? Or at least, why pray to a multitude of gods, as is done in the Vedic and Hindu tradition, when one can do the same with one supreme God, as propounded in some belief systems?

The answer begins in the infinite nature of God. He (She, It – whatever) is beyond name, form or any attribute whatsoever; is at once the source and entirety of our being – implying that He is our essence. All our acts and experiences, however, are carried out through mind which by its nature is finite; our prayers, being mind-born, thus require the duality of the worshipper and the worshipped. And so, when God, the infinite, is perceived through the mind, He appears as finite, with qualities like love, strength, wisdom, etc. It is like getting a peep at a small part of a huge mountain through a window. Prayers are offered to such a God, who in essence, is our inner self but appears separated and defined because of our constrained being, perception and knowledge.

When the divine qualities of God are seen as a personality, then that personification is known as god/ goddess. Thus, depending on one's attitude and stage of evolution on the Spiritual journey, the Infinite God may appear as an infinite number and variety of gods with specific qualities, or as one Supreme God with unbound, unlimited qualities, or even with no qualities whatsoever (*Nirguṇa Brahman*).

Thus, the prayers of the Veda are seemingly towards the gods, but, in reality, they are addressed to God, the Infinite. So, each of the Vedic mantra can be meditated upon or can be used as a prayer. If the prayer is used as a sacred *mantra* for repetition (as in the case of the *Gāyatrī mantra*) then *Oṃ* is added before it.

This section presents certain famous Vedic prayers, which have come down to us from the most ancient times, and continue to be practised even in the present times.

1.
ŚĀNTI MANTRAS

The *Śānti mantras*, mantras for peace and prosperity, are recited before any undertaking, individual or collective. These *mantras* come from the Upaniṣads of the respective Vedas, although some of these lines appear in the Vedas too.

To make a noble undertaking successful, it is always a good idea to have the blessings of the Divine, since inimical subtle forces, invisible to the eyes, are out there prowling to create disturbance in all that is good. So, the sages taught us to pray to the divine power, within and outside, to keep evil forces under restraint.

But how can there be inimical forces in the realm of God who is merciful, loving, etc.? This is because there is no absolute good or bad in the universe. It is our perception that makes us see certain things as opposed to our well-being. A tigress is a protective mother for her cubs but appears dangerous to a potential victim. Such good and bad belong to the empire of the mind, which is the sphere of dualities. God, being infinite consciousness, is beyond any kind of duality, whereas we, the inhabitants of the realm of duality, want things and situations according to our fancy. By praying to the Divine, the forces that we consider noble tend to accumulate around us and make us successful.

True spirituality, however, is beyond duality where there is neither good nor bad, and hence a spiritual seeker has to go beyond every kind of seeking and avoiding. This is the stage that, when aspired for, will ultimately lead to liberation and elevation to God-consciousness, no matter what the starting point is. The aspiration, however, is entirely up to the individual who is always free to choose.

The first of these mantras is for the well-being of the teacher and the learner. It is also used in any gathering before the start of a proceeding to pray for harmony and tranquillity.

ॐ सह नाववतु । सह नौ भुनक्तु ।
सह वीर्यं करवावहै । तेजस्विनावधीतमस्तु मा विद्विषावहै ।
ॐ शान्तिः शान्तिः शान्तिः ॥ Kṛṣṇa Yajurveda

Oṃ saha nāvavatu; saha nau bhunaktu
saha vīryaṃ karavāvahai; tejasvināvadhītamastu mā vidviṣāvahai
Oṃ śāntiḥ śāntiḥ śāntiḥ

Oṃ saha nau avatu *may (He) protect us both!* ***saha nau bhunaktu*** *may (He) bestow upon us the fruit of Knowledge!* ***saha vīryam karavāvahai*** *may we both obtain the energy to acquire knowledge!* ***tejasvi nau adhītam astu*** *may what we study reveal the Truth!* ***mā vidviṣāvahai*** *may we cherish no ill-feeling toward each other!* ***Oṃ śāntiḥ śāntiḥ śāntiḥ*** *Oṃ Peace! Peace! Peace!*

Oṃ May (He) protect us both! May (He) bestow upon us knowledge!
May we both have the vigour to acquire knowledge!
May what we study reveal the Truth!
May we cherish no ill-feeling toward each other!
Oṃ Peace! Peace! Peace!

Oṃ is the highest symbol of God in the Indian tradition, including Hinduism, Buddhism, Jainism and Sikhism. God is the matrix of all objects, ideas and words. In the world, every object is a physical representation of an idea, whose verbal equivalent is a word or some sound.

Thus, in essence, these three (object, idea, word/ name) are one and the same, with the difference lying in the dimension of their state of manifestation, that is, physical, mental and verbal. To a mind, such difference does not matter, and hence it takes all three as a mental wave.

Again, AUM (in Sanskrit, pronounced *aa, oo, mm*) is the matrix of all words, since these three encompass the sound creating mechanism in any living being. Since every object and its name is same (that is, identical), Oṃ represents the entire created and uncreated universe coming from God, both being the matrices of corresponding reality. The silence after 'M' represents the impersonal God, Brahman. Thus, Oṃ is treated as the sound equivalent of God. Any other name for God may be acceptable, but only Oṃ represents God correctly and meaningfully. Every prayer and chant of every mantra necessarily begins with Oṃ.

The *Śānti mantra* then talks about protection of both teacher and the learner.

The expression *tejasvi nau adhītam* – may what we study reveal the Truth – is used since one needs strength to master a subject. All knowledge comes from within, while information comes from outside. So, when a person masters a subject, the knowledge of it comes from within. To bring this knowledge forth from within, one needs strength, which is being prayed for here.

Further, the prayer is for removing any possible ill-feeling that may arise between the speaker and the listener, *mā vidviṣāvahai,* may we cherish no ill-feeling toward each other. There have been instances of jealousy between teacher and disciple, and cases of quarrel, as between Yājñavalkya and his guru Vaiśaṃpāyana, mentioned in the earlier chapter.

The use of *śāntiḥ* three times is to pray for the calming down of three kinds of disturbances that cause internal heat within a person – *ādhyātmika* – pain caused due to health issues, *ādhibhautika* – pain caused due to external causes, and *ādhidaivika* – pain caused by natural forces, like earthquake, flood, etc. It is important that these three disturbances are kept at abeyance during the pursuit of noble acts.

The gods, hundreds of them, find an important place in the Veda. Every prayer is addressed to one of these gods and sometimes to a group of them. The generic term for them is *deva/ devatā*, which can mean 'beings of light, residents of heavens, guides of humanity, established in nobility', etc. The gods, by their very nature, are friendly towards all, so it is in the rightness of things that one wishes for the divine connect, resulting in peace and inner strength through this payer.

ॐ शं नो मित्रः शं वरुणः । शं नो भवत्वर्यमा ।
शं न इन्द्रो बृहस्पतिः । शं नो विष्णुरुरुक्रमः ।
नमो ब्रह्मणे । नमस्ते वायो ।
त्वमेव प्रत्यक्षं ब्रह्मासि । त्वामेव प्रत्यक्षं ब्रह्म वदिष्यामि ।
ऋतं वदिष्यामि । सत्यं वदिष्यामि ।
तन्मामवतु । तद्वक्तारमवतु ।
अवतु माम् । अवतु वक्तारम् ॥
ॐ शान्तिः शान्तिः शान्तिः ॥ KYV

Oṃ śaṃ no mitraḥ śaṃ varuṇaḥ; śaṃ no bhavatvaryamā
śaṃ na indro bṛhaspatiḥ; śaṃ no viṣṇururukramaḥ
namo brahmaṇe; namaste vāyo
tvameva pratyakṣaṃ brahmāsi; tvāmeva pratyakṣaṃ brahma vadiṣyāmi
ṛtam vadiṣyāmi; satyaṃ vadiṣyāmi

tanmāmavatu; tadvaktāramavatu

avatu mām; avatu vaktāram

Oṃ śāntiḥ śāntiḥ śāntiḥ

Oṃ śam naḥ mitraḥ *may Mitra be propitious unto us!* **śam varuṇaḥ** *may Varuṇa be propitious unto us!* **śam naḥ bhavatu aryamā** *may Aryaman be propitious unto us!* **śam naḥ indraḥ bṛhaspatiḥ** *may Indra and Bṛhaspati be propitious unto us* **śam naḥ viṣṇuḥ urukramaḥ** *may Viṣṇu, of wide strides, be propitious unto us!*

namaḥ brahmaṇe *salutation to Brahman!* **namaḥ te vāyo** *salutation to you, O Vāyu!* **tvam eva pratyakṣam brahma asi** *you indeed are the visible Brahman.* **tvām eva pratyakṣam brahma vadiṣyāmi** *you indeed I shall proclaim as the visible Brahman.* **ṛtam vadiṣyāmi** *you indeed, O Vāyu, I shall proclaim as ṛtam* **satyam vadiṣyāmi** *you indeed I shall proclaim as* satyam.

tat mām avatu *may That protect me!* **tat vaktāram avatu** *may That protect the teacher!* **avatu mām** *may It protect me!* **avatu vaktāram** *may It protect the teacher!* **Oṃ śāntiḥ śāntiḥ śāntiḥ** *Oṃ Peace! Peace! Peace!*

Oṃ. May Mitra be propitious unto us! May Varuṇa be propitious unto us!

May Aryaman be propitious unto us! May Indra and Bṛhaspati be propitious unto us!

May *Viṣṇu, of wide strides, be propitious unto us!*

Salutation to Brahman! Salutation to You, O Vāyu!

You indeed are the visible Brahman. You indeed I shall proclaim as the visible Brahman

You indeed, O Vāyu, I shall proclaim as ṝtam. You indeed I shall proclaim as Truth
May It protect me! May It protect the teacher! May It protect me! May It protect the teacher! Oṃ Peace! Peace! Peace!

This prayer, addressed to various gods through their glory, is meant to keep them propitious towards the devotees so that no evil force may touch them, and their strength keeps increasing.

The first god addressed in it is Mitra (lit. friend) who is a god of light, specially connected with the sun, and is quite friendly towards all, as his name indicates. Mitra's great friend is *Varuṇa*. They are often addressed conjointly, and their association is so intimate that Mitra practically has no individuality of his own.

Varuṇa is one of the great gods in the Veda, who is the upholder of *ṛtam* – the physical and moral order – and is also known as one whose laws are established. He binds sinners with fetters (*pāśas*), while he is gracious to the penitent and releases his devotees even from the sin committed by their fathers. These traits of *Varuṇa* are that of a monotheistic God who is like a divine monarch, arousing fear and commanding respect. God with these traits did not find favour with the sages, since such a God miserably fails to explain the inequalities in the world. With time, the idea of monotheism entirely withered away from the Vedic tradition, and instead spiritual ideas on the lines of *ekaṃ sadviprā bahudhā vadanti* – Truth is one, sages speak of it variously, became the keynote of the Veda.

Aryaman (or, *Aryamā*) is a popular god, related to hospitality, Bṛhaspati is the god of learning and wisdom, Vāyu is the god of winds and energy, Indra is the leader of the gods, Viṣṇu is ever attached to Indra, and is famous for his long strides with which he can cover the entire space easily. The characteristics of some of these gods are described in mantras and hymns that are to be discussed later in this work.

Brahman (formless) is the infinite, undifferentiated Consciousness, and hence It can be realized only in the deepest of meditation by dissolving the delusion of separation from It. One can thus become identified with Brahman but can never know It, since there can be no duality of the knower-known in the infinite where all delusions of separation cease to exist.

It should be noted that Consciousness in Hindu religion and philosophy is different from the Western world's ideas about the term, or as commonly understood by expressions, 'conscious-unconscious'. Consciousness in Hinduism is Reality; it alone Exists (*Sat*); it alone is Aware (*Citta*), and it alone is Blissful (*Ānanda*). It can be experienced only when one tastes *mahākāraṇa* (explained earlier) in the state of *samādhi*.

Pratyakṣa Brahman is the supreme reality behind the manifest universe, and is experienced by the sages and the prophets in their meditation and prayers.

Ṛtam is the cosmic order. When God creates, He first manifests His power, which otherwise stays dormant with Him. Once the potential becomes kinetic, *ṛtam*, the cosmic order, comes into effect. Everything in the universe abides by this order. Swami Vivekananda had famously put these three in a prayer, *Oṃ hrīṃ ṛtaṃ* ... implying that the three – God, His Power and His world-order are one and the same, and yet these appear separate. *Ṛtam* is real and truth. Anything that is not *ṛtam* is *anṛtam*, meaning non-existent. In later times, *ṛtam* was adapted to mean *dharma*.

Tat is a pronoun signifying all, so it refers to God or Brahman, as the case might be.

The world is a mix of good and bad for all. Depending on one's orientation, one may choose something over others, while one's actual necessity may be entirely different from what was chosen. This mixing the good and bad, and the resulting choices that we make in life, can create a mental hell for many.

This prayer is for our senses to alight only on the noble, the way a honeybee sucks only nectar from the flowers, as compared to an ordinary fly that sits on a flower as also on garbage. The prayer is also for noble thoughts to enter the mind and for a strong body and firm limbs so that we may become fit to strive for and enjoy whatever we want in life.

Echoing the importance of a strong body and mind, Swami Vivekananda had famously said, 'You will understand the Gita better with your biceps, your muscles, a little stronger. You will understand the mighty genius and the mighty strength of Krishna better with a little of strong blood in you.' (CW: Vol. III)

ॐ भद्रं कर्णेभिः शृणुयाम देवाः । भद्रं पश्येमाक्षभिर्यजत्राः ।
स्थिरैरङ्गैस्तुष्टुवाग्ंसस्तनूभिः । व्यशेम देवहितं यदायुः ।

स्वस्ति न इन्द्रो वृद्धश्रवाः । स्वस्ति नः पूषा विश्ववेदाः ।
स्वस्ति नस्तार्क्ष्यो अरिष्टनेमिः । स्वस्ति नो बृहस्पतिर्दधातु ॥
ॐ शान्तिः शान्तिः शान्तिः ॥ Atharvaveda

Oṃ bhadraṃ karṇebhiḥ śṛṇuyāma devāḥ; bhadraṃ paśyemākṣabhiryajatrāḥ
sthirairaṅgaistuṣṭuvāgṃsastanūbhiḥ; vyaśema devahitaṃ yadāyuḥ
svasti na indro vṛddhaśravāḥ; svasti naḥ pūṣā viśvavedāḥ
svasti nastārkṣyo ariṣṭanemiḥ; svasti no bṛhaspatirdadhātu
Oṃ śāntiḥ śāntiḥ śāntiḥ

Oṃ bhadram *auspicious* ***karṇebhiḥ śṛṇuyāma devāḥ*** *may we, O God, hear with our ears what is* ***bhadram paśyema akṣabhiḥ yajatrāḥ*** *may we, O worshipful gods, see with our eyes what is good* ***sthiraiḥ aṅgaiḥ tuṣṭuvāgṃsaḥ tanūbhiḥ*** *may we, strong in limbs and body* ***vyaśema devahitam yat āyuḥ*** *sing your praise and enjoy the life allotted to us*

svasti na indraḥ vṛddhaśravāḥ *may Indra of great fame be auspicious to us* ***svasti naḥ pūṣā viśvavedāḥ*** *may the omniscient Pūṣān be propitious to us*

svasti naḥ tārkṣyaḥ ariṣṭanemiḥ *may Garuḍa, the destroyer of evil, be well disposed towards us* ***svasti naḥ bṛhaspatiḥ dadhātu*** *may Bṛhaspati ensure our welfare.*

Oṃ śāntiḥ śāntiḥ śāntiḥ *Oṃ Peace! Peace! Peace!*

Oṃ. May we, O God, hear with our ears what is auspicious!
May we, O worshipful gods, see with our eyes what is good!
May we, strong in limbs and body, sing your praise and enjoy the life allotted to us!

May Indra be auspicious to us; may the omniscient Pūṣan be propitious to us
May Garuḍa, the destroyer of evil, be well disposed towards us; may Bṛhaspati ensure our welfare
Oṃ Peace! Peace! Peace!

Indra, Pūṣan and Bṛhaspati are gods with various qualities. *Tārkṣya* is the name of a divine being who was originally seen as a horse-being, but was later seen as a bird and identified with Garuḍa, the divine bird endowed with infinite strength and the power to fly anywhere. The word often comes along with *ariṣṭanemi.*

Ariṣṭanemi tārkṣya is also the name of a Vedic sage.

The best prayers are offered mentally. However, this calls for a level of steady, undivided attention that is beyond the ability of most people, who need something concrete as a medium or platform to offer prayer. For them, the *yajña* presents such a means, performed as it is in front of the sacred fire or before an image, both being tangible and available for their attention to focus on.

ॐ तच्छंयोरावृणीमहे। गातुं यज्ञाय। गातुं यज्ञपतये।
दैवी स्वस्तिरस्तु नः। स्वस्तिर्मानुषेभ्यः ।
ऊर्ध्वं जिगातु भेषजम् । शं नो अस्तु द्विपदे । शं चतुष्पदे।
ॐ शान्तिः शान्तिः शान्तिः ॥ KYV

Oṃ tacchaṃyorāvṛṇīmahe; gātuṃ yajñāya gātuṃ yajñapataye
daivī svasti-rastu naḥ; svastir-mānuṣebhyaḥ
ūrdhvaṃ jigātu bheṣajam; śaṃ no astu dvipade; śaṃ catuṣpade
Oṃ śāntiḥ śāntiḥ śāntiḥ

Oṃ tat śam yoḥ āvṛṇīmahe *we turn towards God and pray for our well-being* ***gātum yajñāya*** *we pray that the yajña get completed successfully* ***gātum yajñapataye*** *we pray that the results of the yajña should come to the sacrificer (master of the sacrifice).*

Daivī svastiḥ astu naḥ *may we enjoy the well-being given to us* ***svastiḥ mānuṣebhyaḥ*** *may there be well-being for humankind* ***ūrdhvam jigātu bheṣajam*** *may they find the means of warding off misfortunes and calamities.*

Śam naḥ astu dvipade *welfare be to our fellow human beings* ***śam catuṣpade*** *welfare be to all animals* ***Oṃ śāntiḥ śāntiḥ śāntiḥ*** *Oṃ Peace! Peace! Peace!*

Oṃ We turn towards God and pray for our well-being
We pray that the yajña gets completed successfully
We pray that the results of the yajña come to the sacrificer
May we enjoy the well-being given to us.
May there be well-being for humankind; may they find the means of warding off misfortunes and calamities
Welfare be to our fellow human beings; welfare be to all animals
Oṃ Peace! Peace! Peace!

Viṣṇu is a god with exceptional qualities, one of which is that He is the god of *yajña*, which, in earlier times, was the most popular way of offering one's devotion to the gods.

The sages here pray for the well-being of all, including fellow human beings and animals. Established in inclusiveness, they knew that the growth of people is not possible unless everything connected with them grow too.

The study of any subject requires understanding of it so that the knowledge becomes useful and applicable. Lucky is the student whose learning descends from the organ of speech to the heart, and thus information gets converted into knowledge.

The study of the Veda, and for that matter any philosophy or scripture, demands a much calmer mind compared to other subjects, and hence this prayer. Here, the learner prays for the grace of the Lord by which his rote learning may become knowledge so that what he has learnt, he can realize as truth by his contemplative mind.

ॐ वाङ् मे मनसि प्रतिष्ठिता
मनो मे वाचि प्रतिष्ठितमाविराविर्म एधि
वेदस्य म आणिस्थः श्रुतं मे मा प्रहासीरनेनाधीतेनाहोरात्रान्
संदधाम्यृतं वदिष्यामि सत्यं वदिष्यामि तन्मामवतु
तद्वक्तारमवत्ववतु मामवतु वक्तारमवतु वक्तारम्।
ॐ शान्तिः शान्तिः शान्तिः ॥ Ṛgveda

Oṃ vāṅme manasi pratiṣṭhitā
mano me vāci pratiṣṭhitam-āvirāvirma edhi
vedasya ma āṇisthaḥ śrutaṃ me mā prahāsīr-anenādhīt-enāhorātrān
saṃdadhāmy-ṛtaṃ vadiṣyāmi satyaṃ vadiṣyāmi tanmāmavatu
tadvaktāram-avatvavatu māmavatu vaktāramavatu vaktāram
Oṃ śāntiḥ śāntiḥ śāntiḥ

Oṃ vāk me manasi pratiṣṭhitā *may my speech be fixed in my mind* ***manaḥ me vāci pratiṣthitam āviḥ āviḥ ma edhi*** *may my mind be fixed in my speech, O self-luminous (Brahman), be manifest unto me*

vedasya ma āṇisthaḥ *(O mind and speech), may you bring to me the Veda* ***śrutam me mā prahāsīḥ*** *may what I* *study from the Veda not leave me!* ***anena adhītena ahorātrān saṃdadhāmi*** *I shall unite day and night for this study*

ṛtam vadiṣyāmi satyam vadiṣyāmi *I shall speak ṛtam, I shall speak Truth*

tanmām avatu *may Brahman protect me* ***tadvaktāram avatu avatu mām avatu vaktāram avatu vaktāram*** *may Brahman protect the teacher, may Brahman protect me, may Brahman protect the teacher*

Oṃ śāntiḥ śāntiḥ śāntiḥ *Oṃ Peace! Peace! Peace!*

May my speech be fixed in my mind
May my mind be fixed in my speech, O self- luminous (Brahman),
be manifest to me
O mind and speech, may you bring to me the Veda!
May what I study from the Veda not leave me!
I shall unite day and night for this study
I shall speak ṛtam; I shall speak Truth
May Brahman protect me; may Brahman protect the teacher!
May Brahman protect me, may Brahman protect the teacher!
Oṃ Peace! Peace! Peace!

Brahman here implies *Saguṇa Brahman* (Brahman that can be realized in this world as God or as any of the gods whom one worships), since prayer can never be addressed to the formless. The prayer here is for the welfare of the student and also for the teacher.

The Veda are not mere words but is the body of the all-important knowledge that acts as guide in this and the other worlds. Hence the prayer is for retaining the knowledge acquired by the learner.

The strength of limbs and inner organs is a must for success in any endeavour. It is much more so in the case of spirituality. A spiritual seeker gives up all material support and so he has to depend only on his body as the vessel that would take him across the world, so he must have a sound body and limbs. This prayer is for a fit body and powerful organs.

ॐ आप्यायन्तु ममाङ्गानि वाक्प्राणश्चक्षुःश्रोत्रमथो बलमिन्द्रियाणि च सर्वाणि ।
सर्वं ब्रह्मौपनिषदं माऽहं ब्रह्म निराकुर्यां
मा मा ब्रह्म निराकरोदनिराकरणमस्त्वनिराकरणं मेऽस्तु ।
तदात्मनि निरते य उपनिषत्सु धर्मास्ते मयि सन्तु ते मयि सन्तु ||
ॐ शान्तिः शान्तिः शान्तिः ॥ Sāmaveda

Oṃ āpyāyantu mamāṅgāni vākprāṇaś-cakṣuḥ-śrotram-atho balam-indriyāṇi ca sarvāṇi
sarvaṃ brahmaupaniṣadaṃ māhaṃ brahma nirākuryāṃ
mā mā brahma nirākarod-anirākaraṇamastv-anirākaraṇaṃ mestu
tadātmani nirate ya upaniṣatsu dharmāste mayi santu te mayi santu
Oṃ śāntiḥ śāntiḥ śāntiḥ

Oṃ āpyāyantu mamāṅgāni *may the limbs of my body be well nourished* ***vāk prāṇaḥ cakṣuḥ śrotram atho balam indriyāṇi ca sarvāṇi*** *as also, my tongue, prāṇa, eyes, ears, and my strength, and other sense-organs be nourished!*

sarvam brahma aupaniṣadam *all indeed is Brahman, as is declared in the Upaniṣads* ***mā aham brahma nirākuryām*** *may I never deny Brahman!* ***mā mā brahma nirākarod anirākaraṇam astu*** *nor may Brahman ever deny me!*

anirākaraṇam me astu *may there never be denial on the part of Brahman, may there never be denial on my part*

tadātmani nirate ya upaniṣatsu dharmāḥ te mayi santu *may all the virtues described in the upaniṣads come to me, who am devoted to that dharma (ātman)* ***te mayi santu*** *may they all be with me!*

Oṃ śāntiḥ śāntiḥ śāntiḥ *Oṃ Peace! Peace! Peace!*

May the limbs of my body be well nourished
also, my tongue, prāṇa, eyes, ears and my strength and other sense-organs, be nourished!
All indeed is Brahman, as is declared in the Upaniṣads; may I never deny Brahman
Nor may Brahman ever deny me; may there never be denial on the part of Brahman; may there never be denial on my part!
May all the virtues described in the Upaniṣads come to me, who am devoted to ātman; may they all be with me!
Oṃ Peace! Peace! Peace!

The *prāṇa* are the sum-total of energy at the cosmic level and is also the energy working within a body at the individual level. A being is considered to be living only if the activity of *prāṇa* is going on within the being. Furthermore, a powerful body and mind is possible only if a person has *prāṇa* working correctly in them. Hence, the prayer for healthy *prāṇa*.

To grow in life and spirituality, one must have a powerful mind, which comes from tranquillity. There can be many ways to attain the peace of mind but the best among them is to stay in deep connect with God.

The beauty of this mantra lies in the statement, *may Brahman never deny me,* which reveals the earnestness on the part of the sage to stay ever-connected with God. This aspect of bonding was later explained in Gita as '*tasyāhaṃ na praṇaśyāmi sa ca me na praṇaśyati,* He who sees me everywhere and sees everything in me, to him I am never lost, nor is he ever lost to me.' (Gita: VI.30)

Such a bond comes in the life of every advanced *sādhaka*. One is reminded of the agonized prayer of Jesus Christ as he was being crucified, 'My God, my God, why hast thou forsaken me?' However, the very next moment, he stopped lamenting, implying the obvious.

The last mantra is one of the finest in the spiritual philosophy of the world, where the sage prays for fullness in life, since everything around is full.

ॐ पूर्णमदः पूर्णमिदं पूर्णात् पूर्णमुदच्यते ।
पूर्णस्य पूर्णमादाय पूर्णमेवावशिष्यते ॥
ॐ शान्तिः शान्तिः शान्तिः ॥ Śukla Yajurveda

Oṃ pūrṇamadaḥ pūrṇamidaṃ pūrṇāt pūrṇamudacyate
pūrṇasya pūrṇamādāya pūrṇamevāvaśiṣyate
Oṃ śāntiḥ śāntiḥ śāntiḥ

Oṃ pūrṇam adaḥ *That (formless Brahman) is full;* ***pūrṇam idam*** *this (Brahman manifested as Creation) is full* ***pūrṇāt pūrṇam udacyate*** *this fullness has been projected from that fullness* ***pūrṇasya pūrṇam ādāya*** *when this fullness merges in that fullness,* ***pūrṇam eva avaśiṣyate*** *all that remains is fullness* ***Oṃ śāntiḥ śāntiḥ śāntiḥ*** *Oṃ Peace! Peace! Peace!*

Oṃ That (formless Brahman) is full; this (Brahman manifested as Creation) is full
This fullness has been projected from that fullness
When this fullness merges in that fullness, all that remains is fullness
Oṃ Peace! Peace! Peace!

Since time immemorial, philosophies of the world have been speculating on the nature and relation of Creation with respect to God. The Upaniṣads see the universe as the manifest Brahman and the source as the formless Brahman, and both are seen as infinite.

More importantly, when the infinite is taken out of infinite then the residue too is infinite, implying that when God creates the universe, He does not become lessened by that much. This mantra thus signifies that Creation and dissolution do not affect the nature of God; He always remains what He is – Infinite.

All these prayers, or some of these, are used before and after any undertaking, individual or collective. At the physical level, these bring prosperity, at the mental level these give peace, and at the spiritual level these connect one with the Divine.

2.
THE UNIVERSAL PRAYERS

Prayers, as explained in the previous chapter, are the verbal connect with the Divine, which can be for one's welfare or out of love for God. Minds tuned to the higher values also pray for nobility, character and strength, which grow from within. The prayers in this section are for inner enrichment, and hence can be practiced by anyone, anywhere in the world, irrespective of gender, occupation and religion.

When two objects interact, there is an exchange of energy, and when two minds interact, there is an exchange of information. These two, energy and information may or may not be related, but the principle of their flow from the higher potential to the lower is common. Also, as with energy, the flow of information may have a destructive effect or a constructive one, depending on how patterned these are. For example, the energy of a storm may destroy a structure, and the instigation by a rogue leader may lead to ruinous consequences.

To make sure that we grow in nobility, the sage prays in this mantra for noble thoughts to flow in the mind from all directions so that we can grow to be what we want to be. This prayer, coming from thousands of years ago, negates the theory that ideas are produced by brain cell activity. Instead, the Hindus believe that even the most creative, inspired expressions of scientists, philosophers, writers, poets and others, are ideas that came to them, without any volition on their part, from source beyond the bounds of their individual personalities.

According to Swami Vivekananda, ideas are attracted to minds that are tuned to them, and hence one must be careful about what one does, speaks or thinks, since a dirty mind will become the resthouse for the garbage of the universe.

He also asserted that a man sitting in a cave thinking of noble things does a great service to the humanity by gifting it the noble ideas that will invariably reach the fit recipients.

One can thus become great simply by choosing consistently to be great!

आ नो भद्राः क्रतवो यन्तु विश्वतः ... | RV I.89.1

ā no bhadrāḥ kratavo yantu viśvataḥ ...

ā naḥ *towards us* ***bhadrāḥ*** *noble* ***kratavaḥ*** *thoughts/ deeds* ***yantu*** *come* ***viśvataḥ*** *from all directions*

May noble thoughts come to us from all directions

The mind, by its very constitution, prefers to run with the sense organs after sense objects, and hence it cannot strive to be noble by its own. If one wants to be noble, one has to pray to be so to God, who is the inner self of all and also the controller of the universe. Hence this prayer.

People argue about what is good and noble, sceptics doubt the idea of goodness, and many modern philosophers question the very existence of morality or goodness. Beyond all this word play and juggling of ideas, it should be known that every act that we perform and every thought that we think, produces a visible external result, and it also impacts our character imperceptibly. The impressions left by these impacts shape our future course of action, and ultimate destiny. Hence the sage prays for *bhadrāḥ*, noble, to come unto us from all directions. Ideas and acts that help us move towards inner enrichment are noble, while everything else is to be shunned.

Kratu is an oft-used word in the Veda, meaning noble deeds. In its particular sense it implies the sacred act of pouring oblation during a *yajña*.

The feeling of the above mantra is carried forward in the next mantra, wherein the sage prays for ideas to be sieved into good and bad, with the bad ones to be cast away forever.

विश्वानि देव सवितर्दुरितानि परा सुव । यद्भद्रं तन्न आ सुव ॥ RV V.82.5

viśvāni deva savitar-duritāni parā suva; yad-bhadraṃ tan-na ā suva

viśvāni deva savitaḥ duritāni parā suva *Savitā, dear God! send all evil far away*

yat bhadram tat naḥ ā suva *bring to us what is good*

Savitā, O dear God! Send all evil far away
and bring to us what is good

In the Veda, *Savitṛ* is sometimes seen as Sun God, but he is mostly described as the god of early morning and evening. At his command the sun rises at dawn, and night falls at dusk. He protects his worshippers and conveys departed spirits to where the righteous dwell. He removes evil dreams and renders men sinless. The famous *Gāyatrī* mantra is also dedicated to *Savitṛ*.

This mantra is also used in *Sandhyā vandana*, the daily ritualistic prayer of the Hindus.

In the Veda, good and evil do not come from any external source as in Abrahamic religions, rather the onus of choosing the good lies entirely with the individual. The goal of life can be only four – *dharma, artha, kāma* and *mokṣa* – all based on noble conduct, as explained in the first chapter. Once the life goal is set, it is dangerous to expose oneself to thoughts that are inimical to one's path of growth. Worse, by exposing oneself to such thoughts, one becomes highly susceptible to stumbles and deviations.

We create our environment and then feed on it for our sustenance. Growth into nobility becomes smooth only when the environment in which we live is conducive, which again is created by us only. Today, when the world is concerned about pollution, global warming, environmental issues, it is worth noting how the sages prayed to be blessed with favourable environment by becoming noble themselves.

मधु वाता ऋतायते मधु क्षरन्ति सिन्धवः । माध्वीर्नः सन्त्वोषधीः ॥
मधु नक्तमुतोषसो मधुमत्पार्थिवं रजः । मधु द्यौरस्तु नः पिता ॥
मधुमान्नो वनस्पतिर्मधुमाँ अस्तु सूर्यः । माध्वीर्गावो भवन्तु नः ॥ RV I.90.6–8; Yajurveda XIII.27–29

madhu vātā ṛtāyate madhu kṣaranti sindhavaḥ; mādhvīrnaḥ santvoṣadhīḥ
madhu naktam-utoṣaso madhumat-pārthivaṃ rajaḥ; madhu dyau-rastu naḥ pitā
madhumānno vanaspatir-madhumām̐ astu sūryaḥ; mādhvīr-gāvo bhavantu naḥ

madhu vātāḥ ṛtāyate *the winds blow sweet for those who hold to ṛtam* ***madhu kṣaranti sindhavaḥ*** *(and) sweet flow rivers* ***mādhvīḥ naḥ santu oṣadhīḥ*** *so may the plants be sweet for us*

madhu naktam uta uṣasaḥ *(may) sweet be the night and dawns be sweet* ***madhumat pārthivam rajaḥ*** *the earth be sweet* ***madhu dyauḥ astu naḥ pitā*** *the space be sweet and sweet be the fatherly heaven to us*

madhumān naḥ vanaspatiḥ, madhumān astu sūryaḥ *may the trees be sweet and sweet be the Sun* ***mādhvīḥ gāvaḥ bhavantu naḥ*** *as also may our cows be sweet for us*

The winds blow sweet for those who hold to ṛtam
(and) sweet flow rivers, so may the plants be sweet for us
(May) sweet be the night and dawns be sweet
the earth be sweet, the space be sweet and sweet be the fatherly heaven to us
May the trees be sweet and sweet be the Sun
as also may our cows be sweet for us

Madhu, sweetness, implies being favourable, which is possible only when a thing is established in nobility. The sage prays that everything on which he depends, and all that surround him, be favourable, noble and sweet.

The word *ṛtam* was explained earlier. It means the universal world order. Here it implies that a person desirous of inner growth must abide by both societal and cosmic laws. The laws made by men may have ulterior motives, but the divine order, as described in the scriptures, always aim at the growth of one and the growth of all. The scriptures are like mother, whose discipline is meant for our own betterment.

Whatever our desires and aspirations, we can never be achievers till we have a powerful mind, which can be powerful only if it is content.

This may sound contradictory, nevertheless it is true. The desire to appear successful or to play to the gallery saps away the inner energies of the mind, even if it applies itself fully to achieving the goal. Gita explains it beautifully as 'Work diligently but without being concerned about the results.' This is contentment, and the sign of a powerful mind.

मनो मे तर्पयत वाचं मे तर्पयत प्राणं मे तर्पयत चक्षुर्मे तर्पयत | YV VI.31

mano me tarpayata vācaṃ me tarpayata
prāṇaṃ me tarpayata cakṣurme tarpayata

manaḥ me tarpayata *content be my mind* ***vācam me tarpayata*** *content my speech;* ***prāṇam me tarpayata*** *content be my prāṇa* ***cakṣuḥ me tarpayata*** *content my eyes*

Content be my mind, content my speech
content be my prāṇa, content my eyes

He, who aspires for the power of the mind, must have his sense organs and the vital forces in full contentment. This prayer is about that.

Prāṇa are the vital forces that work inside the body, making the different bodily functions possible. At the universal level, *prāṇa* provides the universe with energy.

तेजोऽसि तेजो मयि धेहि वीर्यमसि वीर्यं मयि धेहि बलमसि बलं मयि धेह्योजोऽस्योजो मयि धेहि मन्युरसि मन्युं मयि धेहि सहोऽसि सहो मयि धेहि ॥ YV XIX.9

tejosi tejo mayi dhehi vīryam-asi vīryaṃ mayi dhehi balam-asi balaṃ mayi dhehy-ojosyojo mayi dhehi manyur-asi manyuṃ mayi dhehi sahosi saho mayi dhehi

tejaḥ asi tejaḥ mayi dhehi *Thou art powerful, give me power* ***vīryam asi vīryam mayi dhehi*** *Thou art valorous, give me valour,*

balam asi balam mayi dhehi *Thou art strength, give me strength;* ***ojaḥ asi ojaḥ mayi dhehi*** *Thou art energy, give me energy,*

manyuḥ asi manyum mayi dhehi *Thou art passion, give me passion;* ***sahaḥ asi sahaḥ mayi dhehi*** *Thou art forbearance, give me forbearance*

Thou art conquering might, give me conquering might
Thou art powerful, give me power, Thou art valorous, give me valour
Thou art strength, give me strength, Thou art energy, give me energy
Thou art passion, give me passion, Thou art forbearance, give me forbearance

Teja, *vīrya*, *bala* and *oja* generally imply strength and vigour, and are often used interchangeably, but when used simultaneously, these have different connotations.

Manyu means passion. This is the driving force behind strength. However, this is not the passion of the senses, but is born of dharma, righteousness.

Dhehi means to place, which when interpreted, means 'to give'. One gives what one is/ has. God gives what God is – all these qualities and many more. Hence this prayer.

It would be of interest to know that Swami Vivekananda repeatedly asserted the need for a strong body, 'muscles of iron and nerves of steel', an adamantine will and other such qualities for all those striving for religion. It is sad that the land that gave such prayers, suffered for centuries the ignominy of weakness and cowardice.

3.
GĀYATRĪ MANTRA

Two great epical scriptures of India, Rāmāyaṇa by Vālmīki and Mahābhārata by Vyāsa, are known as *itihāsa* (lit. history), meaning these are the history and aspiration of the Indian people, through which the ideals of religion are presented and explained in full. Both these works (not to be confused with popular books on these or tele-serials), are like huge mines of information on the nature, achievements and ideals of the Hindu civilization.

Many stories are common in these two great works, of which the story of Viśvāmitra, the great maverick sage, is one of the more attention-grabbing ones. Viśvāmitra was a *kṣatriya* prince who picked a quarrel with the great sage Vasiṣṭha and lost. To avenge his defeat, he gave up everything and engaged himself in intense *tapasyā*. What happened after that makes such a colourful read in his roller coaster ride of spiritual life. With the power of his *tapasyā*, he created a demon to kill the son of Vasiṣṭha, then went on to create a new heaven, then had a brush with lustful temptations, and was finally venerated as the greatest of sages by Vasiṣṭha, his arch enemy.

With time, Viśvāmitra's eminence grew so huge that out of the ten books in the Ṛgveda, the IIIrd book (*manḍala*) is entirely from his family! And, the most famous mantra of the Veda, the *Gāyatrī* mantra, is ascribed directly to the great sage himself.

For thousands of years *Gāyatrī* mantra has been associated with *yajñopavīta* ceremony (putting on of sacred thread) by Hindu boys at the tender age that marked the start of their Vedic learning. The custom of the Vedic learning has faded but *yajñopavīta* ceremony along with initiation in the *Gāyatrī* mantra continues to be practised by most Hindus.

Sages did not restrict the Veda for any class or gender, so anyone in the world can practise *Gāyatrī* mantra and have *yajñopavīta*. As for the Hindus, they should definitely have these two, along with rituals like *sandhyā vandana*.

(ॐ भूर्भुवः स्वः) तत्सवितुर्वरेण्यं भर्गो देवस्य धीमहि | धियो यो नः प्रचोदयात् ॥ RV III.62.10

(Oṃ bhūrbhuvaḥ svaḥ) tat-savitur-vareṇyaṃ bhargo devasya dhīmahi; dhiyo yo naḥ pracodayāt

***Oṃ bhūḥ bhuvaḥ svaḥ** the universe in totality (the physical, subtle and causal) **tat savituḥ** the effulgent Lord **vareṇyam** worthy of worship **bhargaḥ devasya** the dispeller of darkness **dhīmahi** we meditate upon **dhiyaḥ yaḥ naḥ pracodayāt** may He enlighten our mind*

Oṃ We meditate on the effulgent Lord
Who is the Creator of the universe
Who is worthy of worship
Who is the embodiment of knowledge and light
May (He) enlighten our intellect

This mantra/ prayer is addressed to *Savitṛ* who is celebrated in eleven hymns and in many mantras of different hymns. Derived from the root *su,* meaning to stimulate, *Savitṛ* is the god who energizes all. He is pre-eminently a golden deity, with everything of his being golden, signifying his identification with the morning sun, and raising up his light continually from the east. He removes evil dreams and makes men sinless. He is sometimes identified as the Sun, and at other times a little different. He is also connected with the evening as with the morning, for, at his command night comes and he brings all beings to rest.

Apart from *Ṛgveda*, this mantra also comes in *Yajurveda* and *Sāmaveda.*

The three words, *bhūḥ bhuvaḥ svaḥ* are not from the original Vedic prayer, but are added to make it a complete mantra. By adding *Oṃ* in the beginning of the mantra and also at the end, it becomes the famous *Gāyatrī* mantra.

This mantra is often associated with the goddess *Gāyatrī* who is not a Vedic goddess but is a poetic metre in the Veda. The hymns of the *Ṛgveda* are always metrical, with varying number of lines like three, four or five to a stanza. There are about fifteen metres in it, of which, *Triṣṭubh* (4 x 11 syllables), the *Gāyatrī* (3 x 8) and the *Jagatī* (4 x 12) are more common.

The metres of the Veda are so respected that the later poets refrained from using these, including the *Gāyatrī*. However, some mantras, like *Paramahaṃsa Gāyatrī* and *Sarasvatī Gāyatrī* were composed in this metre.

Oṃ is the symbol of God to represent that He is the matrix of all objects, and is also beyond them. The reason is that every object has a corresponding word for it, and for any mind, the name and the object represented by it are same. Now, as we saw earlier, every word, as sound, is boxed within the three sounds – A, U, M (Sanskrit pronunciation of aa, oo, mm). Of these, A is produced from the throat, M ends at the lips and U is the rolling sound in between. Oṃ is thus the matrix of all words/ names that can ever be produced by any vocal system, human or others, and for the same reason, it is the symbol of God, the manifested. The silence that follows 'Aum' represents the unmanifested/ infinite aspect of God.

Every mantra used as an aid for meditation, or for making it *siddha* (that which has been realized and can give results), has Oṃ at the beginning. It is also used as a symbol of consent.

The first three words, *bhūḥ bhuvaḥ svaḥ*, are the three regions: physical space (*sthūla jagat*), the mid-space (*sūkṣma jagat*) and heavenly space (*kāraṇa jagat*) respectively, along with the worlds associated with these, as explained in the introductory chapters. These spheres are created by God and not by any other being or power, as expressed in the expression, *tat,* which is a pronoun, used in the scriptures to indicate God.

Savituḥ means effulgent, meaning bright like sun, or Sun. It also means God, who is the indwelling spirit, and is the Lord of the universe. This interpretation shows how *Savitā*, the god of dawn (explained above), is in fact the indwelling spirit of all. When we pray to some god/ goddess, the prayer is actually addressed to the supreme God, who is the indwelling spirit of all, and is also the Lord of all.

Vareṇyam means worthy of worship, which is God. *Bhargaḥ* is the dispeller of darkness/ the light of consciousness that impels all into action. Its other meaning is one who burns down all sin, and it also means grain. So, God is the provider of all and everything – physical, mental, spiritual. Thus, Gāyatrī mantra can be used in three different ways – for spiritual realization through meditation on its meaning, as prayer for purity and as oblation in *yajña* for prosperity. People mostly use the mantra for the first two, while the third one is used during *yajña*. People often recite the mantra after bath while offering water to Sun god.

Devasya means the Supreme Lord who created the three regions; *dhīmahi* means 'we meditate upon' (in case the goal is spiritual realization), or 'we offer our prayers' (if the purpose is the other two).

Yaḥ, He (That Divine Light/ God), *pracodayāt* enlighten or goad *naḥ* our *dhī* intellect that guides one to proper action, and righteous conduct, is the prayer.

In Hindu philosophy, mind has four different names (out of many others) used interchangeably depending on the action it performs. These are: *citta* (information collection), *manas* (data sorting), *dhī/ buddhi* (the right understanding and the strength to stay true to that), and *ahaṃkāra* (identification with the object/ goal). This prayer is about getting the right *dhī,* since one can achieve anything in this world, without any intervention by God, if they have proper intellect.

This prayer, thus, can be addressed to an external Supreme God or to the indwelling consciousness. Being impersonal in nature, it can be used by anyone and from any land, culture or faith.

4.
GAṆEŚA, VIṢṆU AND ŚIVA (MAHĀ-MṚTYUÑJAYA) MANTRAS

India worships the Infinite through its infinite qualities in an infinite number of ways. Consequently, there are a huge number of gods and goddesses who are seen as having unique personalities, which, in fact, are like masks on the Infinite. This twin way of worshipping God as infinite and also as personified God has been in continuous practice since the time of the Veda. Here we present three important aspects of the Infinite, worshipped as Gaṇeśa, Viṣṇu and Śiva.

Gaṇeśa mantra

In the spiritual tradition of India, we find that some gods of the Vedic period were not in prominence then but became prominent later. Also, the very nomenclature of some gods changed with time, keeping intact their qualities and traits. Lord Gaṇeśa is one of them. According to one of the traditional stories, Mother Pārvatī had created Gaṇeśa as her spiritual son. Due to some divine mismanagement, the head of Gaṇeśa fell off, after which the head of an elephant was fixed on his body. To appease Mother Pārvatī, the gods blessed that Gaṇeśa would be the first to be worshipped during any puja, physical or mental. He was also given the power to remove all obstacles from the life of those who worshipped him sincerely.

गणानां त्वा गणपतिं हवामहे कविं कवीनामुपमश्रवस्तमम् ।
ज्येष्ठराजं ब्रह्मणां ब्रह्मणस्पत आ नः शृण्वन्नूतिभिः सीद सादनम् ॥ RV II.23.1

gaṇānāṃ tvā gaṇapatiṃ havāmahe kaviṃ kavīnām-upama-śravas-tamam
jyeṣṭharājaṃ brahmaṇāṃ brahmaṇaspata ā naḥ śṛṇvann-ūtibhiḥ sīda sādanam

gaṇānām tvā gaṇapatim havāmahe *we pray to you, the highest among gods* ***kavim kavīnām upamaśravaḥ-tamam*** *the sage of the sages, the king supreme in providing riches*

jyeṣṭharājam brahmaṇām *The best lord of prayers* ***brahmaṇaḥ pate****, O Brahmaṇaspata!* ***ā naḥ śṛṇvan ūtibhiḥ sīda sādanam*** *take a seat at this place of sacrifice to protect us*

We pray to you, O Brahmaṇaspata! the highest among all gods
the sage of the sages, the king supreme in providing riches
The best lord of prayer (please come) on hearing our prayer
come with your protection (for us), and take a seat at this place of sacrifice

The leader or the best among the gods is indicated by *gaṇānām gaṇapatim*. *Gaṇa* means assembly of beings. Later the term came to mean the attendants of Lord Śiva. In this mantra, the word implies the assembly of gods or seers (the great sages who discovered the mantras). The term may also mean 'master of himself'. The expression is now used for Lord Gaṇeśa, who is the first among the worshipped. *Havāmahe,* to invoke, is a popular word in the Veda which was often used to address the gods to come from their abode and be present at the place of prayer/ *yajña.*

The word *kavim,* the wise one, finds regular mention in the Veda. In the present times, *kavi* means a poet but the word actually means one who is a *krāntadarśī* – one who can see the past, present and the future at one go – implying that time as a restrictive factor does not work on them. This quality belongs to God, the creator, but can be used for sages who transcend the limits of time. The sages of the Vedic period were often addressed as *kavi.*

Upama-śravas-tamam means the highest in comparison to all. *Jyeṣṭharājam* is used for the superior among the kings. The way a king provides for his people, the gods too take care of human beings. *Brahmaṇām* here means he who is the best among the knowers of *mantra.* It implies that the god who has been addressed to in this mantra has unparalleled wisdom. The highest wisdom in the Hindu tradition goes to those who can see through the veil of maya. Lord Gaṇeśa has all these qualities. *Brahmaṇaspata* is one who protects riches. The gods are not only the provider but also the protector of the riches that one gets in life.

Through this mantra, Lord Gaṇeśa is requested to come and be present at the place of the worship with his power of protection for the devotee. Wealth, power and also good karma, acquired through unselfish acts and prayers, require growth and protection from loss. This prayer is for that.

Viṣṇu mantra

Lord Viṣṇu is the most important and popular God in Hindu religion. He is the Lord Supreme for his devotees, and incarnates whenever the Vedic dharma is in danger. Of his innumerable avataras, Rama and Krishna are more famous. He is also famous for his three steps with which he can measure the seen and the unseen universe. Two of his steps are visible to men but the third one can be perceived only by the sages, as described here.

तद्विष्णोः परमं पदं सदा पश्यन्ति सूरयः । दिवीव चक्षुराततम् ॥ RV I.22.20

tadviṣṇoḥ paramaṃ padaṃ sadā paśyanti sūrayaḥ; divīva cakṣurātatam

tat viṣṇoḥ paramam padam *that supreme state of Viṣṇu* **sadā paśyanti sūrayaḥ** *the wise one ever see* **divi-iva cakṣuḥ ātatam** *the way one sees the clear sky.*

The wise sages ever see; that supreme state of Viṣṇu
the way one sees the clear sky

The supreme spiritual state is often referred to as *paramam padam* in the Veda and later spiritual literature. Beyond the physical universe and the subtle universe, there is the causal universe (described in the first chapter), known as *kāraṇa jagat*. This is the sphere which can be known, and is ever-known only by *sūrayaḥ*, the greatest of the sages, as clearly as a person with perfect eyes can see the farthest in a clear sky. Thus, God realization is not about some vision (often only a trick of the mind), nor a one-time experience of God, and definitely not about going to heaven after death. To be spiritual means to be able to see God here and now.

Sūrayaḥ is yet another word for sages. The uninterrupted vision/knowledge of God is for the sages who have controlled their passions and are established in the understanding of the spiritual world.

Śiva/ Mahā-mṛtyuñjaya mantra

Creation implies absolute existence becoming (or appearing as) spatial. It is through this process of creation, real or illusory, that objects and beings appear to be, whose chief characteristics is self-preservation by opposing the disintegrating forces acting on them. Living beings do that by continually renewing their bodies, but ultimately lose the battle and disintegrate permanently. The fear of this disintegration is common to all, from sages to the microbes.

To remove this primordial fear of all beings, the sages came up with this beautiful prayer, aimed at removing the fear of untimely death, and at the same time praying for immortality, which is the recurring theme of the Hindu religion. Immortality is not about going to some high heaven but to become one with God by crossing over the ocean of birth and death, the *saṃsāra*. This prayer is considered to be highly effective against fear of death or some severe loss. Oṃ is added at the beginning of the prayer to make it a mantra for *jāpam*.

त्र्यम्बकं यजामहे सुगन्धिं पुष्टिवर्धनम् ।
उर्वारुकमिव बन्धनान्मृत्योर्मुक्षीय मामृतात् || RV VII.59.12

tryambakaṃ yajāmahe sugandhiṃ puṣṭivardhanam
urvārukam-iva bandhanān-mṛtyor-mukṣīya māmṛtāt

tryambakam yajāmahe *we worship Tryambaka (Śiva of the three eyes)* ***sugandhim puṣṭivardhanam*** *whose fame is fragrant, the augmenter of nourishment*

urvārukam iva *as a ripened cucumber* ***bandhanāt mṛtyoḥ mukṣīya mā amṛtāt*** *may he liberate us from death but not from immortality*

We worship Tryambaka (Śiva), whose fame is fragrant
the augmenter of nourishment
May he liberate us from death like a ripened cucumber
but not from immortality

This prayer in the Veda is addressed to Rudra, who was later identified with Śiva. Lord Śiva is easily invoked and is auspicious (*Śiva* means auspicious). He preserves devotees from calamity and bestows blessings. His healing powers are immense and he is the greatest physician of physicians. Lord Śiva has more or less the same qualities as Lord Rudra; only the golden dress of Rudra has now been replaced by *vibhūti* (lit. yogic powers), holy ashes. He is worshipped through a *liṇgaṃ* (meaning, symbol), instead of images that one usually sees for other divinities.

Yajāmahe means to worship. *Tryambakaṃ sugandhiṃ puṣṭivardhanam* are the qualities of Lord Śiva. He is three-eyed, the third eye being the eye of knowledge and wisdom. If he ever opens the third eye, then everything reveals its true form, and thus illusions caused by the forms are burnt down. This idea was taken up by later writers to dramatize stories related to Lord Śiva.

Urvārukam iva bandhanāt implies that the way a cucumber is easily plucked from its stem when it becomes mature, life should end just like that after one has had a full life. Our life should not go waste due to ill health or ill wisdom.

Mṛtyoḥ mukṣīya means to liberate from death. The idea is that we must have a full life and also a fulfilling life. *Mā amṛtāt* is used to indicate that the devotee must not be debarred from immortality.

This prayer shows how life has to be utilized in full so that one enjoys the best here and strives for the highest in the future. Swami Vivekananda has put it beautifully, 'This life is a great chance. What, seekest thou the pleasures of the world? – He is the fountain of all bliss. Seek for the highest, aim at that highest, and you shall reach the highest.' (CW: VI.249).

III

FACETS OF THE DIVINE

From the time that humans started probing the Divine through fear, expectation or love, there was a paradigm shift in the understanding of oneself that transcends the image of being merely a body, and instead unites them with God in various ways. Depending on one's outlook, various schools of thought arose since the beginning of the spiritual history of the world, some of which were born of insightful minds while others were rooted in ignorance.

These outlooks can be broadly classified as: *Animism*, practised in early Shinto religion and by some aboriginal societies, believes that souls inhabit all or most objects; *Totemism*, practised mostly by aborigines, believes in a divine connection between humans and other natural beings; *Polytheism*, as believed by the Greeks and the Romans, believes in multiple gods with human like figures and personal characteristics; *Monotheism*, as practised by Abrahamic religions and by the Vaiṣṇavas in India, believes in one supreme God; *Deism* believes that one God exists but He does not interfere with human life; and *Pantheism* believes that God is equivalent to the physical universe. In addition to these, we have Advaita, Viśiṣṭādvaita and other spiritual outlooks in India that are based on deeper spiritual truths.

Each of these religious systems encourages, or enjoins, its practitioners to feel one with God in its prescribed ways. On the other hand, the Veda – the original fountainhead of spirituality – describe God not in one or two ways, but in every possible way that one can conceive of.

God being infinite, is the repository of infinite qualities. We, humans, cannot comprehend all these qualities, so we often focus on one or some qualities of God and give it a name and also a persona. For example, Sarasvatī is worshipped as the goddess of knowledge, knowing well that God is knowledge. Such personification of a set of qualities is known as god.

Also, God being infinite, He cannot be fully grasped by the human mind, which by its very constitution, is finite. So, the Infinite is perceived variously by different minds, the way one looks at a sight with coloured glasses, and hence there has to be as many ways of looking at God as there are minds, with each of these representations of spirituality known as a god.

These are the two reasons for seeing the Divine as God with form and qualities. It is this God, with a well-defined persona, who is prayed to and who fulfils the wishes of a devotee.

In this section, the first chapter presents the personal aspect of God in which He/ She is seen as our own – the close, personal one, through the prayers addressed to various gods; and the next chapter is devoted to God, the Impersonal.

The selection of these prayers is neither comprehensive nor selective, but is only indicative of what the Veda have to offer.

1.
THE PERSONIFIED GOD

It is in the nature of the human mind to love that form of God, which suits their personality and to love Him with that particular emotion which they themselves have in abundance. The Veda have a huge storehouse of gods and prayers to them through a personal relation that can take care of the spiritual needs of all kinds of people.

This chapter offers a glimpse into the different relationships that a person may have with God.

As father, mother, relative: Indra

This prayer is addressed to Indra to whom nearly one-fourth of hymns of Ṛgveda are addressed.

Indra has many names, which when translated superficially, can give the impression as if he was an invader or the god of the invaders – an idea popularized by Western scholars, which is hopelessly (and, some would argue, mischievously) wrong. As will be seen, the prayers are deeply spiritual in nature, describing the craving of a spiritual mind whose only shelter is God.

In this prayer, Indra is addressed both as father and mother. This idea was later elaborated in other Indian scriptures, as also in popular prayers like *tvameva mātā ca pitā tvameva* – 'God! Thou art father and Thou art mother.'

त्वं हि नः पिता वसो त्वं माता शतक्रतो बभूविथ ।
अधा ते सुम्नमीमहे ॥ RV VIII.98.11, SV 1170 (IV.2.13.2), AV XX.108.2

tvaṃ hi naḥ pitā vaso tvaṃ mātā śatakrato babhūvitha; adhā te sumnam-īmahe

tvam hi naḥ pitā vaso *thou art father, bounteous one* **tvam mātā śatakrato** *you have been our mother, O Indra* **babhūvitha** *to become*
adhā te sumnam īmahe *hence we worship you for happiness*

Bounteous one! You have been our father; and our mother, O Indra hence we pray for your favour

The importance of this mantra can be gauged by the fact that it comes in the other Vedas too apart from the Ṛgveda.

Indra is *Vasu*, the giver of wealth, and *Śatakratu*, the god of many great deeds. He is like a father who protects and provides, and is also the mother who nourishes and takes care. Being the provider and the protector, the prayer to him is for *sumnam,* attaining favour in the form of wealth, peace and happiness.

This kind of relationship is described in the Veda many times. Here we mention a few to give an idea.

इन्द्र क्रतुं न आ भर पिता पुत्रेभ्यो यथा ।
शिक्षा णो अस्मिन्पुरुहूत यामनि जीवा ज्योतिरशीमहि || RV VII.32.26, SV 259, AV XVIII.3.67

indra kratuṃ na ā bhara pitā putrebhyo yathā
śikṣā ṇo asmin-puruhūta yāmani jīvā jyotir-aśīmahi

Give us wisdom, Indra! as a father gives (knowledge) to his sons
Guide us, O Indra! so that we live long and enjoy the light (of existence)

Here, Indra is seen not only as a father who provides material necessities and protection, but is the guide in matters of all knowledge, which is the responsibility of any caring father.

In the next prayer, Indra is seen in many more equivalent relations that ooze with care and love.

त्राता नो बोधि दद्दशान आपिरभिख्याता मर्डिता सोम्यानाम् ।
सखा पिता पितृतमः पितॄणां कर्तेमु लोकमुशते वयोधाः || RV IV.17.17

trātā no bodhi dadṛśāna āpir-abhikhyātā marḍitā somyānām
sakhā pitā pitṛtamaḥ pitṝṇāṃ kartemu lokam-uśate vayodhāḥ

Be Thou our Saviour; you, who look after all
show your grace on the worshippers
And bestow prosperity,
like a friend, father, fatherliest of fathers

Such prayers are addressed to other gods too. In the next prayer to Agni, the sage expresses a very close relation including that of one who is as dear and bright as the sun in the sky.

अग्निं मन्ये पितरमग्निमापिमग्निं भ्रातरं सदमित्सखायम् ।
अग्नेरनीकं बृहतः सपर्यं दिवि शुक्रं यजतं सूर्यस्य ॥ RV X.7.3

agniṃ manye pitaram-agnimāpim-agniṃ bhrātaraṃ sadam-it-sakhāyam
agne-ranīkaṃ bṛhataḥ saparyaṃ divi śukraṃ yajataṃ sūryasya

I consider Agni my father, kinsmen, brother,
and deem him my friend for ever
I honour him as the face of the great deity
(who is like) the adorable sun in the sky

The friend: Indra

माकिर्न एना सख्या वि यौषुस्तव चेन्द्र विमदस्य च ऋषेः ।
विद्मा हि ते प्रमतिं देव जामिवदस्मे ते सन्तु सख्या शिवानि ॥ RV X.23.7

mākirna enā sakhyā vi yauṣustava cendra vimadasya ca ṛṣeḥ
vidmā hi te pramatiṃ deva jāmivadasme te santu sakhyā śivāni

mākiḥ naḥ enā sakhyā vi yauṣuḥ *may this friendship never end* ***tava ca indra vimadasya ca ṛṣeḥ*** *between (you), O Indra and (me), sage Vimada*

vidmā hi te pramatim deva *for we know your attachment, O divine (Indra)* ***jāmivat asme*** *like the love for a sister* ***te santu sakhyā śivāni*** *(may) your benign friendship be*

Never may this friendship be severed
of you, Indra and of sage Vimada

For, we know O God! Of your brother-like love to sister
so with us be your benign friendship

The highest relation with God is of love and sweetness beyond any fear and punishment. God, being our own self, it is our divine right to be happy in the feeling of his ever-presence.

Vimada, the seer of this mantra, prays on behalf of all, that his friendship with Indra may remain ever strong, and that Indra must shower his love on him the way a brother loves *jāmi,* his sister. The overflow of affection in this prayer takes the breath away when God's grace is compared with the love of a brother for his sister.

The noble lady, mother, bride: Uṣā

The Veda have a fair share of goddesses who are seen not only as mother but in many other relations. In this verse Uṣā (lit. dawn) is seen variously as a noble lady, mother and also as a bride.

आ घा योषेव सूनर्युषा याति प्रभुञ्जती ।
जरयन्ती वृजनं पद्वदीयत उत्पातयति पक्षिणः ॥ RV I.48.5

ā ghā yoṣeva sūnary-uṣā yāti prabhuñjatī
jarayantī vṛjanaṃ padvadīyata utpātayati pakṣiṇaḥ

ā gha *to come (daily)* ***yoṣa iva sūnarī*** *like a capable lady* ***uṣāḥ yāti prabhuñjatī*** *Uṣā nourishes all* ***jarayantī vṛjanam*** *(and) makes all beings move (including towards death)* ***patvat īyate*** *makes the biped walk* ***ut-pātayati pakṣiṇaḥ*** *and makes the birds fly up (from their perch)*

Like a noble lady Uṣā comes, carefully tending everything
Rousing all life, she stirs creatures that have feet, and makes the birds fly up

Creation is characterized by time, whose best measure is through sunrise and sunset. Uṣā has been variously described as the mother of sun and the elder sister of night in the Veda. She is also the goddess whose coming and going are the daily markers in life. On her arrival, she goads all to activity. In the process, she also makes all go towards the ultimate disintegration.

How does the goddess manage all this? – Like a noble lady of the house who takes care of everybody and tends to all. At other places she is also seen variously as a mother, and more interestingly, as a bride.

In this mantra, Uṣā is described as the mother who takes care of the whole world.

उच्छन्ती या कृणोषि मंहना महि प्रख्यै देवि स्वर्दृशे ।
तस्यास्ते रत्नभाज ईमहे वयं स्याम मातुर्न सूनवः ॥ RV VII.81.4

ucchantī yā kṛṇoṣi maṃhanā mahi prakhyai devi svardṛśe
tasyāste ratnabhāja īmahe vayaṃ syāma māturna sūnavaḥ

Great goddess (Uṣā)! who destroys darkness, arouses the world to make it visible
We yearn to be thine own, the giver of wealth, as sons are to a mother

The sages felt such closeness to the Divine that they never hesitated in comparing It with the best thing that they found in this world. In this verse, the beauty and brightness of goddess Uṣā is being compared with that of a bride who has been decorated by her mother!

सुसंकाशा मातृमृष्टेव योषाविस्तन्वं कृणुषे दृशे कम् ।
भद्रा त्वमुषो वितरं व्युच्छ न तत्ते अन्या उषसो नशन्त ॥ RV I.123.11

susaṃkāśā mātr-mrṣteva yoṣāvis-tanvaṃ kṛṇuṣe dṛśe kam
bhadrā tvamuṣo vitaraṃ vyuccha na tatte anyā uṣaso naśanta

Bright as a bride decorated by her mother, you show your form that all may see it
Shine yet more brightly O Uṣā! as no other dawn has shone before

The prayer is for dispelling the darkness from the heart of a spiritual aspirant that can be done only by the goddess of light. So the prayer is for the new day to mark a new beginning that may outshine all that was ever before.

Like youth among maidens: Āpa

To be pure means to be divine; so, purity plays a very important role in Hindu religion. At the highest level, spiritual purity is attained by becoming one with God, and at lower level, impurity needs to be cleansed continuously through various means. The books on social conduct, known as *Smṛtis,* have huge elaborations on what constitutes impurity and how to regain purity.

Āpa are the divine waters that give their auspicious fluid to the universe like loving mother; and also purify by carrying away defilement like moral guilt, the sins of violence, cursing, lying, etc. In present day Hinduism, *Āpa* has been replaced with Ganga water, or even simply water, that plays an important role in cleansing the body and the mind. In this verse *Āpa* are compared to maidens.

याभिः सोमो मोदते हर्षते च कल्याणीभिर्युवतिभिर्न मर्यः ।
ता अध्वर्यो अपो अच्छा परेहि यदासिञ्चा ओषधीभिः पुनीतात् ॥ RV X.30.5

yābhiḥ somo modate harṣate ca kalyāṇībhir-yuvatibhir-na maryaḥ
tā adhvaryo apo acchā parehi yad-āsiñcā oṣadhībhiḥ punītāt

yābhiḥ somaḥ modate *those waters with which Soma sports* ***harṣate ca*** *and delights* ***kalyāṇībhiḥ yuvatibhiḥ na maryaḥ*** *as a man (sports) with graceful damsels*

tāḥ adhvaryo apaḥ acchā *O Adhvaryu, approach unto those waters* ***parā ihi yat āsiñcāḥ oṣadhībhiḥ punītāt*** *and purify with herbs what thou has sprinkled*

Those with which Soma sports and delights
as a young man with graceful beauties
Go, unto those Waters, O Adhvaryu
and purify with herbs what you have sprinkled

In this prayer *Soma*, an herbal drink preferred by the gods, is being offered to *Āpa* who are expected to favour the devotees. *Adhvaryu,* the priest who pours oblation during Vedic *yajña,* is being requested to prepare *Soma* that will be offered to *Āpa*, the divine waters. *Soma* will then be as frolicking as a young man amidst *kalyāṇī,* the graceful maidens, which *Āpa* are compared with.

This concept of a young man among the maidens was later elaborated in sacred books like *Bhāgavatam* when Sri Krishna sported with the *gopīs* in the divine dance to bless the world with bhakti.

The chaste wife: Agni

This mantra, dedicated to Agni, looks at God in many different ways – as God, king, guardian, and also as a chaste wife looking after her husband.

देवो न यः पृथिवीं विश्वधाया उपक्षेति हितमित्रो न राजा ।
पुरःसदः शर्मसदो न वीरा अनवद्या पतिजुष्टेव नारी ॥ RV I.73.3

devo na yaḥ pṛthivīṃ viśvadhāyā upakṣeti hitamitro na rājā
puraḥsadaḥ śarmasado na vīrā anavadyā patijuṣṭeva nārī

devaḥ na yaḥ pṛthivīm viśva-dhāyāḥ *(Agni is) on the earth like the god (sun) who holds the universe* ***upa-kṣeti hitamitraḥ na rājā*** *abides like a king, (surrounded by) faithful friends* ***puraḥ-sadaḥ śarmasadaḥ na vīrāḥ*** *in his presence heroes sit in safety* ***anavadyā patijuṣṭā iva nārī*** *is like a blameless, beloved wife*

He (Agni) who on earth is like the god all-sustaining
dwells like a king surrounded by faithful friends
Like men who find safety in his dwelling
and is like a blameless wife dear to her husband

Agni sustains the earth and its beings the way the Sun nourishes the solar system. During *yajña*, he is like the king who is surrounded by his faithful ministers and commanders. He is also like a father with whom children find safety. Above all, he is like a beloved wife who looks after her husband.

In another hymn, Agni is compared to a wife who is like an ornament to all.

दुरोकशोचिः क्रतुर्न नित्यो जायेव योनावरं विश्वस्मै । RV 1.66.5

durokaśociḥ kraturna nityo jāyeva yonāvaraṃ viśvasmai

Agni of unattainable brightness; is like a vigilant sacrificer
He is an ornament to all (in the sacrificial chamber); like a woman in a dwelling

As an infant being kissed: Vena

The idea about Vena, the god who is nearly forgotten now, is not much clear in the Veda. Generally speaking, he is equated with the divine light, which can be the light of the lightning amidst clouds, the light of the moon, sun, etc. Vena is also interpreted as the creator god, Brahmā, since the light of Creation emanates from there, and he is also seen as a god of mid-regions, that is, space.

This mantra is highly mystic and difficult to understand, due to which commentators have explained it differently. In this mantra, Vena is the light amidst clouds, driving on the rays of the sun that appears like a chariot, and which seems to move the particles of space into action. The sage, as if, caresses God like a baby in the lap.

अयं वेनश्चोदयत्पृश्निगर्भा ज्योतिर्जरायू रजसो विमाने ।
इममपां संगमे सूर्यस्य शिशुं न विप्रा मतिभी रिहन्ति ॥ RV X.123.1

ayaṃ venaś-codayat-pṛśnigarbhā jyotir-jarāyū rajaso vimāne
imam-apāṃ saṃgame sūryasya śiśuṃ na viprā matibhī rihanti

ayam venaḥ codayat *(see) Vena urges on* ***pṛśnigarbhāḥ*** *(that which is born of) the womb of the sun (rays of the sun)* ***jyotiḥ jarāyuḥ*** *(Vena, who is born of) the womb of the light (of clouds)* ***rajasaḥ vimāne*** *the waters of the space*

imam apām saṃgame sūryasya *at the confluence of the waters and the sun* ***śiśum*** *like a child.* ***na viprāḥ*** *the sages cherish him* ***matibhīḥ rihanti*** *pray with endearments*

See, Vena, born in light, urges on
the waters of the space, born of the Sun
Sages with hymns caress him as an infant there
where the waters and the sunlight mingle

In the morning sun, Vena appears as the light amidst clouds to goad on the clouds, which are born of water and the sun. The god thus looks like a baby to whom the sage offers prayers, which is like kissing a baby with love.

Pṛśnigarbha is he who was born of Pṛśni and according to later scriptures, means God. However, Sāyaṇācārya explains it as seven bright rays of the sun.

Jyotiḥ jarāyuḥ is the light amidst the clouds, as if in a womb. *Rajasaḥ* is a common term used in the Veda to denote particles, which can be of water, dust or of creation. Here it means the particles of the space where clouds are formed. *Matibhī* means to pray, and *rihanti* means to lick or kiss.

God, the baby: Viśvedevā

This mantra too is a highly mystical mantra that can be interpreted variously. Here the interplay of the gods is compared to the kissing of a baby by her mom and vice-versa. The prayer is offered to Viśvedevā, which is the collective body of the gods so that no one is left out.

This mantra is aimed towards Agni and Vāyu (God of wind), who are two important gods in the Veda, praised for their power, bountiful nature and their friendship. In the world, their togetherness creates many phenomena like thunder, fire, speech etc. that make life possible on this earth.

In this mantra, their interplay is described that can be seen during lightning (thunder being Agni and air being Vāyu), or during speaking (speech being Agni and vital energies being Vāyu).

एकः सुपर्णः स समुद्रमा विवेश स इदं विश्वं भुवनं वि चष्टे ।
तं पाकेन मनसापश्यमन्तितस्तं माता रेळ्हि स उ रेळ्हि मातरम् ॥ RV X.114.4

ekaḥ suparṇaḥ sa samudram-ā viveśa sa idaṃ viśvaṃ bhuvanaṃ vi caṣṭe
taṃ pākena manasā-paśyam-antitastaṃ mātā reḷhi sa u reḷhi mātaram

ekaḥ suparṇaḥ *one beautiful winged (bird)* ***saḥ samudram ā viveśa*** *has entered the ocean of air* ***saḥ*** *he* ***idam*** *this* ***viśvam bhuvanam*** *whole world* ***vi caṣṭe*** *contemplates*

tam pākena manasā *with a mature mind* ***apaśyam*** *I saw* ***antitaḥ tam*** *him from close quarters* ***mātā reḷhi saḥ*** *his mother kisses him* ***u reḷhi mātaram*** *and he (returns) her kiss*

One beautiful winged has passed into the ocean of air
from there he contemplates the whole world
With a mature mind I have beheld him from near
his mother kisses him and he returns her kiss

Vāyu, the wind god, is addressed here as *Suparṇaḥ* (lit. beautiful-winged bird), since he moves about without any support like a bird. This characteristic is of God too, who moves everywhere without any support. God/ Vāyu looks at the world below the way a bird looks below from the sky and thus takes a complete picture of what lies below.

God, who is above and who is also inside the heart, is perceived by the sage in the state of contemplation. That same God moves within the body as *prāṇa* (vital air) with the help of which speech is expressed. Speech has been described as Agni in the Veda, and so it is Agni and Vāyu kising each other like a mother and her baby.

One can thus feel the outpourings of love in these prayers by the greatest of sages who saw God as divine, and also as one's own, in an intense personal relation.

In this verse, we find the word रेळ्हि (rel̲hi) that uses the hard l, which is to be pronounced with the tongue curled backward, as in 'clock', 'clove', etc.

God, the dancer: Indra

श्रिये ते पादा दुव आ मिमिक्षुर्धृष्णुर्वज्री शवसा दक्षिणावान् ।
वसानो अत्कं सुरभिं दृशे कं स्वर्ण नृतविषिरो बभूथ ॥ RV VI.29.3

śriye te pādā duva ā mimikṣur-dhṛṣṇur-vajrī śavasā dakṣiṇāvān
vasāno atkaṃ surabhiṃ dṛśe kaṃ svarṇa nṛtaviṣiro babhūtha

śriye te *to acquire prosperity* ***pādā duvaḥ ā mimikṣuḥ*** *(they) offer adoration at your feet* ***dhṛṣṇuḥ vajrī śavasā*** *you are strong for your enemies, the wielder of the Vajra (thunderbolt)* ***dakṣiṇāvān*** *giver of wealth*

vasānaḥ atkam *clad in a vesture* ***surabhim dṛśe kam svaḥ*** *beautiful as heaven to look on*

na nṛto iṣiraḥ babhūtha *you have been like an active dancer*

For prosperity, your devotees embrace your feet
strong, thunder-armed, gracious in your gifts
Clad in vesture, beautiful as heaven to look on
you have been like an active dancer

Indra is described as the divine dancer since he is always on the move. Mighty and yet attractive to look at, he invites adoration by all. Later the concept of God being a dancer was portrayed elaborately in Krishna's character.

God, the lover: Indra

दोहेन गामुप शिक्षा सखायं प्र बोधय जरितर्जारमिन्द्रम् ।
कोशं न पूर्णं वसुना न्यृष्टमा च्यावय मघदेयाय शूरम् ॥ RV X.42.2

dohena gāmupa śikṣā sakhāyaṃ pra bodhaya jaritar-jāram-indram
kośaṃ na pūrṇaṃ vasunā nyṛṣṭamā cyāvaya maghadeyāya śūram

dohena gām upa śikṣā sakhāyam *draw thy friend to you like a cow to milking* ***pra bodhaya jaritaḥ jāraṃ indram*** *O Singer, wake up God the lover!*

kośam na pūrṇam vasunā ni-ṛṣṭam ā *move the hero (Indra) for the gift of bounty* ***cyāvaya magha-deyāya śūram*** *like the vessel filled with treasure*

Draw thy friend to you like a cow to milking:
O singer, wake up God the lover!
Move the Hero for the gift of bounty
like the vessel filled to brim with treasure

Indra, the God, is seen here as *jāram,* the lover by *jaritaḥ,* the invoker of praise, the sage-poet. In other verses, Indra has been likened to a husband going close to the new wife. The epithet of lover for Indra was so widespread that in later literature he was lampooned as being licentious, which ended his glory as the most popular god, and his popularity was taken over by other portrayals of the Infinite like Vishnu, Rama, Krishna and others.

2.
GOD, THE IMPERSONAL

The previous section gave some idea about how sages felt a strong bond with God, which resulted in some very fine prayers that describe the relation between a devotee and God in endearingly human terms.

This section looks at the impersonal aspect of God as described by the Vedic sages. A more complete description of this aspect comes in the Upaniṣads, but we do come across many verses that clearly indicate how God is both personal and impersonal – a tradition that continues even today. Those familiar with the Indian spiritual traditions know how in India God is worshipped as *Ananta* – the Infinite, but they worship It through Lord Viṣṇu. Sri Ramakrishna put it beautifully, 'Women perform a ritualistic worship known as the *"Ananta-vrata"*, the object of worship being the Infinite. But actually, the Deity worshipped is Viṣṇu. In Him are the "infinite" forms of God.' This is the crux of the multiplicity of gods in Hindu religion – as many minds, so many gods!

God, the unknown: Viśvakarmā

There are many in the world who get curious to know about God, which often leads them to spirituality. This idea has been put beautifully through a prayer to Viśvakarmā, who is the creator God. Viśvakarmā was originally used as an adjective of God, the creator. Later the term was used for the god who can create anything in the world, including tools and weapons. At present, he is worshipped as the god of machinery and tools.

यो नः पिता जनिता यो विधाता धामानि वेद भुवनानि विश्वा ।
यो देवानां नामधा एक एव तं सम्प्रश्नं भुवना यन्त्यन्या ॥ RV X. 82.3, YV 17.27

yo naḥ pitā janitā yo vidhātā dhāmāni veda bhuvanāni viśvā
yo devānāṃ nāmadhā eka eva taṃ sampraśnaṃ bhuvanā yantyanyā

yaḥ naḥ pitā janitā *He who is our creator, our parent,* ***yaḥ vidhātā*** *who is the dispenser of all* ***dhāmāni veda bhuvanāni viśvā*** *who knows the abodes of all beings*

yaḥ devānām nāmadhāḥ *who is the name-giver of the gods* ***ekaḥ eva*** *He is one* ***tam sampraśnam bhuvanā yanti anyā*** *(Him) all wish to know though inquiry*

He who is our creator, our parent, vidhātā
who knows the abodes of all beings
Who is the name-giver of the gods –
He is one; all come to inquire about him

God, the supreme, is our *pitā*, the father who takes care; He is *vidhātā*, the dispenser (of the results of karma) through which He provides for all; He is *dhāmāni veda,* knower of the abode, meaning He knows about all, even about those who live in the high heavens – the gods.

He is also *nāmadhā,* the giver of names. The world – physical, subtle and causal – is the play of *māyā* which shows its effect as name and form in this world. Thus, even gods like Indra are mere name and form, or are like waves in the ocean. Who made them so, and who named them? The answer is God. Thus, every name and form in the universe comes from God only.

People, as also the gods, *sampraśnam,* inquire, wonder who God is, and what is His nature? In the Upaniṣads too the gods are depicted as being unware of the nature of God. Here it is explained that in spite of God being the creator etc., people do not know Him and ask in wonder 'Who is He?'

The one divine existence: Viśvedevā

This is the famous mantra, *ekaṃ sadviprā bahudhā vadanti*, which expresses the truth – 'God is one, but sages call Him by various names.' Indian culture and its outlook towards the world are defined by this mantra that stands for unity amidst diversity. The prayer is addressed to Viśvedevā, who is the collective body of the gods headed by Indra. According to Manu, worship should be offered to them daily.

इन्द्रं मित्रं वरुणमग्निमाहुरथो दिव्यः स सुपर्णो गरुत्मान् ।
एकं सद्विप्रा बहुधा वदन्ति अग्निं यमं मातरिश्वानमाहुः ॥ RV I.164.46

indraṃ mitraṃ varuṇamgnim-āhur-atho divyaḥ sa suparṇo garutmān
ekaṃ sadviprā bahudhā vadanti agniṃ yamaṃ mātariśvānam-āhuḥ

indram mitram varuṇam agnim āhuḥ *they speak of Indra, Mitra, Varuna, Agni* ***atho divyaḥ saḥ suparṇaḥ garutmān*** *and there is the celestial Garutmat, the beautifully winged*

ekam sat viprāḥ bahudhā vadanti *The One Being, the wise call by many names* ***agnim yamam mātariśvānam āhuḥ*** *as Agni, Yama, Mātarisvā*

They speak of Indra, Mitra, Varuṇa, Agni
and there is the celestial Garutmat, the winged one
The wise call that One Being by many names
as Agni, Yama, Mātariśvā

The knowledge of the Divine comes only to those who have immaculate character and a serene mind. Because of their achievements they are known as sages. It is these *vipra*, the learned, who came face to face with the divine beings, and some amongst them realized the Reality behind the multiplicity of gods, namely that Supreme Being. It means that Brahman, the ultimate reality, appears or manifests as various deities.

To remind, these realizations are not from some bygone era, rather anyone can have such realizations, irrespective of their religion and faith.

The gods mentioned in this mantra are famous for their special traits – Indra for splendour, Mitra for saving from death, Varuṇa for saving from sin, Agni as the lighted being. Garutmat (later Garuda) is Suparṇa (lit. one with beautiful wings) who is described as sky born. Mātariśvā is one of the names of the wind god.

God has become all: Ātman

It was mentioned in the introductory chapter how Atharvaveda is a collection of Vedic material, which is not used directly in the *yajña*. This created a misconception amongst the Western scholars that this Veda is a later addition, which is absolutely wrong. The Vedas were organized specifically for the purpose of performing *yajña* in which the Brahmin belonging to Atharvaveda tradition superintended the *yajña*. The content of this Veda is as spiritual as spirituality can be – only that it has no direct bearing on a *yajña*.

There are twenty sections in the Atharvaveda, known as *kāṇḍa*. Of these, some sections deal with Ātman, Brahman and cosmological issues. This mantra expresses how God has become everything.

त्वं स्त्री त्वं पुमानसि त्वं कुमार उत वा कुमारी ।
त्वं जीर्णो दण्डेन वञ्चसि त्वं जातो भवसि विश्वतोमुखः ॥ AV X.8.27

tvaṃ strī tvaṃ pumān-asi tvaṃ kumāra uta vā kumārī
tvaṃ jīrṇo daṇḍena vañcasi tvaṃ jāto bhavasi viśvato-mukhaḥ

tvam strī *thou art woman* ***tvam pumān asi*** *thou art man* ***tvam kumāraḥ*** *thou art boy* ***uta vā kumārī*** *thou maiden*

tvam jīrṇaḥ *thou art the old man* ***daṇḍena vañcasi*** *tottering with the staff* ***tvam jātaḥ bhavasi viśvataḥ-mukhaḥ*** *thou exist in all forms*

Thou art woman, thou art man; thou art boy, thou maiden
Thou art the old man tottering with the staff; thou dost exist in all forms

This mantra, the heartbeat of Indian spiritual outlook, shows how everyone in the universe is the face of the Divine. Later, this idea was further developed into statements like 'Thou art That' and 'I am Brahman'. However, this state of unity is achieved only when all superimpositions from 'thou' and 'that' are removed. It is like melting all jewellery into one mass of gold to remove all distinctions.

One has become many: Indra

Creation is a mystery that cannot be satisfactorily explained by science, philosophy or religion. The Hindus came up with a technical term for this inscrutabilty, *māyā*, to explain the phenomenon of one appearing as many.

Māyā is explained variously by different schools of philosophy in India, ranging from portraying it as an illusion, nothingness, and mirage-like. The term is best understood intuitively by considering how a thing appears as something else, as say, in the case of a desert and mirage. Even after one has known the mirage, it continues to be there, befooling others. The most common example used in Vedanta to explain the concept is of the rope in semi darkness being mistaken for a snake.

Māyā is a statement of fact, but it can never be known. It is like one's desire to see darkness, about which one is very much aware. As one cannot see darkness with the help of either darkness or light, just like that, multiplicity (*māyā*) cannot be explained through multiplicity. However, it ceases to exist once the light of knowledge dawns. *Māyā* is thus neither true, nor false – it simply is a state of being which cannot be denied, nor can it be affirmed through the usual methods of dialectic knowledge.

This mantra expresses how Indra appears as various gods like Agni and others. Just in the same way, God appears as all beings by the power of His *māyā*.

रूपंरूपं प्रतिरूपो बभूव तदस्य रूपं प्रतिचक्षणाय ।
इन्द्रो मायाभिः पुरुरूप ईयते युक्ता ह्यस्य हरयः शता दश ॥ RV VI.47.18

rūpaṃ-rūpaṃ pratirūpo babhūva tadasya rūpaṃ praticakṣaṇāya
indro māyābhiḥ pururūpa īyate yuktā hyasya harayaḥ śatā daśa

rūpam-rūpam prati-rūpaḥ babhūva (*Indra*) *assumes* the *various (divine) forms*

tat asya rūpam *and such is his form* ***prati-cakṣaṇāya*** (*that he appears*) *as various manifestation*

indraḥ māyābhiḥ *Indra through his māyā* ***pururūpaḥ īyate*** *appears in many forms*

yuktāḥ hi asya harayaḥ *horses yoked to his (chariot)* ***śatā daśa*** *are tens of hundreds*

Indra assumes the various (divine) forms
and such is his form that he adopts for his manifestation
Through his māyā Indra appears in many forms
the horses yoked to his chariot are tens of hundreds

The millions of gods that we know in Hindu traditions are actually the manifestations of the one god Indra (actually, God). It is Indra who appears as Agni, Varuṇa, Vāyu, Mitra and others by his divine power, known as *māyā*.

He has many traits, of which one is that his chariot has thousands of horses, meaning that he moves very fast and can reach many places simultaneously. But how? – by taking up various forms, *īyate,* implying that the transformation is not real, but is the effect of *māyā*, his divine power.

God – containing the cosmos yet concealed in the drop: Varuṇa

God in Hindu religion is personified for the sake of prayer and meditation, but the idea that He is larger than the largest and finer than the finest, coming from the Veda, is never lost.

उतेयं भूमिर्वरुणस्य राज्ञ उतासौ द्यौर्बृहती दूरेअन्ता।
उतो समुद्रौ वरुणस्य कुक्षी उतास्मिन्नल्प उदके निलीनः ॥ AV IV.16.3

uteyaṃ bhūmir-varuṇasya rājña utāsau dyaur-bṛhatī dūreantā
uto samudrau varuṇasya kukṣī utāsminn-alpa udake nilīnaḥ

uta iyam bhūmiḥ varuṇasya rājñaḥ *this earth is the possession of Varuṇa, the king* ***uta asau dyauḥ bṛhatī dūre-antā*** *and yonder great space*

uto samudrau varuṇasya kukṣī *and both the seas are his loins* ***uta asmin alpe udake nilīnaḥ*** *(yet) he lies hidden in a drop of water*

This earth is the possession of Varuṇa, the king
and yonder the great space
Both the seas are his loins
and yet he lies hidden in a drop of water

Varuṇa is often extolled as a king, as mentioned in *varuṇasya rājñaḥ.* In some verses this idea was extended to imply a monotheistic God, credited with maintaining the moral order, but the idea did not find favour with the Hindus because of its philosophical inadequacy.

This mantra shows how God is the real king whose majesty extends everywhere and yet He is also in the smallest space.

God, the Ātman

The subject matter of the Upaniṣads is Ātman, which is described as infinite and beyond any duality, like good-bad, birth-death, happiness-misery, etc. The idea of Ātman is present in everyone as the sense of 'I', which is a mere identification with body-mind-ego complex, but the real nature of Ātman, which is infinite, is realized only in the depths of meditation, after which life changes forever.

The greatest of spiritual truths is that 'Ātman is Brahman – the individual is one with the universal', implying that there can be no formal worship or *yajña* at the highest level of spirituality. This made many scholars conclude that the Upaniṣads are the product of 'class struggle' in which *Kṣatriyas* (the warrior class) revolted against the Brahmins!

As can be seen in this and in innumerable such mantras that the vision of Ātman had attained full maturity along with the Vedic rituals itself, although such verses were not used in *yajña*.

अकामो धीरो अमृतः स्वयंभू रसेन तृप्तो न कुतश्चनोनः ।
तमेव विद्वान् न बिभाय मृत्योरात्मानं धीरमजरं युवानम् ॥ AV X.8.44

akāmo dhīro amṛtaḥ svayaṃbhū rasena tṛpto na kutaś-canonaḥ
tameva vidvān na bibhāya mṛtyorātmānaṃ dhīram-ajaraṃ yuvānam

akāmaḥ dhīraḥ amṛtaḥ svayaṃbhūḥ *desireless, wise, immortal, self-existent* ***rasena tṛptaḥ na kutaḥ cana ūnaḥ*** *content with the essence, lacking nothing, is He*

tam eva vidvān na bibhāya mṛtyoḥ *one fears not death who has known Him* ***ātmānam dhīram ajaram yuvānam*** *the Ātman – serene, ageless, youthful*

Desireless, wise, immortal, Self-existent
contented with the essence, lacking nothing, is He
One fears not death who has known Him
the Ātman – serene, ageless, youthful

This verse describes the real nature of Ātman, which is beyond any desire, self-existent, etc. The goal of life is to realize this truth about us and be free of fear of every kind, including death. There is no ageing and no death for us once we realize the truth, and until then we keep revolving on the giant wheel of birth-death, happiness-misery, good-bad and other such dualities.

God, the warp and woof

वेनस्तत्पश्यन्निहितं गुहा सद्यत्र विश्वं भवत्येकनीडम् ।
तस्मिन्निदं सं च वि चैति सर्वं स ओतः प्रोतश्च विभूः प्रजासु || YV XXXII.8

venas-tat-paśyan-nihitaṃ guhā sadyatra viśvaṃ bhavaty-ekanīḍam
tasminn-idaṃ saṃ ca vi caiti sarvaṃ sa otaḥ protaśca vibhūḥ prajāsu

venaḥ tat paśyat nihitam guhā sat *Vena (the sage) beheld That Being in the heart* ***yatra viśvam bhavati ekanīḍam*** *wherein the universe has one dwelling*

tasmin idam sam ca vi ca eti sarvam *therein unites the whole, and therefrom it emanates*

saḥ otaḥ protaḥ ca vibhūḥ prajāsu *far spread is the warp and woof in created beings*

Vena beheld that being in the heart
wherein the universe has one dwelling
There unites the whole, and from there it emanates
far spread is the warp and woof in created beings

The mystics have all asserted that God realization takes place in *guhā*, the spiritual space within the heart. The term is used frequently in the Upaniṣads and also in other scriptures. The visions regarding God may take place outside, but the spiritual knowledge always comes from within, and is perceived variously as divine light, form and others within the heart.

This mantra describes the relation of God with the world. Expressions like transcendent, immanent, etc. fall terribly short in comparison to the expression *otaḥ protaḥ*, inextricably mixed. God is the warp and woof of the universe; He is like milk mixed with water. More importantly, the sage asserts that he saw it so! *Vena* is the sage who realized the spiritual truth that Ātman is Brahman.

God has no equal

न तस्य प्रतिमा अस्ति यस्य नाम महद्यशः ... | YV XXXII.3

na tasya pratimā asti yasya nāma mahad-yaśaḥ ...

na tasya pratimā asti *there is none to compare with Him;* ***yasya nāma mahat yaśaḥ*** *whose glory, verily, is great*

There is none to compare Him with
whose glory, verily, is great

The 32nd chapter of the *Yajurveda* (*Śukla*) from which this mantra has been taken has many verses that describe the impersonal nature of God. This mantra explains how God, expressed by the term *tat,* That, has no *pratimā,* equal. The definition of *pratimā* is *pratimīyate yayā sā pratimā* – that with which something is compared. There is nothing in the universe with which God has a likeness.

Some mischievous people misinterpret it to say that the Vedas prohibit *pratimā,* idol worship, which is not at all the meaning of the mantra.

God is beyond any darkness

वेदाहमेतं पुरुषं महान्तमादित्यवर्णं तमसः परस्तात् ।
तमेव विदित्वाऽतिमृत्युमेति नान्यः पन्था विद्यतेऽयनाय ॥ YV XXXI.18

vedāham-etaṃ Puruṣaṃ mahāntam-āditya-varṇaṃ tamasaḥ parastāt
tameva viditvātimṛtyum-eti-nānyaḥ panthā vidyateyanāya

veda aham *I have known* ***etam Puruṣam mahāntam*** *the great Lord* ***āditya-varṇam*** *effulgent as the sun* ***tamasaḥ parastāt*** *beyond darkness*

tam eva viditvā *by knowing Him alone* ***ati mṛtyum eti*** *one transcends death* ***na anyaḥ panthāḥ*** *no other path* ***vidyate*** *exists* ***ayanāya*** *to immortality*

I have known this great Lord
effulgent as the sun, beyond darkness
By knowing Him alone one transcends death
there is no other way to immortality

The sage here asserts that he has seen *Puruṣam mahāntam*, the great Lord who is superior to all others. God, who lords over all, is *tamasaḥ parastāt*, effulgent like never dying light and is beyond the darkness of *māyā*, mind or and any other kind of duality. Knowledge, characterized by oneness, is light; while ignorance, marked by delusion of multiplicity or duality, is darkness.

The sages, who go into the depths of meditation, realize God as divine light within their hearts, so God is often described as the divine light. The result of this realization is *ati mṛtyumeti*, the transcendence of death, which is not only physical death but also the cycle of birth and death. This happens when one realizes God face to face and thus transcends the empire of the mind. Birth and death are realities within this empire only.

Moreover, *nānyaḥ panthāḥ*, there is no other path to immortality and peace. Whatever religious or spiritual path one may take, *mukti,* liberation from the empire of mind, which extends up to the causal world (explained in chapter 1), and which is characterized by life-death cycle, is possible only once one has gained direct knowledge of that which exists beyond. As we will see below, this is indeed the joyous, inevitable destination for all beings.

In another mantra, God is described as the divine light towards which all are moving – some knowingly, others unknowingly.

ध्रुवं ज्योतिर्निहितं दृशये कं मनो जविष्ठं पतयत्स्वन्तः ।
विश्वे देवाः समनसः सकेता एकं क्रतुमभि वि यन्ति साधु ॥ RV VI.9.5

dhruvaṃ jyotir-nihitaṃ dṛśaye kaṃ mano javiṣṭhaṃ patayat-svantaḥ
viśve devāḥ samanasaḥ saketā ekaṃ kratumabhi vi yanti sādhu

An eternal light, swifter than thought, is stationed
among moving beings to show the way
All the gods, being of one mind and having one purpose
move unimpeded towards the One Intelligence

Thus, the Veda declare that the ascent of the human to the Divine starts the moment aspiration is born in the human heart, poetically expressed here as the eternal, unshakeable *jyoti*. What a beacon of hope for the beleaguered billions of today's world!

The best of the best: Soma

A common man is rarely philosophical in his outlook. So, how to put the idea of greatness of God across to such people? The common methods to do this are to present gods/goddesses as being super powerful, to have stories of their wonderful achievements, and finally to show how God is present in the best of a species.

This mantra compares God with the best of a species. To drive the idea home, examples from different groups are taken.

ब्रह्मा देवानां पदवीः कवीनामृषिर्विप्राणां महिषो मृगाणाम् ।
श्येनो गृध्राणां स्वधितिर्वनानां सोमः पवित्रमत्येति रेभन् ॥ RV IX. 96.6

brahmā devānāṃ padavīḥ kavīnām-ṛṣir-viprāṇāṃ mahiṣo mṛgāṇām
śyeno gṛdhrāṇāṃ svadhitir-vanānāṃ somaḥ pavitram-atyeti rebhan

brahmā devānām *Brahmā (king) among the gods* ***padavīḥ kavīnām*** *greatest among the seers* ***ṛṣiḥ viprāṇām*** *sage among the learned* ***mahiṣaḥ mṛgāṇām*** *bull among the beasts* ***śyenaḥ gṛdhrāṇām*** *falcon among birds* ***svadhitiḥ vanānām*** *axe amongst wood* ***somaḥ pavitram ati eti rebhan*** *Soma passes through the filter with a roar*

Brahmā among gods, the leader of poets
sage among the wise, the bull among the beasts
Falcon amid birds, the axe amidst wood
thus goes Soma singing over the sieve

This mantra is dedicated to Soma, which used to be some kind of herb during the Vedic times, about which practically nothing is known now. The juice extracted from it had divine qualities that gave vigour, health and long life. Soma is treated as a god in the Veda.

Padavīḥ kavīnām means the great among the *kavi*. The word *kavi* is a popular term in the Veda, which means a sage.

The word *padavī* means honorific title. It is explained as 'an honour that does not let one slip down from his position.'

The expression *ṛṣiḥ viprāṇām* means sage among the learned. It is interesting to see the use of two similar expressions, *kavi* and *ṛṣi* here, since both these words have similar connotations. *Kavi* is the sagely poet who can see the complete picture of the universe simultaneously, while *ṛṣi* means one who can see through the veil of time.

By using the best from a group to exemplify the Divine, the attention of the common mind is drawn to the fact that the power of God is well manifested in such members. Later, a devotee realizes that God has become the best, and He is also the ordinary – He alone is.

God's many aspects

मन्ये त्वा यज्ञियं यज्ञियानां मन्ये त्वा च्यवनमच्युतानाम् ।
मन्ये त्वा सत्वनामिन्द्र केतुं मन्ये त्वा वृषभं चर्षणीनाम् ॥ RV VIII. 96.4

manye tvā yajñiyaṃ yajñiyānāṃ manye tvā cyavanam-acyutānām
manye tvā satvanām-indra ketuṃ manye tvā vṛṣabhaṃ carṣaṇīnām

manye tvā yajñiyam yajñiyānām *I deem you as the holiest of the holy,* ***manye tvā cyavanam acyutānām*** *I deem you as the shaker of the unshaken*

manye tvā *I deem you* ***satvanām indra ketum*** *O Indra! the banner of heroes* ***manye tvā vṛṣabham carṣaṇīnām*** *I deem you as the chief of the people*

I deem you as the sacred of the sacred
I deem you as the shaker of the unshaken
I deem you, O Indra! as the banner of heroes
I deem you the chief of the people

God is the shaker of all and the strength of the brave. These qualities are best represented in the personality of Indra, as described here. It is really sad that some mischievous scholars concluded from such mantras that Indra was the leader of the chief warriors of the Aryan!

A similar mantra reads:

यस्मान्न ऋते विजयन्ते जनासो यं युध्यमाना अवसे हवन्ते ।
यो विश्वस्य प्रतिमानं बभूव यो अच्युतच्युत्स जनास इन्द्रः ॥ RV II.12.9

yasmānna ṛte vijayante janāso yaṃ yudhyamānā avase havante
yo viśvasya pratimānaṃ babhūva yo acyutacyutsa janāsa indraḥ

Without whose help people never conquer
whom, in battle, they invoke to give them protection
He of whom all this world is but the copy
who shakes things unshakeable, He, O men, is Indra

Although this prayer is addressed to Indra, the implication is absolutely clear that only God can have these qualities, for it is said here that the universe is fashioned after Him.

This and the earlier chapter give a fair idea about how the sages looked at God, and how those ideas have percolated in the Indian psyche. Even today, the most illiterate Hindu, who had even a little exposure to religion, knows the fundamentals of these truths.

IV

CREATION

Who am I? Wherefrom have I come? Where will I go after death? In short, what is the secret behind creation? This mystery tantalizes a sage, philosopher, scientist, as also a common man and a kid. Unfortunately, there is no definitive answer to it in any branch of knowledge. This, in spite of the fact, that every branch of knowledge must address this question and offer a reasonable solution to build itself up from there.

The inscrutability of the process of creation is best understood by an incident between Einstein and Georges Lemaître (b. 1894), who was a Christian priest, physicist and an astronomer. It was he who first developed a definitive formulation of the idea of an expanding universe, and also of what is now known as the Big Bang theory. Till he expounded his ideas and the mathematics behind it, the world of physics had believed in a static universe as described in the Bible.

Lemaitre had based his conclusions on the Theory of Relativity by Einstein. When he explained his ideas of the expanding universe to Einstein, the great scientist is believed to have said, 'Your math is correct, but your physics is abominable'. Later, even after the ideas of the expanding universe, big bang, etc. became popular Einstein refused to accept them and tried to counter those by introducing a concept known as 'Cosmological constant', which never found favour with other scientists. This shows how ideas about the origin of the universe can be quite complicated even for the best among scientists.

The more interesting thing about the theory of expanding universe is the collapse of equations at a particular point, known as 'singularity', signifying that what happened before that point in time and space cannot be said definitively!

In the Vedas, there are two hymns, *Puruṣa Sūkta* and *Nāsadīya Sūkta,* that describe cosmology and creation from two standpoints. In *Puruṣa Sūkta*, creation is described as having come from God, the Lord, whose external form is one-fourth of the whole manifest universe, while the theory of creation in *Nāsadīya Sūkta* is more impersonal, according to which the creative power existed without vibration (*Ānidavātam*) after the dissolution of the previous cycle (*kalpa*). In that state, there is a kind of equilibrium, which is characterized by absence of any kind of motion. When the process of creation is about to begin, there appears mysteriously the power that disturbs this equilibrium, and the creative process restarts.

The later philosophers and poets took up both these concepts to develop and consolidate their system of thought, the most famous of which are Sāṃkhya, Yoga, Vedanta, and the Purāṇic concepts. Every Indian philosophy takes up one of these two models for their theory of creation and presents a working model of the world based on that. Thus, as can be seen, there is a rich tapestry of schools of thought based on the Veda, which enjoyed total freedom to contradict each other, without incurring any risk of judgment, let alone punishment, for heresy.

1.
NĀSADĪYA SŪKTA
Ṛgveda: X.129

Nāsadīya Sūkta is one of the most beautiful, profound and abstract hymns of the Veda, in which the process of creation, as perceived by the sage, is described poetically. The hymn is logically sound, philosophically complete and spiritually elevating. Swami Vivekananda loved it so much that he had translated it in the verse form.

This hymn indicates how the sages went deep into meditation to come up with truths quite similar to those found in the passages of the Upaniṣads. This also shows how the Upaniṣads did not spring up suddenly but had a steady growth from the time of the earliest composition of the Veda.

Before moving over to the main hymn, let us have a look at the ideas of time and space, which play an important role in the hymn.

Time and space

Philosophical questions regarding time and space have been addressed variously by philosophers all over the world. Greek philosophers defined time as a measure of events, and space as something that held objects. From there, matter came to be defined as something that occupies space.

Newton put all this mathematically as absolute space and absolute time, which meant that space would be present irrespective of the presence of matter, and time would flow uniformly across all of space, whether or not there are objects and phenomena that occur in that space and time. Thus, space and time became fixed like an empty box in which matter was put by God, the watchmaker, who fine-tuned the working of the universe.

Einstein's Theory of Relativity changed it first to a four-dimensional Space-Time continuum, where any object, in order to be located precisely, needed the three spatial coordinates, plus the additional time coordinate to be specified. Subsequently, in his General Theory of Relativity, Einstein added Matter to the melting pot, and sort of made it a Space-Time-Matter continuum. These three were now inter-dependent. Take away one, and the other two will collapse. That is how the absoluteness, as put mathematically by Newton, was done away with.

In India, the Sāṃkhya philosophy looks at the universe as Space-Time-Matter-Mind continuum, with each one of these in a constant interplay with the others. So, one cannot consider anyone in exclusion to others.

The Vedanta philosophy, which is nearest to the philosophy of the Veda, talks about Space-Time-Matter-Mind-Consciousness continuum, implying, space, time, matter and mind to be like waves in the ocean of consciousness. These four appear only when there is creation, but after dissolution, these merge in the ever-existing consciousness like waves merging into a calm ocean.

Thus, there is a fundamental conflict between the approach of Western science and Indian spiritual truth. Where the western approach limits itself to 'external', 'observable' phenomena, Indian seekers were at all times practical and made sure to include *lived experience* in the model they developed, which necessarily dealt with both mind and consciousness, being entities without which there is no one around to develop a theory, let alone try to understand it. Clearly, these two approaches are divided by a gulf, which can never be bridged.

Devatā: Paramātmā

Ṛṣi: Prajāpatiḥ Parameṣṭhī

नासदासीन्नो सदासीत्तदानीं नासीद्रजो नो व्योमा परो यत् ।
किमावरीवः कुह कस्य शर्मन्नम्भः किमासीद्गहनं गभीरम् ॥ 1

nāsad-āsīn-no sad-āsīt-tadānīṃ nāsīd-rajo no vyomā paro yat
kim-āvarīvaḥ kuha kasya śarmann-ambhaḥ kim-āsīd-gahanaṃ gabhīram

na asat āsīt no sat āsīt tadānīm *Existence was not then, nor non-existence* ***na āsīt rajaḥ no vyoma paraḥ yat*** *the world was not, neither was the sky beyond*

kim āvarīvaḥ *what covered it* ***kuha kasya śarman*** *where was it and for whose welfare* ***ambhaḥ kim āsīt gahanam gabhīram*** *was water there, unfathomable depth of water?*

Existence was not then, nor non-existence
the world was not, nor the sky beyond
What covered it, where was it and for whose protection?
was water there, unfathomable depth of water?

The hymn begins with the question, put poetically, *tadānīm,* what was there before Creation? The answer is *na asat āsīt,* non-existence was not there. *Asat* has many meanings like *Prakṛti*, imperceptible objects, absence. Broadly it means, the consciousness associated with absence. For example, if it be said that 'elephant is not here on the table', then it is not only a negation of something but it is also a positive affirmation of a negative fact based on a conscious knowledge that involves sense organs, mind and the process of knowing. The verse here states that no one knows what was there before Creation took place, since all the three organs of knowledge were absent then. Mind is born only after Creation takes place, and senses come much later.

By negating the presence of *asat* before Creation, this mantra contradicts the Sāṃkhya and any other philosophy according to which *Prakṛti* (sum total of matter, energy and mind) has an independent existence.

Does it mean that there was some kind of existence? This too is denied by the statement, *no sat āsīt,* existence was not there. The word *Sat* means existence. Here it means perceptible objects. Since the mind or senses were not there, one cannot say that something was there before Creation.

One meaning of *Sat* is Brahman (since it is pure existence), and another meaning is *Prakṛti* (existence after Creation). The existence of *Prakṛti* has been negated in the previous statement, so does it negate the existence of Brahman too, implying *Śunya* of Buddhists? No. Brahman, the pure consciousness, is never the object of knowledge, since it can be known only during the highest state of *samādhi*, where all functions of the mind stop. So, there can be no discussion on the existence or non-existence of Brahman. What the mantra implies is that what existed before Creation – presence or absence – cannot be comprehended by the mind and can never be expressed in words.

It is to be noted that all references like 'know' and 'before', arise in language, which is by definition bound in subject-object duality, thus making all human language incapable of expressing the state of the non-dual, which is devoid of any qualities including 'time' and 'space'. This will be explained in later verses.

This also explains Advaita – non-dualism, which is not monism. Advaita means pure existence with which a person can become one, but one can never know it. Advaita is neither 0, nor 1; it is beyond all these. Sri Ramakrishna had explained this to Swami Vivekananda with the analogy of ten pots of water in which the sun was reflected, thus making eleven suns (ten reflected and one in the sky). If the pots were broken one by one and finally only one was left, then there would be two suns. But if the last pot too was to be broken, then how many suns remained? Swami Vivekananda had answered, 'one'. Sri Ramakrishna corrected him by telling that what remains after that, cannot be expressed, since there is no one to say what remains. This is Advaita – it is beyond any expression.

Continuing with negation, the mantra says, *na āsīt rajaḥ,* particles were not there. The word *rajaḥ* has numerous meanings implying matter. Here it indicates particles and everything that can be created from them, like the different *lokas* of existence that constitute the three spheres of existence – physical, subtle and causal, as explained in Chapter 1.

The usual concept of heaven and hell are not there in the Veda, instead the prevalent concept, fine-tuned over the period, is of fourteen *lokas* that increase in their subtleness, with *Satya* being the finest – *bhūḥ, bhuvaḥ, svaḥ, mahaḥ, janaḥ, tapaḥ, satya*. The lower *lokas* are *atala, vitala, sutala, rasātala, talātala, mahātala, pātāla*. Sometimes these are also called *bhuvana.* In either case, these being composed of matter, howsoever gross or subtle, are collectively known as *rajaḥ.*

So, was there space? The answer is, *no vyomā paro yat,* there was no sky or space. The way earth is covered by the sky, the *lokas* are enveloped by some kind of space. The mantra negates that possibility. Thus, there neither was matter nor space.

As discussed earlier, whatever approach one may take regarding space from the standpoint of Physics, Newtonian or Einstein's, there was neither the presence, nor the absence of any of the foundational entities postulated in these theories.

So, whatever was there, *kim āvarīvaḥ,* what covered it? Nothing. *Kasya śarman,* for whose well-being? No one's.

Every object is for the use of someone. So where was this creation, and for whose enjoyment? The answer is, for no one, since there was nothing.

The idea of Creation in Hinduism is always from water, often referred to by various words like *salila*. In the *Purāṇas*, the idea was taken further ahead when Lord Viṣṇu was described as sleeping on the causal waters. Were those unfathomable depths of waters there, *ambhaḥ kim āsīt gahanam gabhīram*? The answer is another resounding no.

न मृत्युरासीदमृतं न तर्हि न रात्र्या अह्न आसीत्प्रकेतः ।
आनीदवातं स्वधया तदेकं तस्माद्धान्यन्न परः किं चनास ॥ 2

na mṛtyur-āsīd-amṛtaṃ na tarhi na rātryā ahna āsīt-praketaḥ
ānīda-vātaṃ svadhayā tadekaṃ tasmād-dhānyan-na paraḥ kiṃ canāsa

na mṛtyuḥ āsīt *death was not then* ***amṛtam na*** *nor immortality* ***tarhi*** *at that time* ***na rātryāḥ ahnaḥ*** *not night and day* ***āsīt praketaḥ*** *knowledge could be made out*

ānīt avātam *that One, unmoving* ***svadhayā tat ekam*** *breathed by its own nature* ***tasmāt ha anyat na paraḥ kim cana āsa*** *apart from that nothing did exist*

Death was not then, nor immortality
the night was neither separate from day
That One Thing, unmoving, breathed by its own nature
apart from That nothing did exist

Stephen Hawking, the great physicist, had explained the meaning of 'what existed before Creation (big bang)' as akin to asking, 'what lies south of the south pole?' Such questions make no sense.

But, how to explain such ideas to a common man who wants to know the mysteries of God and Creation? This mantra explains poetically how everything was like a solid mass in which nothing was distinguishable.

There was no death or immortality, *na mṛtyuḥ āsīt amṛtam na*. Every religion talks about becoming immortal by going beyond Creation and being with God. Since there was no Creation, the question of death and immortality do not arise.

Tarhi na rātryā ahna āsīt praketaḥ, day could not be distinguished from night then (day and night here are metaphors for the passage of time). Time is a phenomenon of Creation, born along with mind, matter and space. The previous mantra explained the absence of space, while this one explains the absence of time.

Time, known as *Kāla*, finds a special position in Hindu religion. Everything in the world is credited to time, and hence, going beyond time is the goal of all, which can be effected by God alone. All prayers and spiritual practices are aimed at going beyond time and consequently beyond the cycle of life and death.

So, the Supreme Lord, about whom nothing can be known in that stage, stayed *ānīt,* without breathing, that is, without any kind of movement, since it was the state of *avātam,* no air. In that state of unified existence there was no energy in a differentiated form to make things move. The energy that works within and outside is known as *prāṇa*. Living beings are characterized by the working of *prāṇa* within them and hence they are known as *prāṇī* in India. God is no *prāṇī,* so the question of His breathing or not breathing does not arise, as mentioned here.

How did the Lord then exist? *Tadekam,* that supreme One, alone existed. This word contradicts the independent existence of anything other than God. The possibility of the presence of souls, energy, time, mind, or any other such entity is negated.

That supreme One stayed *Svadhayā,* holding its existence by Itself. God in that state held Himself by His own power. Later scriptures and philosophers came up with terms like *Māyā, Prakṛti, Śakti,* etc. to explain the mystical power of God that creates, sustains and destroys the universe. But in the original state, God stayed with Its own power, internalized within It. Sri Ramakrishna used the example of a snake sitting in a coil, and the snake that moves. Brahman before Creation is like the snake sitting in a coil, holding its power to itself, and It is like a snake that moves when the Creation comes into being. Once the Creation begins, and subjects and objects are born, one can freely use terms that best suit them to describe this power.

Apart from Brahman and His inherent power, nothing else existed, *tasmāt ha anyat na paraḥ kiñcana āsa.*

The first two mantras thus show the non-duality of existence before Creation.

तम आसीत्तमसा गूळ्हमग्रेऽप्रकेतं सलिलं सर्वमा इदम् ।
तुच्छ्येनाभ्वपिहितं यदासीत्तपसस्तन्महिनाजायतैकम् ॥ 3

tama āsīt-tamasā gū̱lham-agrepraketaṃ salilaṃ sarvamā idam tucchyenābhv-apihitaṃ yad-āsīt-tapasas-tan-mahinājāyat-aikam

tamaḥ āsīt tamasā gūḷham *there was only darkness wrapped in darkness* ***agre*** *in the beginning* ***apraketam*** *undistinguishable* ***salilam sarvam āḥ idam*** *as one mass of water (was) all this*

tucchyena *emptiness* ***ābhu apihitam yat āsīt*** *covered by mere nothing* ***tapasaḥ tat mahinā*** *by the power of tapas* ***ajāyata ekam*** *that One was produced*

There was then only darkness covered in darkness
undistinguished as one mass of water
Then That which lay covered by nothing
was produced by the power of tapas

Indian spiritual traditions use many words for the cause of the universe, like *pradhāna, avyakta, adṛśya* and others. Here the term used is *tamaḥ*, darkness, implying what was before it, is not known.

Tamaḥ āsīt tamasā gūḷham agre apraketam, there was then only darkness covered in darkness, meaning that there was the primal cause before Creation, but there was no way to know anything about it, since there was no indication of any kind. *Apraketam* means unknowable due to the lack of any distinguishable sign.

The expression, 'darkness covered in darkness' to describe the intensity of darkness, is a marvellous expression of poetic beauty. It implies that everything that is visible in the universe at present, was covered by māyā in unknowability, the way night covers everything making them unknown and unmanifest. Thus, the objects were present in the form of indistinguishable seeds.

One thus cannot speak of the existence of any 'thing' before Creation, since it will be a contradiction. The best that can be said is that Brahman, abiding in Itself, held within Itself the potential for 'becoming' everything. According to Physics, something similar happens when matter-energy remain as one at the time of Creation, and then slowly become more and more gross to create the universe. Different schools of philosophy use this point to justify their standpoint on Creation.

It was all as water, *salilam sarvam āḥ idam,* before Creation – the two important aspects of the world, cause and effect, were mixed up like milk and water. The word *salilam*, water, is often used to denote the cause of the universe, but it is not the ordinary water, but the cause of everything.

Yat, the cause of the universe, which is also known as *Prakṛti*, was covered in *tucchyena,* emptiness, which cannot be said to be empty or full (as explained earlier). Thus, God alone existed before Creation, with His power which did not have an independent existence.

Now that it was time for creating the universe, God began the process by *tapasaḥ mahinā*, by the power of *tapas,* which is usually translated as the heat born of one-pointed resolve. It can also mean knowledge, as in statements like 'God willed that let there be creation'. The idea of God creating the universe through *tapas* is quite common in Indian literature.

With the beginning of the process of Creation, *tat ekam,* that One, that is, *Prakṛti*, which is the cause of the universe, and which till then was merged in God, became manifest by the power of God's will.

God, the unknown, now appeared as *Saguṇa Īśvara*, the personal God, who creates, sustains and destroys the universe.

कामस्तदग्रे समवर्तताधि मनसो रेतः प्रथमं यदासीत् ।
सतो बन्धुमसति निरविन्दन्हृदि प्रतीष्या कवयो मनीषा ॥ 4

kāmas-tad-agre sam-avartatādhi manaso retaḥ prathamaṃ yad-āsīt
sato bandhum-asati niravindan-hṛdi pratīṣyā kavayo manīṣā

kāmaḥ tat agre sam avartata *in the beginning there was desire* ***adhi manasaḥ retaḥ prathamam yat āsīt*** *which was the first seed of mind*

sataḥ bandhum asati niḥ avindan *the bond of the existent with the non-existent*

hṛdi pratīṣyā kavayaḥ manīṣā *sages having meditated in their hearts have discovered by their wisdom*

In the beginning there was desire
which became the first seed of mind
Sages in their hearts gained the knowledge
of the bond that ties 'sat' with 'asat'

This mantra shows the nature of *avidyā* whose effect is in the form of *kāma* (desires), *karma* (resulting action). *Avidyā* is the link between the existence and non-existence.

Just before the Creation took place, *tat agre kāmaḥ samavartata*, the desire arose in the mind of God for it. This is a tricky point. Why should God, who is self-fulfilled, have any desire? Also, how can one know what was there in the mind of God, since only a superior mind can know another mind? There is no logical answer to this, except that the phenomenon is seen from the standpoint of human beings who always desire first and then convert it into action. To caution, it is always added that God's will is no ordinary desire. When it is said that 'God willed' something, it only means that whatever caused it, is completely beyond our mental comprehension.

When Creation began, the first thing was God's will which was *adhi manasaḥ retah prathamam yat āsīt,* the first seed of mind. Thought, will and mind being inter-dependent, the will of God implies God's mind. *Retaḥ* is a common word used to denote many situations where something comes into being. This seed is again no ordinary seed, but it is that cause which impels the *jīva* (embodied soul in the world) to incur *karma* (impressions left in the mind by the actions performed by an individual), and then work out the fruits of their karma. Here is the early evidence of the Upaniṣadic idea wherein 'That' which 'is', conceives that which is 'not', but appears to be, through the power of māyā.

How do we know all this, and why should we believe what is being said here? The answer is that *kavayaḥ,* the sages, *hṛdi pratīṣyā manīṣā*, gained this knowledge through meditation. *Kavi* is *krāntadarśī,* meaning those who can see things in totality (present, past and future simultaneously). So, God is the true *Kavi.* However, the great sages, who have transcended the limits of their minds, also have this power, so they are addressed respectfully as *Kavi*. These sages gained knowledge about God in their hearts with their pure mind. Since most meditations are done by focussing the mind at the heart centre of *Kuṇḍalinī* (explained in the first chapter), hence this term.

In the Hindu tradition, nothing is taken as mere belief, even if it comes from the Veda itself. Anyone, if so inclined, can replicate the steps sages took, purify one's minds, engage in meditation as they did, and find out for oneself. The correctness of these statements lies in their verifiability.

The most important knowledge that the sages acquired in their meditation is *sataḥ bandhum asati niravindan*, the bond of the existent with the non-existent. Creation is not as real as God is, implying that it does not have a permanent reality, whereas God is permanent and absolutely 'Real', as explained earlier. So, the mystery of how these two came together, cannot be solved by an ordinary mind, but can be known by the penetrating and insightful mind of a sage. *Bandhum,* one who binds, is a beautiful word, since it also means friend, implying friendliness to be the binding chord between two persons. In this case God and Creation get tied up.

Mantras 3 and 4 explain how the will to create came in the mind of God. This idea comes repeatedly in the Veda through various expressions. However, this creation was mental, as explained in *manaso retaḥ*. The two mantras also explain the relationship between *sat* and *asat* – inscrutably bound by māyā, but distinguishable by, and in the hearts of humans – a relation which, otherwise, is quite inexplicable by means of conventional reason and logic.

तिरश्चीनो विततो रश्मिरेषामधः स्विदासीदुपरि स्विदासीत् ।
रेतोधा आसन्महिमान आसन्त्स्वधा अवस्तात्प्रयतिः परस्तात् ॥ 5

tiraścīno vitato raśmir-eṣām-adhaḥ svid-āsīd-upari svid-āsīt
retodhā āsan-mahimāna āsant-svadhā avastāt-prayatiḥ parastāt

tiraścīnaḥ *across* ***vitataḥ raśmiḥ*** *their ray was stretched out* ***eṣām adhaḥ svit āsīt upari svit āsīt*** *whether below or above* ***retaḥ-dhāḥ āsan mahimānaḥ āsan*** *seminal powers made fertile mighty forces* ***svadhā avastāt prayatiḥ parastāt*** *below was strength (matter), and over it was impulse (energy)*

Their ray was stretched out
whether across, or below, or above
Seminal powers made fertile mighty forces
below was strength (matter), and above was impulse (energy)

Once the matter and energy, in whatever form, came into being, these filled up the universe like the sun rays covering the worlds. So how were these spread out? Did these go up or down? Straight or inclined? The answer is that even this remains a mystery. However, what can be said with certainty is that the creative forces had split into two, with one acting on the other.

Retodhāḥ, that which holds the seed, implies the *jīva,* since it leaves seeds to impel creation of its likeness. *Mahimānaḥ,* majestic, when taken conjointly with *retodhāḥ,* these mean male and female principles.

However, these two words are explained differently by sages. Sāyaṇācārya explains these to imply *jīva* and its food, while Swami Vivekananda explains these as energy and matter. In either case, these imply the duality of subject-object.

The duality of subject-object, Pūruṣa-*Prakṛti*, *jīva*-food, energy-matter, was placed in such a way that *svadhā avastāt prayatiḥ purastāt,* below was strength (matter), and over it was impulse (energy).

Interestingly, Swami Vivekananda interpreted it to mean energy and matter, with energy working on itself to create the finest form of matter. This he did quite a few years before Einstein published his Special and General Theories of Relativity! One may wonder how Swamiji came up with this amazing interpretation. The answer would be the same for him, and for all other sages, which is that such knowledge comes in a single, intuitive flash that results in instant and total comprehension. As we know, Einstein, and many among other leading scientists, state the same thing – after all the theorizing on paper, experimentation, and poring over the data, they 'realize' the truth in a single all-illuminating, wordless flash; and only then comes the tedious process of putting the truth on paper for the consumption of the world. Remember what we said in the beginning. Information comes from 'outside'. Knowledge is born 'inside'.

There are mainly two types of Creation theories. The first one is where things came out serially, as in the theory of evolution. The second one is the Creationistic theory, according to which God creates beings one after another, in no particular order. This hymn belongs to the evolutionary category, according to which, *ākāśa* (finest form of matter that gives rise to other forms of matter) comes from *ātman,* implying time, space, matter, consciousness continuum. This has been elaborated in Gita (VII.5) as 'The material Nature or matter is My lower Nature. My higher Nature is the Spirit by which this entire universe is sustained, O Arjuna.'

The development of Creation was so sudden and quick like a flash of lightning (for, it is God's creation), that the series could not be distinguished. Note how uncannily this mirrors contemporary scientific thought on the incredibly rapid expansion and development of the universe in the first few picoseconds after the Big Bang.

को अद्धा वेद क इह प्र वोचत्कुत आजाता कुत इयं विसृष्टिः ।
अर्वाग्देवा अस्य विसर्जनेनाथा को वेद यत आबभूव ॥ 6

ko addhā veda ka iha pra vocatkuta ājātā kuta iyaṃ visṛṣṭiḥ
arvāg-devā asya visarjanenāthā ko veda yata ābabhūva

kaḥ addhā veda *who really knows?* ***kaḥ iha pra vocat*** *who can say* ***kutaḥ ājātā kutaḥ iyam visṛṣṭiḥ*** *from where all this came and how Creation happened*

arvāk devāḥ asya visarjanena *the gods themselves are later than Creation* ***atha kaḥ veda yataḥ ābabhūva*** *so who knows truly whence it has arisen?*

Who really knows, and who can say
from where all this came and how Creation happened
The gods (were) subsequent to the (world's) creation
so, who knows truly whence it has arisen?

Creation is a mystery that can never be explained satisfactorily, *ko addhā veda kaḥ iha pravocat.* And not only

Creation but also its purpose remains a mystery, *kuta ā jātā kutaḥ iyam visṛṣṭiḥ*.

The proposition is that though sages, philosophers and scientists may not be able to explain the mystery of Creation, what about the gods who are the rulers of human destiny? The answer is that not even they have the answer to this mystery, since they came into being after Creation, *arvāk devāḥ asya visarjanena*.

To remind, the gods are the faces of the Infinite. They are also seen as embodied but higher beings. In either case, their presence came into being only after the process of Creation was over, so they cannot say for certain how it all took place.

Here, the sage resists all temptation to hold forth as an oracle of knowledge and acknowledges the limits of knowing. They go so far as to challenge the ability of even deities to transcend this limit, and do so without any fear of being deemed a heretic, even though the Veda focus on the worship of the gods.

इयं विसृष्टिर्यत आबभूव यदि वा दधे यदि वा न ।
यो अस्याध्यक्षः परमे व्योमन्त्सो अङ्ग वेद यदि वा न वेद ॥ 7

iyaṃ visṛṣṭir-yata ābabhūva yadi vā dadhe yadi vā na
yo asyā-dhyakṣaḥ parame vyomantso aṅga veda yadi vā na veda

iyam visṛṣṭiḥ yataḥ ābabhūva *He from whom this creation arose* ***yadi vā dadhe yadi vā na*** *he may comprehend it, or he may not*

yaḥ asya adhyakṣaḥ *he who is its superintendent* ***parame vyoman*** *in the highest heaven* ***saḥ aṅga veda*** *he knows* ***yadi vā na veda*** *or maybe he knows not*

He, from whom this creation arose
may comprehend it, or may not
He who is its superintendent in the highest heaven
he knows, or maybe he knows not

The hymn is addressed to the entire humanity, *aṅga,* human beings, to remind ourselves of the fact that only *yo asya adhyakṣaḥ parame vyoman,* the Supreme being who stays in His own majesty and is the master of the universe, *yadi vā dadhe yadi vā na*, knows that he upholds it, or he may not, meaning He alone may comprehend (hold) why and how Creation happened. Other than God, no one else has, or can have, a clue to the mystery of Creation.

This highly popular hymn on Creation makes the Indian stand on the issue unequivocal. God alone existed before Creation. Why and how it took place, can never be known by the human mind, since the mind came later. The sages realize the nature of Personal God in the depths of their meditation, but cannot know the Impersonal God, since He is beyond mind. Through meditation and *samādhi*, a seeker can be one with It by transcending one's mind, but can never know It, since one would have left the mind behind during *samādhi*.

The important thing to know about this kind of hymn is that the sages were not explaining the physics behind Creation, but were explaining to us the nature of God for contemplation and meditation. The aim of the Veda is to lead humanity to freedom. At times, this requires explanation and narration, which are not at all the subject matter of scriptures, as seen here.

2.
PURUṢA SŪKTA
Ṛgveda: X.90

In spite of a large number of gods, goddesses, gurus and sects in India, three practices are universal here – the use of Oṃ in mantras, repetition of Gāyatrī, and the recital of Puruṣa Sūkta.

Every religion has four essential sets of practices for its followers – rituals, recitals, righteousness and realization. The nature and truth about God, as realized by the sages of a religion, becomes the basis for these four aspects. In the ritual mode, one tries to feel the connect with God through religious acts; in the recital mode, one feels the connect through religious stories, songs, etc.; in the righteousness mode, one tries to practise values and virtues that may cleanse them of worldliness so as to become fit for God realization; and in the realization mode one goes all out to attain God by giving up everything. However, these four are not hidebound; these often overlap.

The realization mode is also characterized by prayers to and meditation on one of the three aspects of God – Qualities, Form, and Divine sport. God is often seen as having qualities like love, mercy, justice, etc., He is described as formless or with various forms, and stories about His great deeds, including Creation, abound in most religious literature. Based on these three aspects, God may have many names. Devotees pray, or do *mantra jāpam* of these names and meditates on the meaning of these for their spiritual growth.

Puruṣa Sūkta belongs to the category of *līlā* – the divine sport of Creation. This hymn presents God as the Divine Creator who not only creates everything but has also become everything. Unlike its counterpart *Nāsadīya Sūkta*, it is far more popular because of its simplicity, sweetness and relatability. Consequently, it is used as a daily prayer, during worship, and also for meditation. Bhakti literature of later periods that describes God becoming everything in the world, owe a lot to this hymn.

According to it, the whole universe has emanated from God, the *Puruṣa*, and is sustained by Him. The material, out of which the world is made, is the body of *Puruṣa*, and the creation of past, present and future is only a partial manifestation of the Supreme Lord. The act of Creation is seen as a *yajña* in which *Puruṣa* is sacrificed. The parts of Him, when cut, became the universe and its beings. This is so because Indian sages saw every noble act as *yajña*, an idea that permeates the Vedic outlook, the Hindu sacraments, the philosophy in Gita, and the life of a Hindu in general.

However, the goal of this hymn is not to explain the process of Creation, but to show how God is behind everything in this universe. Such hymns and prayers, even of later times, imply that anyone who awakens to this mystery of Creation, that is, God alone exists, gets liberated.

Puruṣa Sūkta appears in the Ṛgveda (X.90) with 16 mantras. It is also found in the Yajurveda, Taittirīya Āraṇyaka of the Kṛṣṇa Yajurveda, Sāmaveda and Atharvaveda, with some modifications and redactions. The philosophical aspect of this hymn was later used in the Upaniṣads, and the Puraṇas.

Devatā: *Puruṣa*
Ṛṣi: Nārāyaṇa

सहस्रशीर्षा पुरुषः सहस्राक्षः सहस्रपात् । स भूमिं विश्वतो वृत्वात्यतिष्ठद्दशाङ्गुलम् ॥ 1

sahasra-śīrṣā Puruṣaḥ sahasrākṣaḥ sahasrapāt
sa bhūmiṃ viśvato vṛtvāty-atiṣṭhad-daśāṅgulam

sahasraśīrṣā Puruṣaḥ *thousand headed is Puruṣa* ***sahasrākṣaḥ*** *thousand eyed* ***sahasrapāt*** *thousand footed*
saḥ bhūmim viśvataḥ vṛtvā *He, having covered the earth in all directions* ***ati atiṣṭhat daśāṅgulam*** *exceeds it by ten fingers*

Thousand headed is Puruṣa, thousand eyed and thousand footed He having covered the earth in all directions, exceeds it by ten fingers

God is seen here as Personal God who creates, sustains and reabsorbs the universe. Such a God has to have very special characteristics, which is described as being *sahasra śīrṣā*, having thousand heads. Likewise, He has thousands of eyes and legs. The word 'thousand' is often used in ancient literature to denote largeness. God, being the essence of all, each and everybody, inert or sentient, is part of God's body, and so every head, eye, hand, foot etc. in the universe is an organ of God. This is the best description that can be of God with form. This idea was later taken up in chapter XI of Gita to describe the cosmic form of God.

God is addressed here as *Puruṣa,* one who resides inside the body. The body is often compared to a city because of their many similarities, including that of ownership. The owner and resident of the body-city is God, and He is also the owner-resident of the Universe-city. Whatever happens at the micro level, happens at the macro level too.

God is also *viśvato vṛtvā,* that which envelops everything, and transcends the created and the uncreated universe, spoken figuratively as *atyatiṣṭhat daśāṅgulam,* exceeds by ten fingers. The use of the expression 'ten fingers' is symbolic, since 9 is the ultimate digit in the decimal system, used by the Indians since Vedic times. Ten fingers may also mean that yogis realize Ātman in the heart cavity that is ten fingers above the navel region.

The idea of 'exceeds by ten fingers' was later taken up in the *Bhāgavatam* where Yaśodā, the foster mother of Lord Krishna, tried unsuccessfully to tie him to the mortar. To her surprise, she found that the rope, howsoever long she used, fell short by two fingers in tying him up.

The gist is that whatever the idea about God, He will always be more than what the mind can grasp. The Veda thus see God as innermost being, immanent, transcendent and anything else that one can think of.

पुरुष एवेदं सर्वं यद्भूतं यच्च भव्यम् । उतामृतत्वस्येशानो यदन्नेनातिरोहति ॥ 2

Puruṣa evedaṃ sarvaṃ yad-bhūtaṃ yacca bhavyam
utā-mṛtatva-syeśāno yad-annenātirohati

Puruṣaḥ eva idam sarvam *Puruṣa Himself is all this* ***yat bhūtam*** *(and) that has been* ***yat ca bhavyam*** *and all that is to be*

uta amṛtatvasya īśānaḥ *He is the Lord of immortality* ***yat annena ati-rohati*** *and of all that grows with food*

Puruṣa is verily this all, that has been and that will be
He is the Lord of immortality, and of all that grows with food

God not only creates, but He is also all that has been, is, and will be. There can never be anything that is not divine. This has been beautifully expressed in *yad-bhūtam yacca bhavyam*.

Creation in Indian tradition is accepted as being cyclic. Lord Krishna says in Gita that He never rests for a moment, since the process of Creation is always on; God does not create and then goes to take rest. The expression of past, present and future in this mantra shows that the present cycle of Creation, the *kalpa*, is same as the previous one, and will be like it in future too. Nothing changes in the universe fundamentally.

God is *amṛtatvasya īśānaḥ*, the lord of immortality, which means that He is Lord of gods like Indra too, who have relative immortality. Or it may mean that God alone grants *mukti* or freedom, which is immortality. He is also Lord of *yadannena ati-rohati*, that which mounts (grows) with food, implying living beings, since these outgrow their existing condition to be one with the world through food.

The purport of the mantra is that God is the Lord of all – the gods, human beings, lower animals and others.

एतावानस्य महिमातो ज्यायांश्च पूरुषः । पादोऽस्य विश्वा भूतानि त्रिपादस्यामृतं दिवि ॥ 3

etāvān-asya mahimāto jyāyāṃś-ca pūruṣaḥ
pādosya viśvā bhūtāni tripād-asyāmṛtaṃ divi

etāvān asya mahimā *such is His greatness* ***ataḥ jyāyān ca pūruṣaḥ*** *but Puruṣa is greater still*

pādaḥ asya *a quarter of him* ***viśvā bhūtāni*** *is all created beings* ***tri-pāt asya amṛtam divi*** *three quarters are the immortal in heaven*

Such is His greatness, but Puruṣa is greater still
A quarter of Him is all created beings, three quarters are immortal in heaven

The previous mantra shows how God is the Lord of the gods and beings. He is also all that exists in the universe, so is He nothing but the sum total of all this? No, it is not so. *Etāvān asya mahimā* – the past, present and future universes are manifestations of the Lord's powers, but *Pūruṣa,* the Lord, *ato jyāyāṃś-ca,* is greater than that. How much greater? It says *pādosya viśvā bhūtāni tripād-asyāmṛtam divi,* the Creation is a mere quarter of Him, while three quarters of Him is beyond this.

Different religions perceive God as immanent – encompassing or manifesting in the material world; and as transcendent – to be outside the material world. Here God is seen in both the aspects. This idea of God as being both immanent and transcendental comes repeatedly in Indian scriptures. Lord Viṣṇu is often described as *urukrama,* one with long strides, since He can measure the whole universe in two steps. Gita (X.42) also talks of the universe as being a small part of the Lord.

त्रिपादूर्ध्व उदैत्पुरुषः पादोऽस्येहाभवत्पुनः । ततो विष्वङ्व्यक्रामत्साशनानशने अभि ॥ 4

tripād-ūrdhva ud-ait-Puruṣaḥ pādo-syehābhavat-punaḥ
tato viṣvaṅ-vyakrāmat-sāśanānaśane abhi

tripāt ūrdhva ut ait Puruṣaḥ *by three fourths Puruṣa rises above* ***pādaḥ asya iha abhavat punaḥ*** *one fourth of Him becomes again*
tataḥ viṣvaṅ vi akrāmat *and, He pervades on all sides* ***sāśana-anaśane abhi*** *in all that eats and all that eats not*

By three fourths Puruṣa rises above, one fourth of Him becomes again
He pervades on all sides, in all that eats or eats not

Viṣvaṅ vyakrāmat abhavat punaḥ, God spread pervading all over, that is, He manifested the universe constituting gods, men, etc., in one quarter portion, as He had done repeatedly before in the previous cycles (*kalpa*).

Three fourth of Him remained beyond any transformation. This manifestation of God is in *sāśana,* all that eats, and in *anaśana,* that does not eat, meaning that He becomes the living being and He is also the inert, non-living; He is the food, and He is also the eater.

The idea behind this mantra can be best understood by imagining an unfathomable and unbound ocean in which there are areas that solidify during winter and then melt in summer, as say, at the North Pole. The periodic solidification is like Creation. The huge mass of ice of various shapes and sizes are nothing but the ocean, and yet appears differently. Beyond this being and becoming, the ocean remains what it is – unfathomable, unbound.

तस्माद्विराळ् अजायत विराजो अधि पूरुषः । स जातो अत्यरिच्यत पश्चाद्भूमिमथो पुरः ॥ 5

tasmādvirāḻ ajāyata virājo adhi pūruṣaḥ
sa jāto atya-ricyata paścād-bhūmim-atho puraḥ

tasmāt virāḷ ajāyata *from Him (Pūruṣa) Virāṭ was born* ***virājaḥ adhi pūruṣaḥ*** *Adhi Pūruṣa was born from that Virāṭ*

saḥ jātaḥ *He, who was born (from Virāṭ)* ***ati aricyata*** *extended beyond* ***paścāt bhūmim atho puraḥ*** *(and) then created the earth and beings*

From Him Virāṭ was born, and Adhi Puruṣa was born from that Virāṭ
He, who was born, extended beyond, and created the earth and beings

The process of Creation from Pūruṣa is being described. When Pūruṣa (also known as *Adhi Pūruṣa*) desired that there be Creation, the desire took the form of *Virāṭ*, which is the sum total of the universes seen and unseen. The Vedic pronunciation of *virāḻ* is nearly forgotten now, so it is pronounced in its simplified version as *Virāṭ* or as *Virāj*.

Pūruṣa, who is beyond Creation, now entered Creation and appeared as *Adhi Pūruṣa* who is God with form – the creator, protector and destroyer of the universe. *Adhi Pūruṣa* is described as *dehābhimānī*, who is with a body. Thus, we have two *Pūruṣa* described in this mantra; one before Creation and another after that.

Indian traditions look at God in four forms – *Brahman, Īśvara, Hiraṇyagarbha* and *Virāṭ*, in the order of perceivability. *Virāṭ* is God in the form of the universe (*sthūla jagat*), *Hiraṇyagarbha* is the sum total of the subtle universe (*sūkṣma jagat*), *Īśvara* is the sum total of the causal universe (*kāraṇa jagat*) and Brahman is *mahākāraṇa,* beyond any manifestation.

Brahman, the formless, alone exists but It appears in these three other forms due to the covering power of māyā. Depending on the subtlety of the mind, which identifies itself with the respective world, one sees God accordingly. This is the grand truth/ vision behind this mantra.

Tasmāt virāṭ ajāyata implies that *Virāṭ* or *Virāj* is the cosmic body, which comes into existence in the form of an egg (also known as *brahmāṇḍa*) from *Adhi Pūruṣa* (or simply *Pūruṣa*), the supreme spirit. From this golden cosmic egg *ādi pūruṣa,* God, the Lord of the universe was born. God, thus, by His power, created *Virāj* and entered into it, animating it as the *Dehābhimānī Pūruṣa,* God who is now perceivable by the sages as having a body. The universe is dead matter, and so, unless God enters it and lends Its consciousness, the universe will continue to be inert and ineffective.

This kind of evolution, in which one gives birth to the second, which again gives birth to the first, is known as reciprocal origination, which is often found in the Veda. There are hymns that describe Indra as having been produced from various elements, and in turn Indra produced them. *Taittirīyopaniṣad* (2.6.6) says, '*tatsṛṣṭvā tadevānuprāviśat* –

Having created it, He entered into it.' Later literature like the Purāṇas, describe vividly how God creates the universe, and then Lord appears from it as Brahmā, the creator God.

Thus, *Virāj* is the intermediate state of the Divine between the formless God (*Ādi Puruṣa*) and God with form (*Dehābhimānī*), who created all. All this points at the inscrutability of Creation and are used for prayer or meditation, instead of offering an explanation.

God, who appeared from *Virāj, atyaricyata paścāt bhūmim atho puraḥ,* created the earths, moons, etc., and also the living beings. The sequence of Creation is described in the next mantras.

यत्पुरुषेण हविषा देवा यज्ञमतन्वत । वसन्तो अस्यासीदाज्यं ग्रीष्म इध्मः शरद्धविः ॥ 6

yat-puruṣeṇa haviṣā devā yajñam-atanvata
vasanto asyāsīd-ājyaṃ grīṣma idhmaḥ śaraddhaviḥ

yat puruṣeṇa haviṣā *with Puruṣa as their offering* ***devāḥ yajñam atanvata*** *when the gods celebrated a sacrifice*

vasantaḥ asya āsīt ājyam *then the spring became its ghee* ***grīṣmaḥ idhmaḥ śarat haviḥ*** *the summer its fuel, the autumn its oblations*

When the gods performed the yajña, with Puruṣa as their offering
The spring became its ghee, the summer its fuel, the autumn its oblations

India sees every act of the individual or in the cosmos as a *yajña*. The act of Creation by God too is a *yajña*. But there was nothing other than *Puruṣa* when Creation took place, so how could there be a *yajña*? This is being described.

Yat puruṣeṇa haviṣā, God sacrificed Himself as the offering to Himself into the creative fires of Himself.

Yajñam-atanvata, the *yajña* was performed, by the *devāḥ,* senses of this God. *Devaḥ* (plural *devāḥ*) means god and also the senses. The word comes from the root *div*, which means 'lit'. The gods are lit up with the knowledge of Ātman, while the senses are illuminated by pure consciousness coming through the mind. Indian spiritual philosophy also believes that, due to this similarity, every sense organ has a presiding deity. Thus, the god for eye is the Sun. This mantra explains how God alone existed at the time of Creation, so the gods, who are the senses of the Lord, performed the sacrifice the way it is performed by the sages.

According to another interpretation, the gods, *sādhya* – who are the highest kind of sages, and the *ṛṣis*, the sages of the highest order, were born along with *Virāṭ*. Because Creation is not a one-time affair, but is cyclic, so whatever was in the previous cycle has to be in the new one. Since the gods and sages were there in the previous cycle, they have to be in the present cycle too.

A *yajña* requires many accessories like fire, fuel, oblations, ghee, etc. How was the *yajña* performed by the gods, since nothing was there in the beginning? The mantra describes poetically *vasanto asyāsīd ājyam grīṣma idhmaḥ śarat haviḥ,* the spring became its ghee, the summer its fuel, the autumn its oblations.

Why this particular selection of the seasons for the different organs of *yajña*? It is because the spring brightens Creation as the ghee brightens fire; the summer acted as twigs of the *Palāśa* tree, popularly known as flame of the forest because of its bright red flowers, and was fed to the sacrificial fire to make it hotter; and, autumn, with its brilliant hues, was offered into the fire as *haviḥ,* oblations, which colour the flames of the sacrificial fire. However, these seasons are merely indicative of the passage of time, and the *yajña* was mental, and not a physical one.

All things were created from *Puruṣa*, and not from the sacrifices. The underlying idea is that *Puruṣa* Himself is the variety in Creation.

तं यज्ञं बर्हिषि प्रौक्षन्पुरुषं जातमग्रतः । तेन देवा अयजन्त साध्या ऋषयश्च ये ॥ 7

taṃ yajñaṃ barhiṣi praukṣan-Puruṣaṃ jātam-agrataḥ
tena devā ayajanta sādhyā ṛṣayaś-ca ye

tam yajñam barhiṣi *while performing the rituals of the yajña*
pra aukṣan Puruṣam jātam agrataḥ *they first placed the Puruṣa on kusa and sprinkled Him with water*
tena devāḥ ayajanta *thus the gods conducted the sacrifice*
sādhyāḥ ṛṣayaḥ ca ye *the gods, sadhyas and ṛṣis as well*

In the yajña, they first sprinkled, purifying water on Puruṣa
The gods, sādhyāḥ and ṛṣis, thus conducted the sacrifice

The early beings like the gods, *sādhyas* and the *ṛṣis* who come in every cycle of Creation to be with God, got into the process of Creation through *yajña*. So, they spread *Puruṣa* on the *kuśa* grass to be cut into the pieces, or tied Him like a sacrificial lamb to the sacrificial post and then *tam praukṣan Puruṣam jātam agrataḥ,* first sprinkled water on Him to purify in *yajñam barhiṣi,* the rituals of the *yajña*. This process was contemplated upon and not performed in a physical sense.

The word *barhis* indicates the sacrificial straw. Some scholars consider *Virāṭ, barhis,* and *Prakṛti* to be synonymous, so in that sense all of nature is the stage for this sacrifice in which *Puruṣa* is sacrificed.

With this first act of *yajña* completed, *Puruṣa* was then cut up to create the beings. To remind, these verses are not about some sacrifice but only symbolism to convey that God permeates the Creation.

तस्माद्यज्ञात्सर्वहुतः सम्भृतं पृषदाज्यम् । पशून्तांश्चक्रे वायव्यानारण्यान्ग्राम्याश्च ये ॥ 8

tasmād-yajñāt-sarvahutaḥ sambhṛtaṃ pṛṣadājyam
paśūn-tāṇś-cakre vāyavyān-āraṇyān-grāmyāś-ca ye

tasmāt yajñāt sarva-hutaḥ *from that all sacrificing yajña* **sam-bhṛtam pṛṣat ājyam** *yogurt and ghee were produced*
paśūn tāṃ cakre *He then created the animals* **vāyavyān āraṇyān grāmyāḥ ca ye** *of the air, forest, and village*

From that all sacrificing yajña, yogurt and ghee were produced
He then created the animals, of the air, forest, and village

Puruṣa, the soul of all, was sacrificed in this *yajña*, so it is respectfully called *sarvahutaḥ*, all sacrificing. It was through this *yajña* that all the things of the universe were created. The mention here is made only of the important things like yogurt, ghee, animals and birds, but the mantra implies the creation of everything.

तस्माद्यज्ञात्सर्वहुत ऋचः सामानि जज्ञिरे । छन्दांसि जज्ञिरे तस्माद्यजुस्तस्मादजायत ॥ 9

tasmād-yajñāt-sarvahuta ṛcaḥ sāmāni jajñire
chandāṃsi jajñire tasmād-yajus-tasmād-ajāyata

tasmāt yajñāt sarvahutaḥ *from that ultimate sacrifice sarvahutaḥ* ***ṛcaḥ sāmāni jajñire*** *the ṛcas, sāman were born* ***chandāṃsi jajñire tasmāt*** *chanda were born from that* ***yajuḥ tasmāt ajāyata*** *and so were born yajuḥ*

From that sarvahutaḥ, the ṛcās, sāmāns were born
Chanda originated from that, and yajuḥ were born

This is one of the rare mantras that mention all the four styles of composition in the Veda – *ṛk, sāma, yajuḥ* and *chanda* that characterize the four Vedas – Ṛgveda, Sāmaveda, Yajurveda and Atharvaveda respectively.

The idea is that the Veda and its contents have been the same in the earlier cycle too, and these were produced at the beginning of the Creation, the way these were in the previous cycle. The sages of later times only discovered that knowledge.

तस्मादश्वा अजायन्त ये के चोभयादतः । गावो ह जज्ञिरे तस्मात्तस्माज्जाता अजावयः ॥ 10

tasmād-aśvā ajāyanta ye ke cobhayādataḥ
gāvo ha jajñire tasmāt-tasmāj-jātā ajāvayaḥ

tasmāt aśvāḥ ajāyanta *from the sacrifice horses were born* ***ye ke ca ubhayādataḥ*** *and animals with two rows of teeth*

gāvaḥ ha jajñire *from the sacrifice, cows were born* ***tasmāt tasmāt jātāḥ ajāvayaḥ*** *and were born goats and sheep*

From the sacrifice horses were born, and animals with two rows of teeth
From the sacrifice, cows were born, and were born goats and sheep

The creation of various species on this earth and the heaven were not by some God who went about creating by His will, but was done by the process of divine churning, called *yajña*, in which *Puruṣa* Himself was churned.

This can be best imagined by thinking of the whole universe, with its stars, clusters, galaxies, etc., along with the subtle and the causal worlds being churned for Creation, resulting in the creation of all that is there. Sāyaṇācārya put it beautifully, 'Just as yogurt and butter come forth from undifferentiated, but essential milk, different in nature, yet identical in source.'

The expression, *ye ke ca ubhayādataḥ*, animals with two rows of teeth, is a metaphor used for all kinds of animals.

यत्पुरुषं व्यदधुः कतिधा व्यकल्पयन् । मुखं किमस्य कौ बाहू का ऊरू पादा उच्येते ॥ 11

yat-puruṣaṃ vy-adadhuḥ katidhā vy-akalpayan
mukhaṃ kim-asya kau bāhū kā ūrū pādā ucyete

yat puruṣam vi adadhuḥ *when the gods divided Puruṣa* ***katidhā vi akalpayan*** *into how many parts did they shape him?* ***mukham kim asya*** *what was his mouth,* ***kau bāhū*** *what were his arms* ***kau ūrū pādau ucyete*** *what were thighs and feet called?*

When the gods divided Puruṣa, into how many parts did they shape him?
What was his mouth, arms, and what were thighs and feet called?

The sacrifice, in which *Puruṣa* was sacrificed and was cut into pieces, is the source of Creation, meaning, all that is there in the universe is a manifestation of God only. Even then, what became of the head, thighs, etc. of *Puruṣa* when these were cut up?

This question and the answer that follows are meant for deep meditation on the universe as Virāṭ, the cosmic physical form of God. Sri Ramakrishna once saw that the trees and shrubs were all like a bouquet on the altars of Virāṭ.

ब्राह्मणोऽस्य मुखमासीद्बाहू राजन्यः कृतः । ऊरू तदस्य यद्वैश्यः पद्भ्यां शूद्रो अजायत ॥ 12

brāhmaṇosya mukham-āsīd-bāhū rājanyaḥ kṛtaḥ
ūrū tad-asya yad-vaiśyaḥ padbhyāṃ śūdro ajāyata

brāhmaṇaḥ asya mukham āsīt *the brāhmaṇa was his mouth*
bāhū rājanyaḥ kṛtaḥ *the rājanya were the arms*
ūrū tat asya yat vaiśyaḥ *the thighs became the vaiśya*
patbhyām śūdraḥ ajāyata *the śūdra sprang from his feet*

The brāhmaṇa was his mouth, the rājanya was his two arms
The thighs became the vaiśya, and the śūdra sprang from his feet

Exclusivity and superiority of one caste or species over others is rejected in this hymn by implying that whatever is there, has come from God. Continuing the discourse, the hymn says that the four *varṇa* – *brāhmaṇa* (Brahmins), *rājanya* that is, *kṣatriya* and *śūdra* were born from the different parts of *Puruṣa*.

In the earlier times in India, family and family trade played an important role which led to the concept of *jāti,* the caste, which ensured job for every member of a community, howsoever poor. Customs and religious practices were strictly according to the family tradition, which was known as *kula dharma*, and *jāti dharma,* the practices of the caste.

The specialization of occupation implied that there were thousands of castes whose practices and codes of conduct became unmanageable with time. So, these were classified into the four *varṇa*, whose duties and practices were codified loosely. Slowly, these practices became calcified, leading to privileges and exploitations, which was never the aim of the scriptures. The sages wish us to know that everyone in the society and around us has come from God and will return to Him only.

Some people quote this verse to condemn Hindu religion, citing discrimination in its scriptures. The truth is far from it. God being pure consciousness, it is foolish to say that He has a physical head or feet, and it is mischievous to say that God's feet are inferior to His head. Imagine a figure made of chocolate. Will the head of this figurine be more chocolate-y to its feet in any way?

More importantly, the Veda nowhere talk about different heaven or *mukti* for different *varṇas*. The *varṇas* are the overarching umbrella for socio-economic systems, meant to safeguard the interests of the individual and the society. With time, this also gave rise to super speciality in a trade.

The Veda here only give legitimacy of spiritual equality to all.

चन्द्रमा मनसो जातश्चक्षोः सूर्यो अजायत । मुखादिन्द्रश्चाग्निश्च प्राणाद्वायुरजायत ॥ 13

candramā manaso jātaś-cakṣoḥ sūryo ajāyata
mukhād-indraś-cāgniś-ca prāṇād-vāyur-ajāyata

candramā manasaḥ jātaḥ *the moon was born from His mind*
cakṣoḥ sūryaḥ ajāyata *the sun was born from His two eyes*
mukhāt indraḥ ca agniḥ ca *From His mouth were born Indra and Agni* ***prāṇāt vāyuḥ ajāyata*** *and from His breath Vāyu was born*

The moon was born from His mind, the sun was born from His two eyes
From His mouth were born Indra and Agni, and from His breath Vāyu was born

Since the gods were born in the same process as human beings and others, they are not qualitatively superior to human beings, unless they are seen as the masks of the infinite God.

The sun, moon and others are various popular gods of the Vedic times, who in turn came to be seen as the god of the respective organs of the living beings and also of the natural phenomena connected with them. *Sūrya* is thus the god of the eyes and also of the sun in the sky. This kind of double reference is common in the Ṛgveda, especially in hymns addressed to various deities, which incidentally also contain beautiful imageries of nature.

नाभ्या आसीदन्तरिक्षं शीर्ष्णो द्यौः समवर्तत । पद्भ्यां भूमिर्दिशः श्रोत्रात्तथा लोकाँ
अकल्पयन् ॥ 14

nābhyā āsīd-antarikṣaṃ śīrṣṇo dyauḥ samavartata
padbhyāṃ bhūmir-diśaḥ śrotrāt-tathā lokāṃ akalpayan

nābhyāḥ āsīt antarikṣam *from His navel came the antarikṣa* ***śīrṣṇaḥ dyauḥ sam-avartata*** *from His head the heavens arose* ***patbhyām bhūmiḥ*** *from His feet the earth* ***diśaḥ śrotrāt*** *from ears directions* ***tathā lokān akalpayan*** *thus were the worlds created*

From His navel came the antarikṣa, from His head the heavens arose
From His feet the earth, from ears directions, thus were the worlds created

This mantra describes the creation of various aspects of space, like *antarikṣa*, the intermediary space between the earth and the heavens, *dyauḥ*, the highest space or the heaven, *bhūmi*, the physical space, *diśā*, the quarters, which are described as four and at times as ten, and the *loka*, the various spheres of existence. These terms are the essential coordinates for space.

सप्तास्यासन्परिधयस्त्रिः सप्त समिधः कृताः । देवा यद्यज्ञं तन्वाना अबध्नन्पुरुषं पशुम् ॥ 15

saptāsyāsan-paridhayas-triḥ sapta samidhaḥ kṛtāḥ
devā yad-yajñaṃ tanvānā abadhnan-puruṣaṃ paśum

sapta asya āsan paridhayaḥ *seven fencing-sticks were set* ***triḥ sapta samidhaḥ kṛtāḥ*** *and thrice seven logs of fuel were set*

devāḥ yat yajñam tanvānāḥ *when the gods celebrating the yajña* ***abadhnan Puruṣam paśum*** *bound Puruṣa as the sacrifice*

Seven fencing-sticks were set, and thrice seven logs of fuel set
When the gods celebrating the yajña, bound Puruṣa as the sacrifice

This mantra elaborates further how to visualize God during meditation. *Sapta asyāsan paridhayaḥ,* seven fencing sticks were set, but this being a mental *yajña*, there was no physical enclosure as is needed in a *yajña*. It is only to be imagined.

The seven enclosures are also explained as the seven poetic metres of the Veda: *gāyatrī, uṣṇik, anuṣṭup, bṛhatī, paṃkti, triṣṭup* and *jagatī*. The traditional Hindu belief is that the Veda are the blueprint on which the universe is created, and the metres are the boundaries that define the poetry of the Veda. Hence this expression.

यज्ञेन यज्ञमयजन्त देवास्तानि धर्माणि प्रथमान्यासन् ।
ते ह नाकं महिमानः सचन्त यत्र पूर्वे साध्याः सन्ति देवाः ||16

yajñena yajñam-ayajanta devās-tāni dharmāṇi prathamā-nyāsan
te ha nākaṃ mahimānaḥ sacanta yatra pūrve sādhyāḥ santi devāḥ

yajñena yajñam ayajanta *with the sacrifice, the gods sacrificed to Him* ***devāḥ tāni dharmāṇi prathamāni āsan*** *these were the earliest dharma (the holy rites)*

te ha nākam mahimānaḥ sacanta *the mighty ones assembled in heaven* ***yatra pūrve sādhyāḥ santi devāḥ*** *where the ancient divinities and the Sadhyas abide*

With the sacrifice, the gods sacrificed to Him, these were the earliest dharma
The mighty ones assembled in heaven, where the ancient divinities and the sādhyas abide

Dharma, meaning that which holds, can be physical, mental or spiritual. Dharma is the essence of a being and so the goal of the human life is to be established in its dharma, which is to know one's nature as infinite and divine. The path to this knowledge is also known as dharma.

This mantra states how the first rites of dharma were performed in the highest heavens by the gods and the *sādhyas*, the great sages who were at beginning of Creation, where they abide. Thus, by staying connected to God through *dharmic* acts or through meditation, one can be restored to the living experience of one's divine nature.

The practice of *yajña* continues in Hindu religion only because God had initiated the world order by performing *yajña*.

V

HYMNS TO GOD

It was mentioned in the opening chapter how the Veda have hymns to the gods and goddesses as prayers. When a single verse is taken out from these hymns, it is known as a mantra.

The Veda have thousands of hymns that describe the Divine, express immense love for It, or ask for some favour, which may range from wealth to spiritual enlightenment. Mostly, these prayers are not mere beggarly beseeching, but have a sense of rightful demand born of a deep connect with the Divine.

In the two hymns of Creation, discussed earlier, it was explained how the gods, to whom most prayers are addressed in the Veda, were created only after the universe was created. In Ṛg Veda X.72, we find a beautiful description regarding this, 'Brahmaṇaspati (a creator God) produced the gods the way an iron smith works on his bellows.' Naturally the sages could not care much for this kind of divinities, known as the gods, since these had to be as mortal as men but only with much more power and longevity. So, either they were treated as the face of God, or the impersonal aspect of these divine beings was revered more.

The offerings to the gods were, and are, made through *yajña*. When a *yajña* is performed with a sacred fire, these mantras are chanted with certain rituals in which *svāhā* is used at the end to make offerings to the gods, *svadhā* is used to make offerings to *pitṛs* (ancestors), and *vaṣaṭ* is used to make offerings to both of them while standing.

Here, however, we are concerned more about the spiritual content of these hymns. The names of the gods (known as *devatā*) to whom the prayers are addressed, and the sage (known as *ṛṣi*) who came up with the particular hymn, are mentioned.

To remind, hymns of Ṛgveda are used as prayers during a *yajña*, while hymns of Yajurveda are used to pour oblations into the sacred fire. However, these hymns have independent value as the treasure-house of Indian spiritual wisdom.

1.
AGNI SŪKTA
THE FIRST HYMN
Ṛgveda: 1.1

Devatā: Agni
Ṛṣi: Madhuchanda, son of Viśvāmitra

The worship of Agni, the god of Fire, has been common with the Hindus and the Zoroastrians since the most ancient times. However, whereas Zoroastrians have been exclusive

Fire worshippers, Agni happens to be only one of the gods for the Hindus, who acts as the intermediary between the gods and the humans. The oblations poured into the sacred fire of a *yajña* are carried to the gods in the heavens by Agni, and the resulting prosperity of the devotee is often ascribed to him who is seen as the facilitator of it. Even the mortal remains of the dead are placed on the pyre with the prayer to Agni to carry the soul to the higher worlds.

It was customary for Brahmins to perform various *yajña* all through life, of which the most important was *agnihotra*, which was performed twice daily by everyone who had been initiated into the Vedic way of life through *yajñopavīta*. The fire for the purpose was produced afresh by rubbing of two *araṇī*, the fire sticks. In some homes in India, this practice is still carried out. With time, these practices percolated to the level of the masses, who now offer something into the fire at the time of cooking. A religious Hindu even refrains from blowing at the fire, including candles (so, no birthday candles for the Hindus!) to save Agni from defilement.

According to Yāska, the famous commentator of the Veda, the gods belong to one of the three regions – earth, space and heavens. Agni belongs to the earth region. He has around 200 hymns addressed to him and is second in importance to Indra, who is called his twin brother.

According to legends, the gods generated him as a light for mankind, and placed him among men. Another celestial origin of Agni is in the highest heaven, from where he was brought down by Mātariśvā (wind God), like Prometheus; and the acquisition of fire by man is regarded as a gift of the gods. His origin is also in the aerial waters, and he is conceived as latent in terrestrial waters (*badvānala*).

He has many names, of which *Jātaveda,* knower of all beings, and *Viśvaveda,* knower of everything in the universe, are quite popular. Being produced every morning, as in *agnihotra,* he is young; at the same time no sacrificer is older than Agni, for, it was through sacrifice conducted with his help (ref: *Puruṣa Sūkta* chapter) that Creation came into being.

अग्निमीळे पुरोहितं यज्ञस्य देवमृत्विजम् । होतारं रत्नधातमम् ॥ 1

agnim-īḷe purohitaṃ yajñasya devam-ṛtvijam; hotāraṃ ratna-dhātamam

agnim īḷe *I pray to Agni* ***puraḥ-hitam yajñasya*** *the priest of yajña* ***devam*** *divine* ***ṛtvijam*** *head of the sacrifice;* ***hotāram*** *Hotā* ***ratna-dhātamam*** *the receptacle of riches*

I pray to Agni, the priest of yajña, divine, chief of the sacrifice Hotā, (and) the receptacle of riches

The prayer here to Agni by the worshipper is for overall protection, heroic sons and proper supply of provisions. The pronunciation of *īḷe* is a combination of ḍ and l, so it is pronounced both as *īḍe* and *īle.* The sound produced is similar to the sound of 'l' in clock, clove, flower, etc., with the tongue curled back.

Agni is *yajñasya purohita*, priest of the *yajña*, since he works for the success of a *yajña* the way a priest works for the welfare of a king. The term *purohita* also means to superintend, hence this explanation. Also, Agni being the priest of the gods, the expression implies that.

Being at the centre of the sacrifice, Agni is celebrated as the divine counterpart of the earthly priest, and hence is often addressed as priest, *ṛtvija*. He is also the *Hotā*, the chief during a *yajña* who recites from the Ṛgveda. During a *yajña* there are four priests belonging to the four Vedas: *Hotā* from Ṛgveda, *Udgātā* from Sāmaveda, *Adhvaryu* from Yajurveda and *Brahmā* from the Atharvaveda.

Agni is *deva,* the Divine. The word may mean 'one who makes gifts, one who is bright, one who illumines, or one whose abode is heaven.' Agni fits all these definitions. He is also *ratna dhātamam*, the receptacle of the riches, or the possessor of riches, and hence he is a great benefactor of his worshippers, protecting them and bestowing on them all kinds of favours and prosperity.

Dharma is clear that the ultimate giver is God, who bestows good on people through their *karma,* which can be performed through fulfilling one's duty, as noble acts, as also via rites prescribed in scripture. This prayer is about performing Vedic rites to Agni, the visible aspect of God, who in turn is expected to favour the worshipper.

अग्निः पूर्वेभिर्ऋषिभिरीड्यो नूतनैरुत । स देवाँ एह वक्षति ॥ 2

agniḥ pūrvebhi-ṛṣibhir-īḍyo nūtanair-uta; sa devān eha vakṣati

***agniḥ** may Agni **pūrvebhiḥ** ancient **ṛṣibhiḥ** sages **īḍyaḥ** prayed to **nūtanaiḥ uta** and by the present day (sages); **saḥ** may he **devān ā iha vakṣati** bring the gods at the place of yajña*

May Agni, adored by ancient and present sages
Conduct the gods here

The prayer is to Agni, who has been *pūrvebhiḥ ṛṣibhiḥ īḍyo nūtanaiḥ uta,* the object of worship by the sages of the ancient times as also of the present-day worshippers. The word *ṛṣi* means one who has seen, one who has awakened to the supreme reality. The hymns of the Veda are unquestionably among the greatest works of poetry and prayers known to mankind. Yet they are all this and much more; the Veda are indeed the living expression of eternal spiritual truths realized by the *ṛṣis*.

The prayer points at the importance of tradition in matters of religion, which means that it is not that Agni was not worshipped earlier and suddenly someone has taken to his head to start a new kind of worship: fads that one sees popping up in India every now and then, and then vanishing without a trace.

May that Agni *devān eha vakṣati*, bring the gods here, who are being offered the oblations in the sacred fire.

This may sound quite odd to non-believers, nevertheless it is true. A *yajña* becomes fruitful only when the divine beings come to attend it, attracted by the purity of the sage performing it, correctness of mantras, and perfection in the performance of *yajña*. There are ample stories in the Indian tradition to highlight this.

अग्निना रयिमश्नवत्पोषमेव दिवेदिवे । यशसं वीरवत्तमम् ॥ 3

agninā rayim-aśnavat-poṣameva divedive; yaśasaṃ vīravat-tamam

agninā *through Agni* ***rayim*** *affluence* ***aśnavat*** *(the worshipper) obtains* ***poṣam eva*** *which increases* ***dive-dive*** *day by day*
yaśasam *(which brings) glory* ***vīravat-tamam*** *(and is the) multiplier of humankind*

Through Agni one obtains affluence which increases day by day which brings glory, and increases the family

Agni is being extolled as the god whose worship results in *rayim aśnavat,* obtaining of wealth, *poṣameva dive-dive,* which grows day by day, that is the wealth so acquired does not diminish with time. With the wealth thus obtained, one grows in *yaśasam,* fame, which comes about because of the rich gifts that one may make to the deserving. A wealthy person becomes famous not because of wealth but because of the service that they render to the society with that wealth.

The worship also results in *vīravattamam*, the growth of the family and attendants. A common man in the world wants wealth and enjoyment, both of which are exemplified by a rich family and fruitful associations, as prayed for here.

अग्ने यं यज्ञमध्वरं विश्वतः परिभूरसि । स इद्देवेषु गच्छति ॥ 4

agne yaṃ yajñam-adhvaraṃ viśvataḥ paribhū-rasi; sa id-deveṣu gacchati

agne *Agni!* ***yam yajñam*** *the yajña of which* ***adhvaram*** *unobstructed* ***viśvataḥ pari-bhūḥ asi*** *you protect from all sides*
saḥ it deveṣu gacchati *assuredly reaches the gods*

Agni, the unobstructed yajña, of which you are the guardian on every side
Assuredly reaches the gods

It is not surprising that people perform good work; it is a wonder that a noble work at all gets completed, given the host of inimical forces continuously trying to cause disruption and ruin the work. There are innumerable stories in the sacred epics where sages used to face major disruptions while performing *yajña*. The great sage Viśvāmitra had to face so many interruptions that he had to take Sri Rama with him to protect his *yajña*. Even in the present times, it is a part of the ritual during every *pujā* by the priest to throw water around him, uttering *raṅ* and imagining a circle of fire around him for protection from inimical forces.

The prayer here praises Agni that he being the *viśvataḥ paribhūrasi*, protector from all sides, the *yajña* gets performed *adhvara,* unobstructed. The result is that the offering *saḥ it deveṣu gacchati* assuredly reaches the gods. Thus, Agni accepts oblations, assures protection, and makes the delivery confirmed.

The word *paribhūrasi* also has a special significance during a *yajña* when four different fires are lit in the four cardinal points, east, west, south and north, known respectively as *āhavanīya, mārajālīya, gārhapatya, agnīdhrīya.*

अग्निर्होता कविक्रतुः सत्यश्चित्रश्रवस्तमः । देवो देवेभिरागमत् ॥ 5

agnir-hotā kavi-kratuḥ satyaś-citraśravas-tamaḥ; devo devebhir-ā-gamat

agniḥ *May Agni* ***hotā*** *the Hotā* ***kavi-kratuḥ*** *the foremost among the wise* ***satyaḥ*** *true* ***citra-śravaḥ-tamaḥ*** *of most wonderful glory*

devaḥ *the Divine* ***devebhiḥ*** *with the gods* ***ā gamat*** *may come here*

May Agni, the Hotā, the wise, true, of most wonderful glory
The Divine, come here with the gods.

Agni is described in this mantra the way one would describe God – Truth, Glory, Conscious; he is also described as God with a personality who is the provider and fulfiller of wishes. Agni is like the *hotā*, the chief priest, belonging to Ṛgveda, and he is *kavi-kratu*, the wise performer of the sacrificial rites. Kratu implies prowess, which implies the power of Agni as the great divine priest.

Satya, Truth, is a common term used for the gods, while *citra-śravastama* means one who has the most wonderful acquisition in the form of glory or wealth.

Agni is then prayed to bring all the gods at the place of the *yajña* to make it meaningful. A *yajña* is not performed to a faceless and bodiless god but to the living presence of the divinities.

यदङ्ग दाशुषे त्वमग्ने भद्रं करिष्यसि । तवेत्तत्सत्यमङ्गिरः ॥ 6

yad-aṅga dāśuṣe tvam-agne bhadraṃ kariṣyasi; tavet-tat-satyam-aṅgiraḥ

yat aṅga *in totality* ***dāśuṣe tvam agne*** *you will grant to the sacrificer, O Agni* ***bhadram kariṣyasi*** *good you will give*

tava it tat satyam aṅgiraḥ *that shall indeed be your own, O Aṅgirasa*

Whatever good thou, Agni, will grant to the sacrificer
That shall indeed be your own, O Aṅgirasa

Agni has many names related to his origin and deeds. One of them is *Aṅgirasa* or Atharvan, who have different lore to explain the origin. One of them being that he was a sage who sprang from burning charcoals, and hence the word became another name of Agni. According to another account, the sage officiated as Agni during his absence due to some reason, or it may be that the sage *Aṅgirasa* mastered the art of creating fire by rubbing woods for the rituals and hence his name became synonymous with Agni.

Aṅga means limb and it also implies totality of limbs, that is, the whole. Here it is being said that whatever (in totality) noble things you will grant to the sacrificer as a result of the *yajña,* that shall, O Agni, indeed be yours, that is, the credit will go to you. Or it may also mean that this result will be further used for a future *yajña*.

उप त्वाग्ने दिवेदिवे दोषावस्तर्धिया वयम् । नमो भरन्त एमसि ॥ 7

upa tvāgne dive-dive doṣāvastar-dhiyā vayam; namo bharanta emasi

upa tvā agne *(we) approach you Agni* ***dive-dive*** *every morning and evening* ***doṣāvastaḥ*** *daily* ***dhiyā vayam*** *we (come) with a mind dedicated to you*

namaḥ bharantaḥ ā imasi *with reverential homage*

We come to you every day, both morning and evening, with prayer, O Agni
With reverential homage

The beauty of this mantra lies in the fact that the worshipper here is not begging for favours, rather he is certain that his desires for prosperity will be fulfilled as a natural matter of course from his daily worship of Agni, morning and evening, with all reverence. In Hindu tradition this approach is of much importance which we find repeated at many other places, as say, in the *Iśopaniṣad* (mantra 15).

Bhakti is thus an act of love, and the expectation from the beloved is also out of love. There is no shop-keeping attitude in it, nor a beggarly cribbing about it.

राजन्तमध्वराणां गोपामृतस्य दीदिविम् । वर्धमानं स्वे दमे ॥ 8

rājantam-adhvarāṇāṃ gopām-ṛtasya dīdivim; vardhamānaṃ sve dame

rājantam *the resplendent* ***adhvarāṇām*** *sacrifices* ***gopām*** *the protector* ***ṛtasya*** *of ṛta* ***dīdivim*** *the constant illuminator* ***vardhamānam*** *ever increasing* ***sve dame*** *in your abode*

You, the resplendent, the protector of sacrifices, the constant illuminator of ṛta
And ever increasing in your abode

Agni used to be worshipped by the devoted at a particular place known as *yajñaśālā*, which later transformed into the household worship room. The place for public worship evolved into temples. The sacred fire grows in *yajñaśālā* due to the pouring of oblations, hence the term *vardhamānam sve dame.*

He is also being praised for his qualities as resplendent, protector of sacrifices from evil powers, and most importantly, he is the constant illuminator of *ṛta*, which here means the results of *karma* of an individual. Here Agni is being extolled as God who is *vidhātā* – the Lord who makes sure that the results of *karma*, good or bad, comes to its performer.

स नः पितेव सूनवेऽग्ने सूपायनो भव । सचस्वा नः स्वस्तये ॥ 9

sa naḥ piteva sūnavegne sūpāyano bhava; sacasvā naḥ svastaye

saḥ naḥ pita iva *like a father* ***sūnave*** *to a son* ***agne*** *Agni* ***sū-upāyanaḥ bhava*** *be of easy access to us*

sacasva *be ever present* ***naḥ*** *us* ***svastaye*** *for our welfare*

Agni, be of easy access to us, like father to son
and be ever present with us for our welfare

The prayer concludes with the request to Agni to be ever present with the devotee for his welfare, the way a father is always there for his son. This father-son relation is a recurring theme in the Veda.

Thus, this prayer is not about any demand, but as a loving offering to one's dear Lord.

2.
VIṢṆU SŪKTA
THE SUPREME LORD
Ṛgveda: 1.154

The Veda have hundreds of gods as masks of the Divine. With the onward journey of the Indian Spiritual traditions for thousands of years, some of them got confined to the pages of history, some were accommodated as lesser gods, while some of them, like Indra, lost relevance but continued to be worshipped.

However, two popular gods of the Vedic times, Agni and Viṣṇu, continue to be important even today. Agni became the all-pervasive god in the Hindu way of life, finding a place in every *yajña*, including marriage; while Viṣṇu became the ruler of Hindu spiritual hearts through his *avatāra*, which are said to be ten, twenty-four, or even innumerable. This hymn is dedicated to that great Lord.

It may be asked by sceptics that if the Veda are eternal and were given out by the Creator, an idea espoused by some schools of Vedic philosophy, then why have people tinkered with the ideas to make them look to be of human origin? The fact is that the Veda are the perception of countless masters who received these insights while immersed in intense states of meditation, and as the meditation deepened, so did their perception of God, culminating in what we find in the *Upaniṣads.* The Veda are thus a living testament to the evolution of human consciousness and not just a fossil record of seers bygone.

In terms of the number of hymns, Viṣṇu, meaning all-pervasive, occupies a subordinate position in the Ṛgveda, but becomes 'the God' in later spiritual literature. Being God, he is the creator and sustainer of the universe, which he does effortlessly in three steps, which may refer to the creation of the three *lokas*. He is described as the younger brother of Indra, and he is ever ready to help him, as also humankind, in any crisis. An interesting feature of his nature consists in his three steps, connected with which are his exclusive epithets 'wide-going' (*uru-gāya*) and 'wide-striding' (*uru-krama*), with which he traverses the entire universe. RV I.22.18 mentions, 'In observance of laws from here (from heaven), Viṣṇu the infallible guardian, took three steps.'

This quality of the Lord was later elaborated in the story of the king of the *daitya* clan, Bali, when Viṣṇu incarnated as a dwarf Brahmin and asked for three steps of land from him. When Bali agreed to give that, the Lord expanded his form and measured the entire universe in two steps and put his third step on the head of Bali, as requested by the shocked king. Thus, was vanquished a potential threat to the devas.

Two of his steps are visible to men, but the third or the highest can be seen only by the sages, as explained in the earlier chapter on prayer to Lord Viṣṇu. This idea is repeated further in RV VII.99.1, 'O Viṣṇu! Men do not comprehend your greatness, as you are growing through your own self beyond all measure. We, human beings, know from the earth only two regions of the Universe, i.e., the earth and the sky, whereas O God! You know the highest region of the

Universe'; and in RV VII.99.2, 'None of those who are born or who were born in the past has reached the farthest limit of your greatness.'

This hymn, dedicated to Lord Viṣṇu, describes His special qualities, with a general prayer for the worshipper.

Devatā: Viṣṇu
Ṛṣi: Dīrghatmā aucathyaḥ

विष्णोर्नु कं वीर्याणि प्र वोचं यः पार्थिवानि विममे रजांसि ।
यो अस्कभायदुत्तरं सधस्थं विचक्रमाणस्त्रेधोरुगायः ॥ 1

viṣṇor-nu kaṃ vīryāṇi pra vocaṃ yaḥ pārthivāni vimame rajāṃsi
yo askabhāyad-uttaraṃ sadhasthaṃ vicakramāṇas-tredhorugāyaḥ

viṣṇoḥ *of Viṣṇu* ***nu kam*** *right now* ***vīryāṇi*** *the great deeds* ***pra vocam*** *I will recite* ***yaḥ*** *who* ***pārthivāni*** *earth/ universe* ***vimame*** *arrange/ specially constructed* ***rajāṃsi*** *the elements*

yaḥ *he, who* ***askabhāyat*** *(created space as) pillars of support* ***uttaram*** *higher* ***sadha-stham*** *dwelling* ***vi-cakramāṇaḥ*** *traverse* ***tredhā*** *thrice* ***uru-gāyaḥ*** *of wide strides/ praised by the greats*

Earnestly I now recite the acts of Viṣṇu
who made the three worlds with elements
and fixed their support for dwelling
Traversing thrice with wide strides
and hence is praised by the greats

It is in the nature of human beings to ponder over their origin at the individual and the universal level. Two hymns, *Nāsadīya Sūkta* and *Puruṣa Sūkta* – exclusively dedicated to this discussion – were explained earlier. This verse presents aspects of the universe by praising Lord Viṣṇu, who is described as the creator of the three universe, *sthūla jagat, sūkṣma jagat* and *kāraṇa jagat* with the help of *rajas* – the material particles. The highest of these *loka* is known variously as *Satya loka, Viṣṇu loka*, etc. The fourth state of existence, *mahākāraṇa*, is not material in nature, and hence there is no question of its creation.

The sage proclaims that he is going to narrate *viṣṇoḥ nu kaṃ vīryāṇi pra vocam*, the qualities of the great Lord Viṣṇu, *yaḥ pārthivāni vimame rajāṃsi,* who created the universe with the material particles. The word *pārthivāni* is a derivative of *pṛthvī*, meaning earth, but here it implies every sphere of existence where individuality is retained. Individuality implies 'I-ness', which is indicative of the activity of mind. The mind, in Indian tradition, is treated as material, and hence even the highest of the heavens is material in nature, since the individuality of a person continues to exist there.

The Lord then made sure that these spheres do not go loose by way of their material nature, so he created the highest of these spheres, *Viṣṇu loka,* as described in *yo askabhāyat uttaram*, He, who created the highest sphere as the pillar of support for other spheres. The worlds exist because the highest heaven exists as their fulcrum. The spheres are *sadhastham*, where souls reside, with their individuality retained. To reach *mahākāraṇa*, one has to merge one's individuality in the universal by giving up all thoughts of the self.

The Lord is not an indifferent creator; he is *vicakramāṇaḥ tredhā*, one who moves around the universe and can cover it in three mere steps. He is thus all-pervasive and attainable, all through spiritual practices.

The idea of three steps that we come across associated with the Lord, seems to have come from the *Puruṣa Sūkta*, where it was described how the Lord creates the universe and is yet beyond it by three quarters. To remind, these statements are not to be taken literally, but as aids to meditation.

The word *urugāyaḥ* generally means 'one with wide strides.' It can also mean 'one whose glory is sung by the great sages,' as explained by Sāyaṇācārya. This meaning is closer to the nature of the great Lord. The sages of the past and the present sing his glory because of his tremendous prowess and kindness, along with many other qualities, as will be explained in the next verses.

प्र तद्विष्णुः स्तवते वीर्येण मृगो न भीमः कुचरो गिरिष्ठाः ।
यस्योरुषु त्रिषु विक्रमणेष्वधिक्षियन्ति भुवनानि विश्वा ॥ 2

pra tad-viṣṇuḥ stavate vīryeṇa mṛgo na bhīmaḥ kucaro giriṣṭhāḥ
yasyoruṣu triṣu vikramaṇeṣv-adhikṣiyanti bhuvanāni viśvā

pra *towards* ***tat*** *that* ***viṣṇuḥ*** *Viṣnu* ***stavate*** *to sing in praise* ***vīryeṇa*** *might* ***mṛgaḥ*** *a lion* ***na bhīmaḥ*** *mighty* ***kucaraḥ*** *deadly to his enemies/boundless* ***giriṣṭhāḥ*** *residing in a mountain*

yasya *whose* ***uruṣu*** *wide* ***triṣu*** *three* ***vikramaṇeṣu*** *steps* ***adhikṣiyanti*** *to take shelter* ***bhuvanāni*** *beings* ***viśvā*** *of the worlds*

Viṣṇu is glorified due to his might
who is leonine, boundless, praised by the sages
And because in his three wide strides
abide the being of the worlds

Pra tat viṣṇuḥ stavate vīryeṇa, the sage continues to narrate the glory of the mighty Lord, who is *mṛgo na bhīmaḥ,* like a ferocious lion, *kucaraḥ,* deadly to enemies, *giriṣṭhāḥ,* whose praise is sung by the sages

The adjectives used in this line can be quite misleading, since some of these do not match with the personality of the Lord as we know him. Many Western scholars, looking at the literal meaning of the Sanskrit words, came up with translations that are simply preposterous, which includes expressions like 'Viṣṇu is *giriṣṭhāḥ,* lives in mountain caves, and is *kucaraḥ,* cruel ... etc.' Unfortunately, many Indian translators have re-translated these English expressions into Indian languages.

The interpretation, as has come down to us traditionally, says in clear terms that the Lord is unsurpassable in his strength, with which he vanquishes the demons, as narrated in innumerable religious stories of India. This strength is compared to that of a mountain lion who lords over all animals. The term *kucaraḥ* means 'engaged in killing', but according to Sāyaṇa it means 'one who moves through the world unhindered.' Anyone familiar with the Indian traditions would know this to be indeed correct, since the Lord can measure the universe in three steps.

This power to move through the lokas effortlessly makes Lord Viṣṇu incarnate from time to time in various species to give it the evolutionary push. This idea was later taken up in Buddhism to narrate the stories of Jātaka in which Buddha is born in various species on the way to becoming the perfect being. Explaining this, Sri Ramakrishna used to say 'God has different forms, and He sports in different ways. He sports as Isvara, deva, man, and the universe. In every age He descends to earth in human form, as an Incarnation, to teach people love and devotion.'

The word *giriṣṭhāḥ* too has a different meaning than understood by the scholars. The root *gir* means words, and hence the word here means 'the Lord whose praise is sung by the sages.' Thus, Lord Viṣṇu is being praised here as leonine in strength, possessing the power to move through the world, and one whose praise is sung by the sages. The word can also mean that the Lord resides in the cave of the heart of all, which is quite a common expression in spiritual traditions.

Yasya uruṣu triṣu vikramaṇeṣu, the three steps of the Lord, *adhikṣiyanti,* is the shelter, of *bhuvanāni,* all beings, of *viśvā*, the universe. *Bhuvana* also means the spheres of existence. However, that does not change the intent of the verse, since a sphere of existence implies that beings exist there, and includes them in its reference. Thus, the Lord is the shelter of all beings, high or low, believers and non-believers.

प्र विष्णवे शूषमेतु मन्म गिरिक्षित उरुगायाय वृष्णे ।
य इदं दीर्घं प्रयतं सधस्थमेको विममे त्रिभिरित्पदेभिः ॥ 3

pra viṣṇave śūṣametu manma girikṣita urugāyāya vṛṣṇe
ya idaṃ dīrghaṃ prayataṃ sadhastham-eko vimame tribhirit-padebhiḥ

pra viṣṇave *towards Viṣṇu* ***śūṣam*** *strength* ***etu*** *to reach* ***manma*** *prayers* ***giri-kṣite*** *speech* ***uru-gāyāya*** *whose praise has been sung by many* ***vṛṣṇe*** *bountiful*

yaḥ *who* ***idam*** *this* ***dīrgham*** *huge* ***prayatam*** *fixed* ***sadhastham*** *place of dwelling* ***ekaḥ*** *alone* ***vimame*** *to arrange* ***tribhiḥ*** *three* ***it*** *(it is an adverb)* ***padebhiḥ*** *steps*

May this prayer born of strength reach Viṣṇu
the celebrated lord, great and bountiful
Who holds the heights of the universe
and creates it just in three steps

Prayers must not end up being empty words. This verse shows how the sage expects his prayer to reach the Lord by the strength acquired through the rigours of religious practices.

The sage prays, may *manma,* the prayers, born of a heart full of devotion and uttered with all sincerity, *etu* attain (reach) *pra viṣṇave,* Lord Viṣṇu. To reach somewhere, a force/ strength is required, which is expressed by the word, *śūṣam,* strength born of performing *yajña*. The word *śūṣam* means strength, which has been acquired by the rigours of the performing of religious rituals by the sage, indicating that the prayers of a devotee are answered only if he/ she has worked towards achieving the results, or else even the trivial prayers of a child will have to be answered by God, and most days will end up being off-days since kids pray for school holiday all the time! There might also be plenty of death due to ill-wishers. All this does not happen since prayers are answered only if there is the strength of rigorous spiritual practices behind them.

Where does God reside? The answer is given by this beautiful expression, *girikṣita*, one who stays in the highest heavens or one who resides in the prayers of the devotees. God does not become visible to the ordinary, but he is always available in word form, that is, as Veda, for all. The word may also mean that he is attainable only in the highest heavens. God thus resides in the hearts of beings, in words, and in the highest heavens. Bhakti literature of India talks of four kinds of *mukti* for a devotee who reaches such heaven – *sālokya, sārupya, sāmīpya, sāyujya* – residing in that heaven, nearness, similar appearance, and merging into the Lord.

He is also *urugāyāya,* one whose praise has been sung by many sages, which shows the importance of continuity of tradition. He is also *vṛṣṇe*, one who showers gifts on the devotees. After all, of what use would be a miserly God to a devotee!

Some Western scholars have translated *urugāyāya vṛṣṇe* as 'the bull with a huge body,' something that simply does not make sense in the context.

Yaḥ, Viṣṇu, is the ultimate of strength, since he *ekaḥ,* single handed, *vimame,* created, (and) *prayatam*, fixed *idam dīrgham* this huge *sadhastham*, place of residence for being.

The expression *dīrgham prayatam* means huge designated place, and *sadhastham* means place of dwelling, implying the immensity of Creation, in which there is no confusion amongst beings of various spheres regarding their abode.

How did he create this infinite universe? – By taking *tribhiḥ*, three, *it* (an adverb) *padebhiḥ* steps. Lord Viṣṇu is thus inextricably associated with his three steps – a description that is used to express various ideas linking God with Creation.

The idea is that the prayer to the Lord, whose greatness has been described, should reach him by the power of one's commitment towards him.

यस्य त्री पूर्णा मधुना पदान्यक्षीयमाणा स्वधया मदन्ति ।
य उ त्रिधातु पृथिवीमुत द्यामेको दाधार भुवनानि विश्वा ॥ 4

yasya trī pūrṇā madhunā padāny-akṣīyamāṇā svadhayā madanti
ya u tridhātu pṛthivīm-uta dyām-eko dādhāra bhuvanāni viśvā

yasya *whose* ***trī*** *three* ***pūrṇā*** *full/ perfect* ***madhunā*** *divine* ***padāni*** *step/ creation* ***akṣīyamāṇā*** *inexhaustible* ***svadhayā*** *sustaining elements* ***madanti*** *to make happy*

yaḥ u *he, who* ***tri-dhātu*** *three elements* ***pṛthivīm*** *earth* ***uta*** *and* ***dyām*** *space* ***ekaḥ*** *alone* ***dādhāra*** *to hold* ***bhuvanāni*** *the lokas* ***viśvā*** *universe*

Him, whose three places are filled with sweetness
imperishable, giving joy to beings all
He, who alone upholds the earth, sky, universe
that are made of three elements

This verse, as also the earlier ones, is related to the next verse as subject and predicate are in a sentence. Here the Lord is being praised as the one who creates and sustains the universe, while the next one will be the prayer to attain the highest heaven from where there is no return.

Yasya trī padāni, whose (Lord Viṣṇu) three steps are *madhunā pūrṇā,* nectarine and perfect. The word *pada* has many meanings and connotations, but here it implies Creation. The adjective *tri,* three, added to it implies the three steps of the Lord, signifying the limits of Creation, or the three kinds of *loka* – gross, subtle, causal, as explained earlier. The twin expressions of *madhunā pūrṇā* imply sweetness and perfection in the steps of the Lord, or in the creation. These two qualities are *akṣīyamāṇā,* inexhaustible, and so beings of various spheres *madanti,* experience joy, or get maintained *svadhayā,* by their inherent sustaining power.

The idea is that God provides for all and sustains them by providing food for them, suitable for the sphere where one might be residing. The word *svadhayā* means inherent power but can also mean food, which creates inherent power in a living being to sustain itself against the onslaught of nature to rupture its existence.

Yaḥ, who (Viṣṇu) then *dādhāra,* upheld (continues to uphold), *ekaḥ u,* all alone, *bhuvanāni viśvā,* the lokas of the universe. The lokas are fourteen in number, including *pṛthivīm,* the earth and in *uta dyām,* space. The idea is that whatever is in the universe is sustained by the Lord.

The *lokas,* universe and Creation are made up of *tridhātu,* three elements: earth, water and fire. Usually, we find the mention of five elements as the fundamental building blocks of the universe, but sometimes the numbers are brought down to three as in the *Chāndogya upaniṣad* (6.3.3).

The next verse states what is expected of the Lord by the devotee through the prayer.

तदस्य प्रियमभि पाथो अश्यां नरो यत्र देवयवो मदन्ति ।
उरुक्रमस्य स हि बन्धुरित्था विष्णोः पदे परमे मध्व उत्सः ॥ 5

tadasya priyamabhi pātho aśyāṃ naro yatra devayavo madanti
urukramasya sa hi bandhuritthā viṣṇoḥ pade parame madhva utsaḥ

tat asya priyam abhi pāthaḥ *that cherished abode* ***aśyām*** *may I attain* ***naraḥ yatra devayavaḥ*** *where the devotees desirous of attaining the highest* ***madanti*** *rejoice*

urukramasya *(Viṣṇu) of wide stride* ***saḥ hi bandhuḥ*** *he alone is the well-wisher* ***itthā*** *thus* ***viṣṇoḥ pade parame*** *the supreme abode of Viṣṇu* ***madhvaḥ utsaḥ*** *(which is) the fountainhead of supreme joy*

May I attain that cherished abode
where devotees live and rejoice
From there springs, in the supreme abode of Viṣṇu –
the well-wisher of all, the stream of joy

This and the next verse is the prayer of the sage to the Lord, through which he expresses his desire to attain the highest heaven, termed variously as *parama pada, brahma loka,* etc.

Aśyām, may I attain, *tat asya priyam abhi pāthaḥ,* the abode of the Lord which is so much cherished, by *naraḥ yatra devayavaḥ* his devotees who aspire for the highest heaven from where there is no return. The word *pāthaḥ* is translated variously but here it means the heavenly abode. The devotees there *madanti*, enjoy the bliss which is both material and spiritual, as one would expect in any heaven that has been created involving matter, howsoever fine.

Viṣṇoḥ pade, that abode of the Lord, *urukramasya*, of he, whose strides are wide, *saḥ hi bandhuḥ itthā,* (and) who is the friend and well-wisher of all. (That abode) is *parame madhvaḥ utsaḥ* the spring of joy for all those who attain that state. The word *itthā* is often used in the Veda to stress the importance of the idea that is being conveyed.

The devotees of the Lord, who wish to attain the highest, worship him variously and thus purify themselves to attain the abode of that joy which knows no letting up. There is also no fear of hunger, thirst, old age, death, etc. in that *loka.*

A common man does not want *mukti,* liberation, which is the cessation of all desires, but wants best of both the worlds. The Veda, in this hymn and numerous others, talk about the fulfilment of such a wish of the devotees. This is continued in the next verse.

ता वां वास्तून्युश्मसि गमध्यै यत्र गावो भूरिशृङ्गा अयासः ।
अत्राह तदुरुगायस्य वृष्णः परमं पदमव भाति भूरि ॥ 6

tā vāṃ vāstūnyuśmasi gamadhyai yatra gāvo bhūriśṛṅgā ayāsaḥ
atrāha tadurugāyasya vṛṣṇaḥ paramaṃ padamava bhāti bhūri

tā vām *may you two (for whom prayer has been offered)* ***vāstūni*** *restful place* ***uśmasi*** *desired* ***gamadhyai*** *that you wanted to* *go* ***yatra*** *where* ***gāvaḥ*** *light* ***bhūri-śṛṅgāḥ*** *bright* ***ayāsaḥ*** *widespread*

atra aha *here* ***tat*** *that* ***urugāyasya*** *who has been praised by many (Viṣṇu)* ***vṛṣṇaḥ*** *fufiler of desires* ***paramam*** *supreme* ***padam*** *abode* ***ava bhāti*** *shines* ***bhūri*** *with splendour*

May you find rest in that cherished loka
where the divine light spreads wide
For, this loka of Lord, the benevolent
shines with great splendour

A *yajña* is performed for oneself, and at times, for a *yajamāna*, the host (client). When performed for a client, the prayers are for their well-being, as in this prayer, which is meant to be recited during a *yajña*. This concluding verse blesses the *yajamāna* with the prayer by the sage/ priest that the couple may go to the highest heaven.

Nearly every *yajña* was, and continues to be, performed in the presence of both husband and wife. The story goes that when Sri Rama was performing the famous *aśvamedha yajña,* his consort, Sita, was in exile. So, the priests suggested that either he remarry or have a golden statue of Sita made for the purpose of *yajña*. Sri Rama refused to remarry and instead a golden statue of the Divine Mother was made.

The hymn concludes with, *vām*, you two (husband and wife), *gamadhyai*, go to *tā vāstūni* that abode of happiness, which you *uśmasi*, desired. After having a full life of pleasure and achievement on the earth, people want to have a continuation of all that after death too. *Yatraḥ*, that heaven has *gāvaḥ bhūriśṛṅgāḥ ayāsaḥ*, a wide spread of splendour in the form of bright light.

This is one of the verses that met a tragic fate in the hands of the translators. The abode of the Lord is being praised here as being full of light but some translators will have nothing of it, instead they find in these words the Lord to be a big bull and his heaven 'full of cows with large horns'! The problem in all such cases is that the translators relied on certain literal translations of Sanskrit words and let go of many other meanings that fit well. When the context and the tradition is not paid attention to, one then has to end up with this kind of blunder.

The word *bhūriśṛṅgāḥ gāvaḥ* appears to some translators to mean 'cows with large horns', implying that the couple will go to that heaven where the Lord is like a big bull and his place is full of cows with big horns! How preposterous! They forget that Lord Viṣṇu is never associated with cows! Indian traditions always associate the higher heavens with light, and the beings of those heavens as having bodies which are made of light element. To attain that, one has to perform spiritual austerities, or perform certain *yajña*. This prayer is about this.

Why desire for such a heaven? Because *atra aha tat urugāyasya vṛṣṇaḥ paramam padam*, that is the abode of the Lord who is benevolent and whose praise has been sung by many sages of the past, and which is *ava bhāti bhūri*, full of splendour.

3.
SARASVATĪ SŪKTA
GODDESS OF LEARNING
Ṛgveda: VI.61

Mother Sarasvatī, the goddess of learning, is worshipped universally by the Hindus, and the first learning of letters by a Hindu child is invariably done with a prayer to Sarasvatī. Etymologically, the word may mean waters and also speech. In the Veda, it appears both as a reference to a river and as a goddess. At times, the word refers to the Sarasvatī, the river and at other, it is described as the best of mothers, of rivers, of goddesses, who cleanses all and takes away defilement.

In the Nadī Sūkta, RV X.75, Sarasvatī as a river finds a place with Gaṅgā and Yamunā, while in RV X.64.9 there is call for the aid of three great rivers – Sindhu, Sarasvatī and Sarayu. At another place, the sage prays:

बृहदु गायिषे वचोऽसुर्या नदीनाम् । सरस्वतीमिन्महया सुवृक्तिभिः स्तोमैर्वसिष्ठ रोदसी ॥
RV VII.96.1

bṛhadu gāyiṣe vacosuryā nadīnām; sarasvatīm-in-mahayā suvṛktibhiḥ stomair-vasiṣṭha rodasī

– Chant, Vasiṣṭha, a powerful hymn to her who is the most mighty of rivers; worship, Vasiṣṭha, with well-selected praises, Sarasvatī, who is both in heaven and earth.

Over the period, Sarasvatī has been viewed as 'waters that purify', 'that which purifies', '*vāc* – speech that purifies', 'knowledge that purifies', and the goddess that embodies knowledge, arts, music, melody, language, creative work and anything whose flow purifies the self of a person. It is in this last aspect that the goddess is worshipped in the present times.

महो अर्णः सरस्वती प्र चेतयति केतुना । धियो विश्वा वि राजति ॥ RV.I.3.12

maho arṇaḥ sarasvatī pra cetayati ketunā; dhiyo viśvā vi rājati – Sarasvatī, the mighty ocean, illumines with her light; she brightens every intellect

In one of the more sublime expressions, Sarasvatī is described as the mother who nourishes all with knowledge. This verse is so important that it is repeated in the other Vedas too. Due to its importance, the verse is explained here fully.

यस्ते स्तनः शशयो यो मयोभूर्येन विश्वा पुष्यसि वार्याणि ।
यो रत्नधा वसुविद्यः सुदत्रः सरस्वति तमिह धातवे कः ॥ RV.1.164.49, AV 7.10.1, YV 38.5

yaste stanaḥ śaśayo yo mayobhūr-yena viśvā puṣyasi vāryāṇi
yo ratnadhā vasuvid-yaḥ sudatraḥ sarasvati tam-iha dhātave kaḥ

yaḥ te stanaḥ śaśayaḥ *that abundant breast of yours* ***yaḥ mayaḥ-bhūḥ*** *nourishing* ***yena viśvā puṣyasi vāryāṇi*** *with which you nourish the world*

yaḥ ratnadhāḥ *that which is the receptacle of wealth* ***vasuvit yaḥ*** *dispenser of riches* ***sudatraḥ*** *the giver of good* ***sarasvati*** *Sarasvatī!* ***tam iha dhātave kaḥ*** *lay bare for us*

Sarasvatī! That abundant breast of yours, the source of well-being
with which you nourish the world –
The receptacle of treasure, wealth, and fortune
you lay that bare now for us

Unlike a mother of any creature with limited resources, Mother Sarasvatī can nourish the entire universe. This power is implied through *śaśayo stanaḥ* – abundant breasts, which is not about worldly food but about knowledge.

Those who strive for knowledge and attain it, acquire *vasuvidyaḥ sudatraḥ* – riches and fortune. Knowledge is power, wealth, fame – everything. These do not come through any divine intervention, but only through one's effort, aided by the grace of God. So, the worshipper prays to the Divine Mother that he too may be blessed to attain all that he desires, and hence she has to *dhātave kaḥ* – get into the act of breastfeeding.

Ṛṣi: Bharadvāja, son of Bṛhaspati
Devatā: Sarasvatī

In this hymn (ṚV VI.61), Sarasvatī, the goddess of learning, is physically represented by the river, and also by the goddess. The words used in the hymn seem to swing from one aspect of Sarasvatī to the other but in reality, the prayer is to the goddess only.

Bharadvāja, the sage-poet of this hymn, is one of the great sages of India. In Ramayana, we come across him (or some descendant of his) who lived near the *saṅgama* (confluence) of Ganga, Yamunā and the invisible Sarasvatī (near Prayagraj). The sage was renowned for his spiritual powers and simple way of living. It is described there how he created heavenly luxuries by the power of chants from the Veda for the army of Bharata, the brother of Sri Rama.

इयमददाद्रभसमृणच्युतं दिवोदासं वध्र्यश्वाय दाशुषे ।
या शश्वन्तमाचखादावसं पणिं ता ते दात्राणि तविषा सरस्वति ॥ 1

iyam-adadād-rabhasam-ṛṇacyutaṃ divodāsaṃ vadhryaśvāya-dāśuṣe

yā śaśvantam-ācakhādāvasaṃ paṇiṃ tā te dātrāṇi taviṣā sarasvati

iyam *she* ***adadāt*** *gave* ***rabhasam*** *powerful* ***ṛṇa-cyutam*** *to make one free of debts* ***divaḥ-dāsam*** *Divodāsa* ***vadhri-aśvāya*** *to Vadhryaśva* ***dāśuṣe*** *performer of religious acts*

yā *she* ***śaśvantam*** *innumerable* ***ācakhāda avasam*** *self-centred and hoarder* ***paṇim*** *Paṇis* ***tā*** *them* ***te dātrāṇi*** *your bounty* ***taviṣā*** *huge* ***sarasvati*** *Sarasvatī*

She gave to the worshipper, Vadhryaśva, a son Divodāsa
endowed with speed, and acquitting the debt
She, who destroyed the hoarder, self-centred Paṇis
and great are your bounties, Sarasvatī

The verse refers to an ancient story according to which there was a sage named *Vadhryaśva,* who fell under mortal debt from which he was released by his great son, *Divodāsa* who became a successful king. Later, *Divodāsa* became a legendary figure, with different stories centering him, incorporated in the epical works. According to Valmiki's Ramayana, he was the brother-in-law of king Daśaratha, father of Sri Rama. This verse praises Goddess Sarasvatī for the success of *Divodāsa* in the past.

Paṇis literally means those who are self-centred. In some mythological stories of the Veda, they, as also *dasyus* and *vṛtras*, are narrated to be some kind of robbers or dark forces who stole the cows of the noble persons including the sage Aṅgirasa who performed *yajña* to get his cows back. Then, with the intervention of Indra, the robbers were subdued and the cows liberated.

This legend reads like any other story of the victory of good over evil. But, are the Veda really about such commonplace legends, stories, glorification of some heroes as one finds in European folklore? Impossible. Indian tradition is full of stories between *dharma* and *adharma*. That is why most Indian mystics and philosophers refuse to take the story at face value and assert that it is a deep spiritual reality, according to which a spiritual person loses his inner light (*go*, lit. cows, but it also means light) to the darker aspects of his mind. He then performs inner *yajña*, which helps him get back his spiritual powers.

This indeed makes sense. The mantra explains that the rise of *Divodāsa* and the destruction of *Paṇis* happened because of the grace of Sarasvatī on the worshippers. The hymn here wishes for her grace to be on those who pray to her.

The next verse is addressed to Sarasvatī, the river.

इयं शुष्मेभिर्बिसखा इवारुजत्सानु गिरीणां तविषेभिरूर्मिभिः ।
पारावतघ्नीमवसे सुवृक्तिभिः सरस्वतीमा विवासेम धीतिभिः ॥ 2

iyaṃ śuṣmebhir-bisakhā ivārujat-sānu girīṇāṃ taviṣebhir-ūrmibhiḥ

pārāvataghnīm-avase suvṛktibhiḥ sarasvatīmā vivāsema dhītibhiḥ

iyam *this* ***śuṣmebhiḥ*** *by its vigour* ***bisakhāḥ iva*** *like a digger of lotus stems* ***arujat*** *to break like* ***sānu*** *ridge* ***girīṇām*** *of the mountains* ***taviṣebhiḥ*** *huge* ***ūrmibhiḥ*** *waves*

pārāvat-aghnīm *slayer of the peaks* ***avase*** *support* ***suvṛktibhiḥ*** *by prayers* ***sarasvatīm*** *Sarasvatī* ***ā vivāsema*** *to serve* ***dhītibhiḥ*** *sacred acts*

With her mighty waves she breaks down the precipices of the mountains
like a digger breaking mud for the lotus stalks
We pray for our protection with prayers and rites
to Sarasvatī, the breaker of both her banks

Sarasvatī, the goddess, is best represented by the mighty river named after her. This river breaks through the mountain, jumps over precipices and seems to wash away its banks by its mighty flow. The prayer is to that might.

Even at the superficial level, this verse demonstrates a sophisticated understanding of the processes of geological erosion, unmatched in contemporary literature, if any.

Nevertheless, a deeper meaning, with spiritual implications, would be that we pray to the Goddess that the flow of knowledge to her devotees stays unimpeded. Even the most ignorant can overcome his dense ignorance the way a digger breaks through the mud.

सरस्वति देवनिदो नि बर्हय प्रजां विश्वस्य बृसयस्य मायिनः ।
उत क्षितिभ्योऽवनीरविन्दो विषमेभ्यो अस्रवो वाजिनीवति ॥ 3

sarasvati devanido ni barhaya prajāṃ viśvasya bṛsayasya māyinaḥ
uta kṣitibhyo-vanīr-avindo viṣamebhyo asravo vājinīvati

sarasvati *Sarasvatī* ***devanidaḥ*** *the revilers of the gods* ***ni barhaya*** *to destroy* ***prajām*** *folks* ***viśvasya*** *wide-spread* ***bṛsayasya māyinaḥ*** *offspring of Bṛsaya, the deluder*

uta *and* ***kṣitibhyaḥ*** *men* ***avanīḥ*** *land (taken away by the asuras)* ***avindaḥ*** *to get back* ***viṣam*** *water* ***ebhyaḥ*** *for men* ***asravaḥ*** *to rain* ***vājinīvati*** *powerful*

Destroy, Sarasvatī, the revilers of the gods
the offspring of the universal deluder, Bṛsaya
Giver of sustenance, you have acquired (recovered) for men the lands
and have showered water upon them

This verse has reference to an ancient lore, according to which Tvaṣṭā, one of whose names is Bṛsaya, had lost his son, Viśvarūpa, to Indra. To take revenge, Tvaṣṭā performed a sacrifice so that his son may be able to kill Indra. During the *yajña*, Sarasvatī made the priest pronounce the mantra a bit wrongly to mean ‘may he be born of whom Indra is the slayer'. So, even before Vṛtra was born, he was fore-doomed by the wrong accentuation to be put to death by Indra. This story is often used to lay stress upon the importance of correctness of pronunciation and intonation of the Vedic mantra, as mentioned in the first chapter.

The *asuras* are the enemies of the gods, and they want to be victorious all the time. The gods get quite frightened whenever a powerful asura is born in that clan. They then have to take help of the Divine to get back whatever the asuras took away from them.

viṣamebhyo asravo vājinīvati – Sarasvatī is being described here as one who made the victory of Indra possible against the *asura*. She has also made it possible for men to live on the banks of the river named after her. It may also mean that she makes it possible for men to be wise and spiritual when she rains her grace on them.

The use of metaphor is quite liberal in this hymn.

प्र णो देवी सरस्वती वाजेभिर्वाजिनीवती । धीनामवित्र्यवतु ॥ 4

pra ṇo devī sarasvatī vājebhir-vājinīvatī; dhīnāmavitry-avatu

pra *especially* ***naḥ*** *our* ***devī sarasvatī*** *goddess sarasvatī* ***vājebhiḥ*** *with vigour* ***vājinī-vatī*** *the goddess of vigour;* ***dhīnām*** *intellect* ***avitrī*** *the protector* ***avatu*** *protect*

May Goddess Sarasvatī, rich in power, give us vigour
and protect us by enriching our intellect

This mantra reminds one of the beautiful Gāyatrī mantra, whose import is same as of this one.

Sarasvatī is *vājinīvatī*, full of vigour. The word *vāja* has many meanings, ranging from food grains to strength and vigour. However, taking the second line into consideration, the meaning of *vāja* and its derivatives has to be vigour and strength.

dhīnām avitry avatu – Sarasvatī is the goddess of intellect too, so the sage prays that his intellect be protected and also enhanced.

This mantra is used as prayer for a bright intellect.

यस्त्वा देवि सरस्वत्युपब्रूते धने हिते । इन्द्रं न वृत्रतूर्ये ॥ 5

yastvā devi sarasvaty-upabrūte dhane hite; indraṃ na vṛtratūrye

yaḥ *whosoever* ***tvā*** *to you* ***devi sarasvati*** *Devī Sarasvatī* ***upabrūte*** *prays* ***dhane hite*** *for welfare*; ***indram na*** *like Indra (did)* ***vṛtra-tūrye*** conquest of enemies

Devī Sarasvatī, be gracious unto those who pray to you
the way you protected Indra in the battle

It refers to a layered statement, which may be pointing at Indra's battle with Vṛtra, the famous Puranic king of the *asura* race; or it may simply be talking about the fight of good against evil. The word *vṛtra-tūrye* means 'the conquest of enemies', which may have evolved with time into the character of King Vṛtra. In either case, the prayer is to Mother Sarasvatī since she helped Indra win the war by increasing his mental powers.

The prayer is for the Mother to be gracious unto those who pray to her the way she had been to Indra.

त्वं देवि सरस्वत्यवा वाजेषु वाजिनि । रदा पूषेव नः सनिम् ॥ 6

tvaṃ devi sarasvaty-avā vājeṣu vājini; radā pūṣeva naḥ sanim

tvam *you are* ***devi sarasvati*** *Goddess Sarasvatī* ***ava vājeṣu vājini*** *the goddess of wealth, splendour and strength;* ***rada*** *to distribute* ***pūṣā-iva*** *like Pūṣan* ***naḥ*** *to us* ***sanim*** *desirable*

Goddess Sarasvatī, strong in wealth and power; bless us as Pūṣan does

Pūṣan is the God who nourishes the universe. Here the sage prays to Goddess Sarasvatī to be as benevolent as *Pūṣan*.

As explained earlier in this hymn, *vāj* means both worldly gains and strength. One can thus interpret the verses depending on one's mentality.

Note also how *rada* becomes *radā* in the mantra because of the rules of poetry.

उत स्या नः सरस्वती घोरा हिरण्यवर्तनिः । वृत्रघ्नी वष्टि सुष्टुतिम् ॥ 7

uta syā naḥ sarasvatī ghorā hiraṇya-vartaniḥ; vṛtraghnī vaṣṭi suṣṭutim

uta *and* ***syā*** *that* ***naḥ*** *our* ***sarasvatī*** *Sarasvatī* ***ghorā*** *powerful* ***hiraṇya-vartaniḥ*** *riding golden chariot;* ***vṛtraghnī*** *destroyer of enemies* ***vaṣṭi*** *to desire* ***su-stutim*** *special prayers*

May the powerful Sarasvatī, riding in a golden chariot, the destroyer of enemies; be pleased by our prayers

The sage wishes that his prayers be especially accepted by Sarasvatī, who is *ghorā* powerful, and *vṛtraghnī*, the destroyer of the enemies that lurk within our minds as desires and other emotions. The greatest enemy of the mind are emotions, which are neither positive nor negative – these are what these are, emotions. To keep them under check, the mind needs to be extra powerful. The prayer to Mother is for that.

Sarasvatī is described as *hiraṇya-vartaniḥ*, riding a golden car. This adjective is used for other gods too in the Veda.

यस्या अनन्तो अह्रुतस्त्वेषश्चरिष्णुरर्णवः । अमश्चरति रोरुवत् ॥ 8
सा नो विश्वा अति द्विषः स्वसॄरन्या ऋतावरी । अतन्नहेव सूर्यः ॥ 9

yasyā ananto ahrutas-tveṣaś-cariṣṇur-arṇavaḥ; amaś-carati roruvat
sa no viśvā ati dviṣaḥ svasṝr-anyā ṛtāvarī; atannaheva sūryaḥ

yasyāḥ *whose* ***anantaḥ*** *infinite* ***ahrutaḥ*** *undeviating* ***tveṣaḥ*** *bright* ***cariṣṇuḥ*** *moving* ***arṇavaḥ*** *waters;* ***amaḥ*** *strength* ***carati*** *proceed* ***roruvat*** *loud roar*

sā *may she* ***naḥ*** *us* ***viśvā*** *all* ***ati*** *to take across* ***dviṣaḥ*** *inimical* ***svasṝḥ*** *born together* ***anyāḥ*** *other* ***ṛta-varī*** *rivers* ***atan*** *constantly* ***ahā-iva*** *like a day* ***sūryaḥ*** *the Sun*

May she whose unbounded water, swift-moving with a rapid rush
comes onward with tempestuous roar
Overcome all our adversaries
and bring to us her laden sisters (Ganga and other rivers)
as the ever-rolling sun overcomes the days

The prayer in this verse is for Sarasvatī, the fast flowing, to take us near other rivers like Ganga, which were born with it, and also to take us beyond the reach of our adversaries. This crossing is compared to the Sun crossing the day smoothly.

It is natural for many to think that this prayer to the river is for making the crossing smooth to reach other rivers, which are in the north of Sarasvatī. But, when seen in the light of Indian tradition of prayers, the meaning is to take one across the impurities of the world to the purity of the soul effortlessly.

As explained earlier, Sarasvatī is both the goddess of learning and the river, and hence the prayer may be to either, but in either case it will be focusing on purification of oneself.

उत नः प्रिया प्रियासु सप्तस्वसा सुजुष्टा । सरस्वती स्तोम्या भूत् ॥ 10

uta naḥ priyā priyāsu saptasvasā sujuṣṭā; sarasvatī stomyā bhūt

uta naḥ priyā priyāsu *and, dearest among the dear ones* ***sapta-svasā*** *seven Vedic metres, or seven rivers* ***sujuṣṭā*** *beautiful* ***sarasvatī*** *Sarasvatī* ***stomyā*** *applaudabe* ***bhūt*** *to be*

May Sarasvatī, who has seven sisters, who is dearest of dear, and has been well adored
Be ever adorable

Sapta-svasā, of seven forms, may mean the seven rivers, addressed as sisters, which are: *Gaṃgā, Yamunā, Godāvarī Sarasvatī, Narmadā, Sindhu Kāverī*. It may also mean the seven metres of the Veda – *Gāyatrī, Uṣṇik, Anuṣṭup, Bṛhatī, Paṅkti, Triṣṭup, Jagatī*. These metres being the seven sisters of Sarasvatī imply that knowledge and their medium of expression are born together.

Sarasvatī was adored by the sages of the past, and so the sage prays that may she remain adorable to them too, that is, they may ever remain vigilant about praying to the goddess of knowledge.

आपप्रुषी पार्थिवान्युरु रजो अन्तरिक्षम् । सरस्वती निदस्पातु ॥ 11

āpapruṣī pārthivāny-uru rajo antarikṣam; sarasvatī nidaspātu

āpapruṣī *by own radiance* ***pārthivāni*** *related to earth* ***uru*** *spread wide* ***rajaḥ antarikṣam*** *the loka of all spheres* ***sarasvatī*** *Sarasvatī* ***nidaḥ*** *derision* ***pātu*** *save*

May Sarasvatī, who fills with radiance the expanse of earth and heaven
Defend us from the deriders

The prayer is simple. The sage does not want to face ridicule from his critics, whether right or wrong. Only the goddess of knowledge can give one the brilliance to keep such deriders silent.

त्रिषधस्था सप्तधातुः पञ्च जाता वर्धयन्ती । वाजेवाजे हव्या भूत् ॥ 12

triṣadhasthā saptadhātuḥ pañca jātā vardhayantī; vāje-vāje havyā bhūt

tri-sadhasthā *abiding in the three worlds* ***sapta-dhātuḥ*** *comprising seven elements* ***pañca jātā*** *the five types of beings* ***vardhayantī*** *nourishing* ***vāje-vāje*** *in vigour* ***havyā bhūt*** *worthy of prayer*

Abiding in the three worlds, comprising seven elements, nourishing the five types of beings
She is worthy of our prayers for vigour

The physical nature of the goddess is being described, which comprise *triṣadhasthā*, the three spheres – *sthūla jagat, sūkṣma jagat, kāraṇa jagat; saptadhātuḥ*, seven elements that constitute a body – *Rasa*: Plasma/ lymph fluid; *Rakta*: Blood; *Māṃsa*: Muscles, *Meda*: Fat; *Asthi*: Bone; *Majjā:* Bone marrow; *Śukra*: Reproductive fluid; *pañca jātā* – the five types of beings, as accepted in Hindu religion, are – *deva* (gods), *gandharva, nāga, pitṛ* and *nara* (human beings). These are known as *pañca jana*. These five belong to different spheres of existence.

Sarasvatī, the goddess, nourishes the five kinds of beings through seven elements in the three spheres. So, here the prayer is to her to give us vigour. Also, she being the nourisher of all is truly worthy of worship.

प्र या महिम्ना महिनासु चेकिते द्युम्नेभिरन्या अपसामपस्तमा ।
रथ इव बृहती विभ्वने कृतोपस्तुत्या चिकितुषा सरस्वती ॥ 13

pra yā mahimnā mahināsu cekite dyumnebhir-anyā apasām-apastamā
ratha iva bṛhatī vibhvane kṛtopa-stutyā cikituṣā sarasvatī

pra yā *she who is* ***mahimnā*** *in glory* ***mahināsu*** *amongst the glorious* ***cekite*** *to be known* ***dyumnebhiḥ*** *in glory* ***anyaḥ apasām*** *among waters* ***apaḥ-tamā*** *fast flowing*

rathaḥ-iva *like a chariot* ***bṛhatī*** *huge* ***vi-bhvane*** *all-pervasive* ***kṛtā*** *to make* ***upa-stutyā*** *praiseworthy* ***cikituṣā*** *those who know* ***sarasvatī*** *Sarasvatī*

She who is distinguished in glory among the glorious
she who is the fastest among the fast
She who has been created to go everywhere as a chariot
she, Sarasvatī, is to be glorified by the wise

The words used in the verse can be used to address a river, as also the goddess. The overall meaning of it is that Sarasvatī is to be worshipped by the devotees, knowing well her qualities as the most glorious and omnipresent. She is the fastest because she is present everywhere.

The use of *kṛtā* signifies the origin of *Sarasvatī* from Brahmā or Prajāpati.

सरस्वत्यभि नो नेषि वस्यो माप स्फरीः पयसा मा न आ धक् ।
जुषस्व नः सख्या वेश्या च मा त्वत्क्षेत्राण्यरणानि गन्म ॥ 14

sarasvaty-abhi no neṣi vasyo māpa spharīḥ payasā mā na ā dhak
juṣasva naḥ sakhyā veśyā ca mā tvat-kṣetrāṇy-araṇāni ganma

sarasvati abhi naḥ neṣi *guide us, Sarasvatī, to glory* ***vasyaḥ*** *ample riches* ***mā*** *not* ***apa spharīḥ*** *to retard growth* ***payasā*** *water* ***mā*** *not* ***naḥ*** *us* ***ā dhak*** *to overwhelm*

juṣasva *accept* ***naḥ*** *our* ***sakhyā*** *friendly prayers* ***veśyā*** *residence* ***ca*** *and*

mā *not* ***tvat*** *from you* ***kṣetrāṇi*** *place* ***araṇāni*** *inferior* ***ganma*** *to go*

Lead us, Sarasvatī, to glory; refuse us not thy grace
overwhelm us not with flooding
Accept our prayers, be at our habitations
and make us not go away from you

Since Sarasvatī has been personified as the river, the words chosen here are metaphorical. On the face of it, the prayer wishes that the river may not cause damage due to flooding, and that one may not have to leave his place of stay. But the real intent is to pray to the goddess so that her grace, in the form of knowledge, always be there; that the flood of evil thoughts and deeds from the surroundings may not divert the devotee from his chosen path of spirituality.

4.
INDRA SŪKTA
LEADER OF THE GODS
Ṛgveda: VII.31

Indra is the most famous god of the Vedic times who has around 250 hymns, which is about one-fourth of the Ṛgveda, dedicated to him. The picture that we get of him from these hymns makes him appear quite anthropomorphic on the physical side, and having deep mythological imagery. He is the face of God, the overlord and also the god of the thunderstorm who vanquished the demon *Vṛtra* who had held up the waters. The fight is more of spiritual symbolism than an actual fight. However, later literature created many interesting stories centring on it.

Indra has been described as a born being, with two hymns dedicated to the subject, and many more references to it. Lover of the drink *Soma* that often intoxicates him, he drives in a golden chariot whose horses are Hari, which might be their name or probably because they are of yellowish-brown colour. He wields *vajra*, fashioned by Tvaṣṭṛ, with which he vanquishes all kinds of enemies.

Great cosmic actions, like settling the quaking mountains and plains, are also attributed to him. He stretches out heaven and earth like a hide; he holds asunder heaven and earth as two wheels are kept apart by the axle; he makes the non-existent into the existent in a moment.

Indra has such names and adjectives that made him look like a great conqueror for the Aryans in the eyes of the Western scholars. These scholars often and conveniently let go of the fact that while the Veda do use elements from the surroundings where the sages dwelt, these are not mere praise for any marauding conqueror (in the form of Indra), instead the hymns are inspired expressions of the connect of the Vedic people with the Divine.

The power and popularity of Indra went down with time, probably because the sages saw too much of the human in him. In the present times he remains confined to rituals during formal worship, which shows how the Hindus are not content to see human traits even in the masks of the Infinite – they aspire to see God as God, the Divine.

This hymn is from the seventh book of the Ṛgveda, which belongs to the family of sage Vasiṣṭha. The family had considerable influence during the Vedic period and also in the Ramayana and Mahabharata periods, with the name of the sage and some incidents of his life coming in both the epics. He is also famous for his epic rivalry with sage Viśvāmitra, who gave the world the incomparable *Gāyatrī mantra.*

Devatā: Indra
Ṛṣi: Vasiṣṭha

In this hymn (ṚV VII.31), dedicated to Indra, the sage, probably Vasiṣṭha himself, or someone from his family, prays to God by praising him and then asking for favours. It describes the scene at the site of a *yajña* where the sage tells the priests to chant in adoration of Indra through a description of his personality and achievements.

To remind, the goal of *karma* in the form of prayer and *yajña* is to purify one's mind through acts dedicated to God. This purification is meant to lead a person ultimately towards *jñāna,* God realization, as elaborated in books like Gita. As a by-product, *karma* is seen as the pathway to gain riches in earthly life and sojourns in heaven after death.

प्र व इन्द्राय मादनं हर्यश्वाय गायत । सखायः सोमपाव्ने ॥ 1

pra va indrāya mādanaṃ haryaśvāya gāyata; sakhāyaḥ somapāvne

pra *(an adverb)* **vaḥ** *you all* **indrāya** *for Indra* **mādanam** *joyful* **hari-aśvāya** *one who has horse named Hari, or one who has tawny horses* **gāyata** *sing* **sakhāyaḥ** *o friends!* **somapāvne** *drinker of Soma*

Sing, friends, a joyful hymn to Indra, the lord of Hari, the horses, and the drinker of Soma

The priests are here addressed as *Sakhāyaḥ,* which can mean simply friends or 'friends of Indra,' since the priests come regularly to pray to Indra and are thus in regular contact with him. What a loving relation!

The sage says *sakhāyaḥ,* o dear friends, *vaḥ,* you *indrāya pra gāyata,* sing the praise of Indra, *somapāvne,* who loves to drink Soma, and is *hari aśvāya,* who has horses named Hari. The word may also mean golden horses. Indra is often referred to as *hariaśvāya*. The sage further adds that the song has to be *mādanam,* pleasing to him. To make someone happy, one must choose to say what is pleasing to the listener.

शंसेदुक्थं सुदानव उत द्युक्षं यथा नरः । चकृमा सत्यराधसे ॥ 2

śaṃsed-ukthaṃ sudānava uta dyukṣaṃ yathā naraḥ; cakṛmā-satyarādhase

śaṃsa it uktham *sing the praise* ***sudānave*** *to the bounteous giver* ***uta dyukṣam*** *bright* ***yathā*** *as* ***naraḥ*** *other people* ***cakṛma*** *chant the praise* ***satya-rādhase*** *one with true gifts*

To him, the Bounteous, sing brilliant praise
as others do to the giver of true gifts

The request to the priests to sing in praise of Indra continues. It says *śaṃsa it uktha* chant the prayers to Indra, who is *sudānave* liberal in granting favours to the devotees, and who is *satyarādhas* one who bestows real gifts or blessings. Indra is thus liberal and true in gift giving.

What kind of prayer it should be? It is explained, *yathā naraḥ,* as other people, that is, other priests, belonging to other families, chant *uta dyukṣam* bright or scintillating prayers, in the same way we too should *cakṛma*, offer our prayers.

There is a note of competitive encouragement in this as one would expect from a priest who expects to get favours from God and from those for whom they are performing the *yajña*.

त्वं न इन्द्र वाजयुस्त्वं गव्युः शतक्रतो । त्वं हिरण्ययुर्वसो ॥ 3

tvaṃ na indra vājayustvaṃ gavyuḥ śatakrato; tvaṃ hiraṇyayurvaso

tvam *thou* ***naḥ*** *us* ***indra*** *Indra* ***vājayuḥ*** *giver of grains* ***tvam gavyuḥ*** *be thou giver of cattle* ***śatakrato*** *O Śatakratu* ***tvam hiraṇya-yuḥ vaso*** *O Vasu, give us gold*

Do thou, Indra, be giver of grains, Śatakratu, give us cattle; O Vasu, give us gold

The prayer here is for the well-being in the world, which is characterized by getting grains, gold and cattle. When people outgrow worldly desires of this kind, only then they start desiring for *mukti*.

The sage prays *tvam naḥ indra vājayuḥ*, give us grains, O Indra, *tvam gavyuḥ śatakrato*, give us cattle *Śatakratu*. The term *Śatakratu* is used for Indra since he performed one hundred *yajña* when he was on the earth as a human. Thus, Indra also came to be seen as a post that could be attained by anyone who performed one hundred *yajña*. This makes Indra a highly anthropomorphic god, with a good share of jealousy and love for the good things in life, and yet being referred to as the face of the infinite.

At the level of anthropomorphism, a superficial parallel could be drawn between the gods of the Veda and the Greco-Roman pantheon. The resemblance however ends there, as the Veda go infinitely beyond this rather mundane plane to envision the ultimate, unknowable, indescribable Brahman upon, in and through whom all of Creation rests.

Indra is also known as *Vasu*, meaning one who gives shelter. He is prayed to as *tvam hiraṇyayuḥ vaso*, give us gold (wealth) O Vasu, the giver of shelter to all.

वयमिन्द्र त्वायवोऽभि प्र णोनुमो वृषन् । विद्धि त्वस्य नो वसो ॥ 4

vayam-indra tvā-yavobhi pra ṇonumo vṛṣan; viddhī tvasya no vaso

vayam *we* ***indra*** *Indra* ***tvāyavaḥ*** *are devoted to you* ***abhi pra nonumaḥ*** *pray intensely* ***vṛṣan*** *one who showers wishes* ***viddhī*** *know* ***tu*** *verily* ***asya*** *this* ***naḥ*** *our* ***vaso*** *O Vasu!*

Devoted to you, showerer (of gifts) we glorify you, Indra
be cognizant, O good lord, of this prayer by us

The priests wish that Indra make take cognizance of their prayers and fulfil them, so they add, *vayam indra tvāyavaḥ* we are devoted to you, O Indra, and *abhi pra nonumaḥ* we pray to you, *vṛṣan*, the showerer of gifts, *viddhi tu asya naḥ vaso iti*, so please take a note of our prayers, O Vasu.

The prayer may seem childish in nature but it is not so. Even in bhakti literature we come across prayers where a saint prays to their Lord to make a note of the prayer and not forget them.

मा नो निदे च वक्तवेऽर्यो रन्धीरराव्णे । त्वे अपि क्रतुर्मम ॥ 5

mā no nide ca vaktaveryo randhīra-rāvṇe; tve api kratur-mama

mā naḥ nide *subject us not up to the reviler* ***ca*** *and* ***vaktave*** *to the abuser* ***aryaḥ*** *O Lord!* ***randhīḥ*** *in the control of* ***arāvṇe*** *miserly* ***tve*** *to you* ***api kratuḥ*** *prayers* ***mama*** *mine*

Lord, subject us not up to the reviler, to the abuser, to the miserly May my prayers reach you

The list of demands of the priests does not seem to end! The prayer now says *aryaḥ*, Lord! *mā naḥ nide ca vaktave,* do not subject us to the revilers and abusers, and not even to the *randhīḥ arāvṇe,* control of the miserly.

Brahmins have been vilified throughout the ages, starting Vedic times itself, for reasons varying from their learning to their poverty. In this verse, the priest is worried for their self-respect and self-preservation, so they pray that they may not face abusers, revilers and the miserly hosts. Even in the present times, it is not unusual to see how a *yajamāna*, the person for whom the *yajña* is performed, makes fun of the priest and refuses to pay liberally. To avoid these problems, many temples nowadays have fixed rates for the performance of rituals!

Moreover, say the priests *tve api kratuḥ mama*, may my prayers reach you. The word *kratu* has been explained earlier, which means noble deeds, particularly related to *yajña.*

त्वं वर्मासि सप्रथः पुरोयोधश्च वृत्रहन् । त्वया प्रति ब्रुवे युजा ॥ 6

tvaṃ varmāsi sa-prathaḥ puroyodhaś-ca vṛtrahan; tvayā prati bruve yujā

tvam varma asi *you are the armour* ***saprathaḥ*** *great on all sides* ***puraḥ-yodhaḥ*** *great warrior* ***ca vṛtrahan*** *and the slayer of the demon vṛtra* ***tvayā*** *with your* ***prati bruve*** *I make counter replies (to detractors)* ***yujā*** *help/ association*

You are our armour, O Indra! great (that you are),
and victor in the battle, slayer of Vṛtra
With you as ally, I counter the detractors

One idolizes what one aspires for, and hence one worships that God whom he idolizes for knowledge, protection, wealth, etc. Indra being bounteous, majestic and valorous, he is often prayed to by the sages for protection and wealth.

In this verse the sage says how he is often attacked by detractors, philosophically or verbally, and that he is able to counter them simply because he worships Indra, the powerful.

O Indra! *tvam varma asi*, you are like armour, for our protection from the enemies and detractors. You are *saprathaḥ*, great on all sides, meaning you are great in every sense, and you are *puraḥyodhaḥ ca*, a valiant warrior who faces his enemies from the front, and thus he became *vṛtrahan*, the slayer of the great *asura*, warrior *Vṛtra* who is said to be the demon of drought. By slaying him, Indra released the waters for the earth.

The sage says that being your worshipper, who have the aforesaid qualities, *prati bruve*, I am able to counter people in arguments, *tvayā yujā*, because of my association with you. The Sanskrit language has many expressions for discussions, like *vāda, vivāda, jalpa, prativāda*, etc. *Prati bruve* belongs to the same category in which an opponent is countered logically, which requires both knowledge and wit. To have these two qualities, one needs intellect which is a gift of God.

महाँ उतासि यस्य तेऽनु स्वधावरी सहः । मम्नाते इन्द्र रोदसी ॥ 7

mahāṃ utāsi yasya tenu svadhā-varī sahaḥ; mamnāte indra rodasī

mahān uta asi *you verily are great* ***yasya*** *whose* ***te*** *yours* ***anu*** *(adverb)* ***svadhāvarī*** *abounding with food* ***sahaḥ*** *strength* ***mamnāte*** *adore* ***indra*** *Indra* ***rodasī*** *heaven and earth*

You verily are great; heaven and earth abounding with food, adore
Indra, your strength

The praise for Indra continues by saying that Indra, you are great, heaven and earth are abounding in food that sustains all beings and hence they praise your strength. *Indra* Indra, *mahān uta asi*, you are great, *svadhāvarī rodasī*, the heaven and earth abounding in food, that sustain the beings and hence *yasya*, you whose *sahaḥ* strength, *te*, they *anu mamnāte*, praise.

The strength of Indra is thus sung by heaven and earth too. *Rodasī* is a very interesting word, since it often means 'to cry', but the Veda always use it to mean *dyāvāpṛthivyau* – heaven and earth, which are dual divinities, meaning these two are named and addressed together.

तं त्वा मरुत्वती परि भुवद्वाणी सयावरी । नक्षमाणा सह द्युभिः ॥ 8

taṃ tvā marutvatī pari bhuvadvāṇī sayāvarī; nakṣamāṇā saha dyubhiḥ

tam *your (appreciation)* ***tvā*** *with you* ***marutvatī*** *sung by the sages* ***pari bhuvat*** *surround you* ***vāṇī*** *adoration* ***sa-yāvarī*** *go with you,* ***nakṣamāṇā*** *to reach* ***saha*** *with* ***dyubhiḥ*** *radiance*

May the praise of your adorers, accompanying you, such as you are
And spreading around with radiance, reach you

The adorations, in the form of prayers that are sung by the sages and the priests, sparkle with radiance and spread wide to reach Indra wherever he goes. The idea is that wherever Indra may be, these prayers should reach him.

Indra, *tam,* the adorations (as mentioned in the previous verses) addressed to you, *tvā sayāvarī saha* go with you wherever you go. May these *dyubhiḥ* radiant, *marutvatī vāṇī* prayers specially addressed to Indra by the priests, *nakṣamāṇā* reach you *pari bhuvat* from all directions.

The word *marutaḥ* means the singer of praise and *marutvatī* means 'that which belongs to Indra.' Later stories have forty-nine *marutas* who are companions of Indra. Indeed, it is very difficult to understand the religious stories of the Hindus without having some knowledge of the Veda.

ऊर्ध्वासस्त्वान्विन्दवो भुवन्दस्ममुप द्यवि । सं ते नमन्त कृष्टयः ॥ 9

ūrdhvāsas-tvānv-indavo bhuvan-dasmam-upa dyavi; saṃ te namanta kṛṣṭayaḥ

ūrdhvāsaḥ *ascend* ***tvā anu*** *towards you* ***indavaḥ*** *moon or Soma* ***bhuvan*** *to be or become* ***dasmam*** *who can be seen, or who is beautiful* ***upa dyavi*** *abiding in heaven* ***sam*** *together* ***te*** *you* ***namanta*** *make pranams* ***kṛṣṭayaḥ*** *people*

The offerings ascend up to you, Indra – the abider in heaven and of godly aspect
And so men bow before you

Indra is being glorified as *ūrdhvāsaḥ tvā anu indavaḥ bhuvan*, Soma ascends toward you, when offered by us, the priests, during a *yajña,* and you are *dasmam upa dyavi*, visible in the high heaven, that is, you have the godly appearance. It is for you that Soma is produced on the earth and *sam te namanta kṛṣṭayaḥ*, people bow down before you in reverence to make *praṇāms* (salutations).

The expression *upa dyavi dasmam* is quite interesting. There are many kinds of heaven, which are categorized variously. According to one such, there are four major spheres – *Sūryaloka, Candraloka, Dyuloka* and *Brahmaloka*. These grow in subtleness progressively and can be ascended through noble deeds and pure minds. Indra is seen near *Dyuloka*, implying that *Brahmaloka*, the sphere of God is subtler than his sphere.

The word *dasmam* means visible and also 'one who has many accomplishments.' The expression would then mean that Indra lords over the creatures while staying in *Dyuloka*.

The word of interest here is *kṛṣṭi*, meaning people. It is one of those words that have undergone a lot of semantic changes. Originally, the word meant cultivated ground, then an inhabited land, next its inhabitants, and lastly any race of men. The English word 'culture' has come from *kṛṣṭi*, meaning qualities specific to them that have been acquired by working on them the way one works on a field to cultivate it.

प्र वो महे महिवृधे भरध्वं प्रचेतसे प्र सुमतिं कृणुध्वम् ।
विशः पूर्वीः प्र चरा चर्षणिप्राः ॥ 10

pra vo mahe mahivṛdhe bharadhvaṃ pracetase pra sumatiṃ kṛṇudhvam
viśaḥ pūrvīḥ pra carā carṣaṇiprāḥ

pra vaḥ *you (priests)* ***mahe*** *great (Indra)* ***mahi-vṛdhe*** *the giver of great wealth* ***bharadhvam*** *offer (Soma)* ***pra-cetase*** *one with bright mind* ***pra su-matim*** *beautiful prayers* ***kṛṇudhvam*** *perform*

viśaḥ *people* ***pūrvīḥ*** *many* ***pra cara*** *to go* ***carṣaṇi-prāḥ*** *for the wishes*

Bring offerings to the great (Indra), the giver of great (wealth)
offer prayers to the wise Indra, fulfiller of desires of men
Come (O Indra) to the people (who are) offering many (oblations)

The first line of the verse is towards the worshipper and the second one towards the worshipped. It says *pra sumatim kṛṇudhvam*, offer beautiful prayers, *pra vaḥ mahe mahi-vṛdhe bharadhvam*, to the great lord Indra who increases the wealth of the worshipper, and who is *pra-cetase*, of bright intellect.

Indra is addressed in prayer as *carṣaṇi-prāḥ* the fulfiller of wishes of people, *pra cara*, to go towards *viśaḥ pūrvīḥ*, people who are making the offering.

उरुव्यचसे महिने सुवृक्तिमिन्द्राय ब्रह्म जनयन्त विप्राः ।
तस्य व्रतानि न मिनन्ति धीराः ॥ 11

uruvyacase mahine suvṛktim-indrāya brahma janayanta viprāḥ;
tasya vratāni na minanti dhīrāḥ

uru-vyacase *wide-pervading* ***mahine*** *great* ***su-vṛktim*** *prayers* ***indrāya*** *to Indra* ***brahma*** *grains* ***janayanta*** *producer* ***viprāḥ*** *the wise*

tasya *their* ***vratāni*** *protection* ***na minanti*** *is not destroyed* ***dhīrāḥ*** *the wise gods*

The sages who offer prayers and grains (offering during yajña) for the wide-pervading and mighty Indra
The protection (by Indra) of such people cannot be breached even by the gods

The greatness of Indra is being extolled as *brahma janayanta su-vṛktim viprāḥ*, the wise ones who offer grains and prayers, *uru-vyacase mahine indrāya*, to Indra who is wide-pervading and mighty, *tasya vratāni*, their protection (by Indra), *na minanti dhīrāḥ*, cannot be breached even by the gods.

The word *brahma janayanta*, is explained as producer of grains, implying those who make sacrificial offerings. Most *yajña* require offerings like *puroḍāṣa*, which are made of grains.

Suvṛktim means that which causes to bend. Since prayers make the gods favourable towards a devotee, hence the term.

Thus, the verse implies that Indra is so powerful that if he becomes favourable, then no one can harm the worshipper. This kind of an idea, when applied to God, is unacceptable to the higher minds, since God does not favour any. Unfortunately, people make the mistake of asking for favours from God, which was originally intended to be addressed to the gods, who are as limited as human beings when compared to the infinite God.

इन्द्रं वाणीरनुत्तमन्युमेव सत्रा राजानं दधिरे सहध्यै ।
हर्यश्वाय बर्हया समापीन् ॥ 12

indraṃ vāṇīranuttam-anyum-eva satrā rājānaṃ dadhire sahadhyai; haryaśvāya barhayā samāpīn

indram *for Indra* ***vāṇīḥ*** *offer the words* ***anutta-manyum*** *whose wrath is irresistible* ***eva*** *verily* ***satrā rājānam*** *the lord of the whole universe* ***dadhire*** *to hold (the enemies)* ***sahadhyai*** *to overcome*

hari-aśvāya *whose horses are Hari* ***sam*** *together* ***āpīn*** *friends/kinsmen* ***barhaya*** *to encourage (to pray)*

Prayers to Indra, the lord of the universe whose wrath is irresistible
enable the devout to overcome detractors
Urge your friends, (O friends!) to worship the lord of tawny horses

Indra is the lord of the universe. Prayers offered to him enable a person to overcome his foes, so one should encourage his friends and kinsmen to pray to Indra. Implying this, the sage tells the priests that Indra is *anutta-manyum*, one whose wrath cannot be countered by anyone. This makes him supreme. Further, he is *satrā rājānam*, the lord of the universe, meaning God. So, *indram vāṇīḥ*, prayers offered to Indra *eva dadhire*, make it possible for a person to *sahadhyai*, overcome (the detractors).

The priests used to have (and continue to have) enemies, and even sages have detractors. Only when a person realizes his oneness with the supreme that one goes beyond taking a note of these problems. One may then ask why have such prayers, instead of going all out for self-knowledge, which is beyond these issues. The answer is that the talk of self-knowledge for most people is like baby's prattle; rarely does one come across a true aspirant for self-knowledge. Most people only want a safe and good life, and hence such prayers.

The sage adds *barhaya*, to encourage, *sam āpīn*, one's kinsmen to pray to *hari-aśvāya*, Indra, whose horses are Hari or whose horses have golden coat.

Thus ends this hymn to Indra. Most hymns in the Veda to Indra have more or less the same tone, with certain adjectives and demands changed.

One may ask 'why all these *yajña* and prayers?' Aren't they all mere superstition? Hasn't modern science demonstrated that human prosperity is the direct result of human endeavour and nothing else? Of what use then are these hymns and prayers which extoll superstitious incantations over honest labour?

The answer is that nowhere is it said that *yajña* are a substitute for action. All of the Veda are intended to establish just the opposite, which is that you are divine, and hence invoke the Divine in all that you do. At various stages of evolution of thought, the Divine may be personified as an Indra or a Viṣṇu or a Śakti, indeed, as all of them. Take your pick according to your own personal make up. The sacred Gita is but the culmination of this living monument of human divinity that places performance of duty as an offering to God at the same level as the performance of the holiest of *yajña*.

Did it actually work? Indeed, yes. The Veda delivered extraordinary success in all spheres of human endeavour. The history of ancient India is a testimony to that.

5. DEVĪ SŪKTA MOTHER GODDESS Ṛgveda: X.125

One of the most popular sacred books of India is *Caṇḍī*, which is also known as *Devī māhātmya* and *Durgā Saptaśatī*. It consists of seven hundred verses and is recited in every temple dedicated to Śakti (universal mother), as also by millions of devout Hindus daily, who believe that a recital of the book gives inner power to overcome obstacles of every kind in life, and also leads one towards mukti.

This fact is beautifully exemplified in its story of a king and a businessman, both disillusioned and devastated, who wander into a hermitage where the sage narrates to them the greatness of the mother of the universe, who is known variously as Śakti, Divine Power, Māyā, etc. and who manifests in the universe as Durgā, Kālī and other such goddesses to save the noble from the unholy. At the end of the narration, they are asked to recite Devī Sūkta, which they do, and finally they get what they aspired for – the businessman got *mukti* and the king became the king of the universe. It is thus that the greatness of Devī Sūkta, coming from a tradition of thousands of years, became universally known and appreciated, which otherwise would have remained confined in the hands of the Brahmins who recited and studied the Veda.

Of all the gods and goddesses that are worshipped in India, three are universal – Śiva, Śakti and Viṣṇu (along with his avatāra and their accompanying characters) – with all three having their roots in various hymns of the Veda. This hymn, dedicated to Śakti, is the fountainhead of all later Śakti worship.

This hymn is also unusual because of two important reasons – the first is that it is composed by a female sage, *Vāgāmbhṛṇī*, (*Vāk*, daughter of the sage *Ambhṛṇa*). India had such a high level of culture that women walked shoulder to shoulder with men in all walks of life, including the composition of Vedic hymns. So, it becomes painful when ignorant preachers try to push women out of Vedic learning. The second reason is that the hymn is not towards any god, as is usual in the Veda, but is towards the same *Vāgāmbhṛṇī*! The great commentators concluded that the hymn is addressed to *Paramātmā*, the Supreme Self; that the sage, after going into the deepest of meditation where all functioning of the mind stops, realizes herself as one with Ātman, the supreme self. This Truth is embodied in the immortal Statement in the Upaniṣads: '*aham brahma asmi.*'

What follows after that, is expressed in this hymn – the sage exclaims how she is the force that drives the universe, the gods, etc., as will be explained. The exhilaration, born of such realization, is unmatched in this world where lust and gold rule the roost. It also shows how the Veda are the storehouse of spiritual wisdom of India, and how anyone can attain such wisdom.

The content of this hymn is poetically sublime, philosophically sound, spiritually intense and universally applicable.

Devatā: Vāgāmbhṛṇī/ Paramātmā
Ṛṣi: Vāgāmbhṛṇī, Vāk, daughter of the sage Ambhṛṇa

अहं रुद्रेभिर्वसुभिश्चराम्यहमादित्यैरुत विश्वदेवैः ।
अहं मित्रावरुणोभा बिभर्म्यहमिन्द्राग्नी अहमश्विनोभा ॥ 1

ahaṃ rudrebhir-vasubhiś-carāmy-aham-ādityair-uta viśvadevaiḥ
ahaṃ mitrā-varuṇobhā bibharmy-aham-indrāgnī aham-aśvinobhā

aham rudrebhiḥ vasubhiḥ carāmi *I move the Rudras, the Vasus* ***aham ādityaiḥ uta viśvadevaiḥ*** *(I move) the Ādityas and the Viśvedevās*

aham mitrāvaruṇā ubhā bibharmi *I alone hold Mitra – Varuṇa both* ***aham indrāgnī*** *I (hold) Indra – Agni* ***aham aśvinā ubhā*** *I (hold) the Aśvin twins*

I move (with) the Rudras, the Vasus
the Ādityas and the Viśvedevās
I alone hold Mitra-Varuṇa, Indra-Agni
and the Aśvin twins

The *ṛṣikā* (female sage) Vāk, daughter of sage Ambhṛṇa, after having gone through the rigours of learning, contemplating, meditating and then realizing her oneness with the universal, breaks out in joy to find that she alone exists, as pure consciousness, and that the forces of nature, the gods, divinities and the nature, which she had considered to be lording over her till then, were like specks before her real self, nay, the very identity of these gods was dependent on her alone.

This truth is realized by every spiritual seeker who reaches the state of *mahākāraṇa* to know that they are one with Brahman – the support and substratum of everything that there is in the three worlds of *sthūla jagat, sūkṣma jagat* and *kāraṇa jagat*.

The gods Rudra, Vasus, Ādityas, Viśvedevās, Mitra, Varuṇa, Indra, Agni, Aśvins are some of the important gods of the Veda. Of these Rudra are eleven, Vasus are eight, Ādityas are twelve, Viśvedevās are the collective gods, and Aśvins are twins. Mitra – Varuṇa and Indra – Agni are considered to be friends and they often come in the Veda as dual divinities. The functions of each of these gods and groups of divinities are various but they all are engaged in doing good to the world and maintaining the world order. If need be, they even subdue evil forces when they cross the boundary.

Vāk declares, *aham carāmi*, I have become, all the gods, whose names have been mentioned in the previous paragraph. The word *carāmi* may also mean to yoke into action, which will then imply that Vāk is identifying herself with Śakti, the universal Mother, who is seen as the power that makes everything in the world move. Brahman and Its power, Śakti, being non-different, it is perfectly alright to see the verse in both ways. Either way, Vāk is the ruler of the world in every sense of the term. So, the acts of the gods, howsoever powerful, are due to Vāk.

The tradition of worship of Śakti, both in the Purāṇas and Tantra, has its root in this hymn, starting this verse.

The sage further declares that *(aham) bibharmi*, I hold or maintain, the gods, meaning she is the substratum of all the divinities, since she is non-different from Brahman.

Vāk also means speech/ word. A word is non-different from idea, so some commentators interpret the hymn accordingly.

अहं सोममाहनसं बिभर्म्यहं त्वष्टारमुत पूषणं भगम् ।
अहं दधामि द्रविणं हविष्मते सुप्राव्ये यजमानाय सुन्वते ॥ 2

ahaṃ somam-āhanasaṃ bibharmy-ahaṃ tvaṣṭāram-uta pūṣaṇaṃ bhagam
ahaṃ dadhāmi draviṇaṃ haviṣmate suprāvye yajamānāya sunvate

aham somam āhanasam bibharmi *I support Soma, the cherished/ destroyer of foes* **aham tvaṣṭāram uta pūṣaṇam bhagam** *I (also support) Tvaṣṭā, Pūṣan and Bhaga*

aham dadhāmi *I bestow* ***draviṇam*** *wealth* ***haviṣmate*** *containing haviḥ (sacred offerings)* ***suprāvye*** *loved by the gods* ***yajamānāya*** *those who perform yajña* ***sunvate*** *(who) prepare/ press Soma.*

I hold Soma, the cherished
I also support Tvaṣṭṛ, Pūṣan and Bhaga
I bestow wealth upon him who perform yajña
in which oblations are made, loved by the gods

Soma had a special place in the Vedic culture. It was some kind of herb about which we do not know anything in the present times. When crushed, the herb gave out juice which was part intoxicant and part medicinal. Because of this and other properties, Soma juice was quite coveted and was religiously offered to the gods during a *yajña*. When the gods had their share of the drink, they used to become unbeatable, and so the credit for their victory often went to Soma.

Soma is also the god of the moon and, at times, synonymous with it. However, in this and other such verses, Soma means the juice.

The sage Vāk says *aham somam āhanasaṃ bibharmi*, I uphold Soma, the cherished. The word *āhanasam* means that which is pressed, as in the case of grapes. It can also mean 'destroyer of foes', since the gods destroy their foes after drinking Soma. She is also the support of *tvaṣṭāram uta pūṣaṇam bhagam*, the divinities named *Tvaṣṭā, Pūṣan* and *Bhaga*. Of these, *Tvaṣṭā* is the god of constructions, including machines and weapons, *Pūṣan* is equated with the Sun who nourishes the world, and *Bhaga* is the god of wealth and fortune. These, and all other gods, owe their existence in Brahman and perform their duties due to Brahman. Vāk, being non-different from Brahman, utters that she alone has become all of them and functions through them.

Moreover, the Brahmins and devotees who acquire good fortune and wealth by performing *yajña* with devotion, owe their good fortune to Vāk only. Thus, she is also the vidhātā, God who gives the results of karma. All this is expressed in *aham draviṇam dadhāmi,* I bestow wealth to *yajamānāya,* those who perform *yajña* with *haviṣmate* containing the sacred offering for the *yajña* which are *suprāvye* loved by the gods by *sunvate,* pressing of Soma juice. It is the belief of the devout that all good come in life only through the proper performance of *yajña*. Vāk is emphatic that good fortune to a devout comes only because of her, since she is the Supreme Lord.

अहं राष्ट्री सङ्गमनी वसूनां चिकितुषी प्रथमा यज्ञियानाम् ।
तां मा देवा व्यदधुः पुरुत्रा भूरिस्थात्रां भूर्यावेशयन्तीम् ॥ 3

ahaṃ rāṣṭrī saṃgamanī vasūnāṃ cikituṣī prathamā yajñiyānām
tāṃ mā devā vyadadhuḥ purutrā bhūristhātrāṃ bhūryā-
veśayantīm

aham rāṣṭrī *I am the queen* ***saṃgamanī*** *bestower* ***vasūnām*** *wealth* ***cikituṣī*** *knower* ***prathamā*** *the first* ***yajñiyānām*** *of the worshipped*

tām *thus* ***mā*** *me* ***devāḥ*** *the gods* ***vi adadhuḥ*** *to do* ***purutrā*** *variously* ***bhūristhātrām*** *in many ways* ***bhūri*** *many* ***āveśayantīm*** *to enter*

I am the queen of the universe, bestower of wealth
knower (of Brahman), the foremost of those worthy of worship
As such the gods have put me in many places
abiding in manifold conditions, entering into numerous (forms)

Being established in the knowledge of Brahman, Vāk realizes that she is the foremost among the worshipped, she is the giver of the wealth to all, and she has entered everything in the universe to make their existence possible. The common perception that various gods do all this is transcended by Vāk, and of course, by everyone who has such realization.

She says, *aham rāṣṭrī*, I am the queen sovereign of the universe, meaning, I am the mother Goddess of the universe who creates, sustains, provides for, and destroys the universe. She is *saṅgamanī* (one who unites) *vasūnām*, the bestower of wealth to the deserving; and is *cikituṣī*, having known Brahman. Because of this she is *prathamā yajñiyānām*, the foremost among the worshipped during a *yajña*. This position is usually reserved for Indra, who is the leader of the gods, but Vāk identifies herself with Brahman, and hence she deserves to be the first among the gods to be worshipped.

Vāk is one with the universe, so she says that *bhūri āveśayantīm*, I have entered all life forms as their soul. *Tām*, it being so, *devāḥ vi adadhuḥ purutrā*, the gods have established *mā bhūristhātrām*, me variously in many places, implying that whatever the gods do, are essentially the worship of her only.

The acts of the gods and men, knowingly or unknowingly, are the worship and adoration of the mother of the universe, that is, Vāk.

मया सो अन्नमत्ति यो विपश्यति यः प्राणिति य ईं शृणोत्युक्तम् ।
अमन्तवो मां त उप क्षियन्ति श्रुधि श्रुत श्रद्धिवं ते वदामि ॥ 4

mayā so annam-atti yo vipaśyati yaḥ prāṇiti ya īṃ śṛṇotyuktam
amantavo māṃ ta upa kṣiyanti śrudhi-śruta śraddhivaṃ te vadāmi

mayā saḥ annam atti *he who eats food, does so through me* ***yaḥ vipaśyati*** *he who sees* ***yaḥ prāṇiti*** *he who breathes* ***yaḥ īm śṛṇoti uktam*** *he who hears what has been spoken*

amantavaḥ *those who are ignorant* ***mām*** *of me* ***te*** *they* ***upa kṣiyanti*** *get destroyed* ***śrudhi*** *listen!* ***śruta*** *celebrated ones* ***śraddhivam*** *worth listening to* ***te*** *them* ***vadāmi*** I tell

He who eats food, sees, breathes,
and hears that is spoken, does so through me
Those who are ignorant of me perish
you, who have ears, listen—
I tell you that which is deserving of Śraddhā

Vāk shows how she is responsible for everything in the universe, *mayā saḥ annam atti*, all those who eat food, that is, all living beings do so through me, *yaḥ vipaśyati yaḥ prāṇiti ya īm śṛṇoti uktam*, all that sees, breathes, and hears the uttered. Every act of a living being is carried out because of the power of the Mother Goddess, who resides in every being as the power of each organ and also as the *prāṇa*, the vital energy working within a body to keep it alive, apart from her being the soul.

Then there is note of caution for the ignorant of spiritual truths. She says, *amantavaḥ mām te upa kṣiyanti,* those who are ignorant of me, perish. Life goes even for the atheists, but blessed are those who have knowledge of spiritual truths and of the Divine Mother who is the origin and sustainer of all. The word *upa kṣiyanti* imply the fall from spiritual state, which, of course, is not eternal. Anyone can take the royal road to spirituality at any time in life, but blessed are they who are on the path.

So, *Vāk says, śruta*, o celebrated ones! *śrudhi,* listen to *te vadāmi* what I tell you. The words that she tells are *śraddhivam*, credible, that is, worth attaining with the help of strength born of *śraddhā.* The word *śraddhā,* which is quite common in the Hindu tradition, means the power of a person to hold on to an ideal born of imbibing the words of teachers, elders and scriptures. It is *śraddhā* that becomes the impelling force towards goodness and greatness. In the famous *Kaṭhopaniṣad*, there is a story of the young boy Naciketā, who happily went to the abode of Yama, the king of death, by the power of his *śraddhā*. What Vāk is going to tell, is worth listening to with complete śraddhā, since one can then attain anything in the world with that.

अहमेव स्वयमिदं वदामि जुष्टं देवेभिरुत मानुषेभिः ।
यं कामये तन्तमुग्रं कृणोमि तं ब्रह्माणं तमृषिं तं सुमेधाम् ॥ 5

ahameva svayamidaṃ vadāmi juṣṭaṃ devebhiruta mānuṣebhiḥ
yaṃ kāmaye tantamugraṃ kṛṇomi taṃ brahmāṇaṃ tamṛṣiṃ taṃ sumedhām

aham eva svayam *verily, I myself* ***idam vadāmi*** *say this* ***juṣṭam devebhiḥ*** *(and my words are) pleasing to gods* ***uta mānuṣebhiḥ*** *and to men*

yam kāmaye *whomsoever I desire* ***tam tam*** *them* ***ugram kṛṇomi*** *I make mighty* ***tam brahmāṇam*** *I make them Brahmin* ***tam ṛṣim*** *I make them a sage* ***tam sumedhām*** *I make them wise*

Verily, I myself say this
and my words are pleasing to gods and men
whomsoever I desire I make mighty
I make him a Brahmin, a sage or a person wise

The effect of Vāk is all-pervasive. She asserts that *aham eva svayam idam vadāmi*, verily I myself say this. The assertion in these words is not mere self-confidence but the reality of truth. Further, *juṣṭam devebhiḥ uta mānuṣebhiḥ,* these words are so pleasing to the gods and men of knowledge since they all go by this truth and make themselves blessed.

What is that truth? *Yam kāmaye tam tam ugram kṛṇomi,* whomsoever I wish, I make him mighty or superior over everyone else. Further, *tam brahmāṇam tam ṛṣim tam sumedhām,* I make him a Brahmin, a sage or one of brilliant mind.

Thus, every achiever in this world owes their success to the Divine Mother, who is none other than Vāk.

अहं रुद्राय धनुरा तनोमि ब्रह्मद्विषे शरवे हन्तवा उ ।
अहं जनाय समदं कृणोम्यहं द्यावापृथिवी आविवेश ॥ 6

ahaṃ rudrāya dhanurā tanomi brahmadviṣe śarave hantavā u
ahaṃ janāya samadaṃ kr̥ṇomy-ahaṃ dyāvā-pr̥thivī āviveśa

aham rudrāya dhanuḥ ā tanomi *I bend the bow for Rudra* ***brahmadviṣe*** *the enemies of the noble* ***śarave*** *to hurt* ***hantavai u*** *to kill*

aham *I* ***janāya*** *for people/ devotees* ***samadam*** *conflict* ***kr̥ṇomi*** *to act* ***aham dyāvāpr̥thivī ā viveśa*** *I pervade heaven and earth*

I bend the bow for Rudra to slay
the demonic enemies of the noble
I battle the enemies of my devotees
Indeed, I pervade heaven and earth

Mother Durgā is the most famous and revered goddess who destroyed demons whenever they crossed boundaries to attack the noble. In her impersonal form she is worshipped as Śakti, the divine power of God, who makes the incarnation of God possible and helps God in vanquishing the enemies of Creation.

Here Vāk says, *aham rudrāya dhanuḥ ā tanomi,* I am the power that strung the bow of Lord Śiva when he fought the famous demons who were the sons of Tārakāsura at the city of Tripura. The demon king had three cities of iron, silver and gold that extended up to the heavens. According to a boon, he could be killed only if someone destroyed the three cities with one arrow. So, Lord Śiva was requested to perform the task, which he did with his bow. At that time, the Earth became his chariot with the Sun and Moon as the wheels, Brahmā held the reins, Mount Meru became the bow, Vāsuki, the serpent king was the bow string, Viṣṇu was the arrow and Agni was the tip of the arrow, etc.

It was not a mere battle but a fight to kill, *brahmadviṣe śarave hantavai u,* to hurt and slay the demonic forces that are against good people. The word *brahmadviṣa*, literally means those who are against the Brahmins, but the implied meaning is 'those who are noble (of high learning and character) people.'

The noble ones are by nature gentle and so they cannot fight the cruel, and hence the Divine Mother has to often appear to subdue the unholy, *aham janāya samadam kṛṇomi,* I get into fights for the protection of my devotees. *Janāya* means people but here it implies the devotees.

Being one with Brahman, *aham dyāvāpṛthivī ā viveśa*, I pervade the whole of earth and space. *Dyāvāpṛthivī* is a compound word containing *dyu* and *pṛthivī*, space and earth. These two are also known as dual divinities since the two are mostly addressed as a compound in the Veda.

अहं सुवे पितरमस्य मूर्धन्मम योनिरप्स्वन्तः समुद्रे ।
ततो वि तिष्ठे भुवनानु विश्वोतामूं द्यां वर्ष्मणोप स्पृशामि ॥ 7

ahaṃ suve pitaram-asya mūrdhan-mama yonir-apsvantaḥ samudre
tato vi tiṣṭhe bhuvanānu viśvotāmūṃ dyāṃ varṣmaṇopa spṛśāmi

aham suve *I brought forth* ***pitaram*** *the father-like (sky)* ***asya*** *its* ***mūrdhan*** *as its (supreme being) head* ***mama yoniḥ*** *my origin* ***apsu*** *waters* ***antaḥ samudre*** *in the midst of the ocean (God)*

tataḥ *due to this* ***vi tiṣṭhe*** *I enter* ***bhuvanā anu viśvā*** *all the being in the universe* ***uta*** *and* ***amūm dyām*** *reach the heavens* ***varṣmaṇā*** *heights* ***upa spṛśāmi*** *I touch*

I brought forth the father-like sky
on the crown of this (Supreme Being)
My place of origin is in the midst of waters
from where I spread through all beings
and touch the heaven with my body

Vāk is all pervading – she reaches from the ocean to the sky, nay, she created the sky, who is considered to be the father, according to some scriptural sayings, since everything proceeded from it. She says, *aham suve pitaram asya mūrdhan,* I gave birth to the heavens and put it as the head of God. It was mentioned in the *Puruṣa Sūkta* how God, the personal, is seen as having thousands of heads. Here the word head is used in that sense. The first born in the process of Creation is *ākāśa*, which has the dual meaning of sky and space particles. Being the first born, it is referred to here as the head of God.

These descriptions are meant for the purpose of meditation.

Where did Vāk originate? She answers, *mama yoniḥ* my origin is *apsu antaḥ samudre* in the midst of the waters of the ocean. *Samudra* is a popular word for God due to the similarity of hugeness. She is born of God, is the inseparable power of God, and manifests whenever there is Creation. This idea of Śakti, being inseparable from God and manifesting at every instance of creation, is universally accepted in Hinduism. Thus, Vāk is both sage and mother goddess.

What was the result? *Tataḥ vi tiṣṭhe bhuvanā anu viśvā*, thus, I entered all being that are in the universe. She, being the power behind everything, has entered all. *Uta amūm* and thus, *dyām varṣmaṇā upa spṛśāmi*, I touch the highest heavens with my body. Wherever there is some *loka,* there are beings – which are all the body of Vāk, so figuratively, she touches heaven with her body.

The crux is that Vāk, being the consciousness in the world, enters every mind and thus becomes the body of the being, which forms the universe. Nothing in this creation is outside of her.

To remind, this kind of realization can come to anyone who, through *sādhanā,* transcends the *māyā* of separation from Brahman.

अहमेव वात इव प्र वाम्यारभमाणा भुवनानि विश्वा ।
परो दिवा पर एना पृथिव्यैतावती महिना सं बभूव ॥ 8

aham-eva vāta iva pra vāmy-ārabhamāṇā bhuvanāni viśvā
paro divā para enā pṛthivyaitāvatī mahinā saṃ babhūva

aham eva *verily, I myself* ***vātaḥ iva*** *like the wind that blows* ***pra vāmi*** *(I) engage* ***ārabhamāṇā*** *initiate* ***bhuvanāni viśvā*** *the beings in the universe*

paraḥ divā *beyond the space* ***paraḥ enā pṛthivyā*** *beyond this earth* ***etāvatī*** *such is* ***mahinā*** *greatness* ***sam babhūva*** *have become*

Like the wind that blows
I set in motion all the created things
(I am) beyond the sky and the earth
and I have become all this, in my own splendour

Vāk, the universal mother, is the cause that makes the effects possible and then she herself becomes the effect. The idea that God creates the universe and then enters it is quite common in the Veda – He is the material cause, efficient cause, the effect, and yet He is beyond all this.

Vāk, the sage, says *aham eva vātaḥ iva*, like the wind that blows on its own, *pra vāmi ārabhamāṇā,* I set in motion *bhuvanāni viśvā,* all the created beings of the universe. Why does she do so? It is her will. The will of God cannot be questioned, nor can it be reasoned with, since God is well beyond mind, and hence the question itself becomes absurd. God explained is no God.

She says further, *paraḥ divā paraḥ enā pṛthivyā,* I am beyond space and also beyond this earth – I am neither matter nor mind; I am beyond all this. Even then *etāvatī mahinā*, it is due to her power/ splendour that *sam babhūva*, she has become everything, says she.

In brief, Vāk, the sage, after having realized her oneness with Brahman, expresses that she is the cause and effect of everything in the universe, she is the essence of all, and yet she is beyond all this.

Thus, is woman exalted by the Veda, coeval with the Godhead itself; thus is the feminine celebrated in India, the most ancient of all civilizations.

6.
HIRAṆYAGARBHA SŪKTA
CREATOR GOD
Ṛgveda: X.121

A father commands respect traditionally since for nearly all of humanity and across much of history until modern times, the father has played the role of creator, provider, guide and protector of the family; and so it is natural that God, or any other divinity, bringing forth these characteristics for the whole of humanity, will be adored with reverence. Let this not make one conclude that the Veda advocate only patriarchy, since one comes across some extremely sublime hymns dedicated to Mother power, some of which have been selected for this work. Through all this, one finds that the sages saw God as Divine first and foremost, and had no particular preference for seeing God as male or female.

The Veda have many hymns in which Indra and other divinities are prayed to as father. Of these, Prajāpati, the progenitor of beings, continues to be adored in later scriptures too under various names of which Brahmā is the most common. This hymn is an offering to Prajāpati, who is also known as Hiraṇyagarbha.

Who or what is Hiraṇyagarbha? When God, the formless, wanted to create, his desire became his creative power, known variously as *Avidyā, Māyā, Śakti*, etc. God now appeared as the Lord of all and was known as *Īśvara*, God with a form. Prayers and worship are offered to *Īśvara*, since God, the formless, is infinite and everywhere, so who will pray to whom and where!

With the process of Creation on, the creator God appeared as holding the cosmic golden egg in his womb and thus came to be known as Hiraṇyagarbha – *Hiraṇya* means gold and *garbha* is womb. This womb contains the seeds for all that is going to be created in a particular cycle. Hiraṇyagarbha is one with God, since there is no creation yet, but to distinguish the Lord's creative aspect, he is referred to separately.

The moment Hiraṇyagarbha appeared, it spread throughout, creating and sustaining the various spheres – physical, subtle and causal – by its divine power. After that, the physical objects and beings were born.

In the *Upaniṣads,* he is addressed as *Sūtrātmā,* the Soul of the Universe; in the *Manusmṛti* (1.9) Hiraṇyagarbha is described as Brahmā. However, in some other sacred books, Brahmā is described as emerging from Hiraṇyagarbha.

In this Sūkta, Hiraṇyagarbha is addressed as *Kaḥ,* meaning Prajāpati, as explained by Sāyaṇācārya, according to whom *Kaḥ* means 'the unknown; one who desires; happiness, bliss' etc., which all indicate the word to mean Prajāpati. Unfortunately, some scholars translated *Kaḥ* to mean 'whom', which is a literal translation of the word, changing the meaning of the hymn such that it appears more like a poetry than a sacred hymn.

The sage of this hymn is *Hiranyagarbha* who was the son of Prajāpati. There are quite a few hymns in the Veda like this, making one wonder how the name of the God and of the sage came to be the same!

Devatā: Kaḥ; Prajāpati
Ṛṣi: Hiraṇyagarbha Prājāpatya

हिरण्यगर्भः समवर्तताग्रे भूतस्य जातः पतिरेक आसीत् ।
स दाधार पृथिवीं द्यामुतेमां कस्मै देवाय हविषा विधेम ॥ 1

hiraṇyagarbhaḥ sam-avartatāgre bhūtasya jātaḥ patir-eka āsīt
sa dādhāra pṛthivīṃ dyām-utemāṃ kasmai devāya haviṣā vidhema

hiraṇyagarbhaḥ sam avartata agre *Hiraṇyagarbha was in the beginning* ***bhūtasya*** *of the beings* ***jātaḥ*** *when born* ***patiḥ ekaḥ āsīt*** *became the sole lord*

saḥ *he* ***dādhāra*** *upheld* ***pṛthivīm*** *the earth* ***dyām uta*** *the heaven* ***imām*** *this* ***kasmai*** *to Ka* ***devāya*** *the Divine* ***haviṣā*** *oblations* ***vidhema*** *offer*

In the beginning was Hiraṇyagarbha
when born, he became the sole lord of beings
He upheld this earth and heaven
let us offer oblation to the divine Ka

The sage wishes to offer the oblations to Ka, the creator God, also known as Prajāpati and Hiraṇyagarbha, who is the first manifestation of God in the relative world. This is being described as *agre hiraṇyagarbhaḥ sam avartata*, in the beginning Hiraṇyagarbha existed, who when *jātaḥ*, born, *bhūtasya patiḥ ekaḥ āsīt*, became the sole lord of the created beings.

The role of the creator God continued as *saḥ dādhāra pṛthivīm dyām uta imām* he upheld this earth and the sky above by his powers. It is his power behind the forces of nature that keep things the way these appear to us. And so, *kasmai devāya haviṣā vidhema*, let us offer oblations to Ka, Prajāpati.

More reasons for his worship follow.

य आत्मदा बलदा यस्य विश्व उपासते प्रशिषं यस्य देवाः ।
यस्य छायामृतं यस्य मृत्युः कस्मै देवाय हविषा विधेम ॥ 2

ya ātmadā baladā yasya viśva upāsate praśiṣaṃ yasya devāḥ
yasya chāyāmṛtaṃ yasya mṛtyuḥ kasmai devāya haviṣā vidhema

yaḥ He, who is ***ātmadāḥ*** the giver of soul ***baladāḥ*** the giver of strength ***yasya viśve upāsate praśiṣam*** whose commands all beings obey ***yasya devāḥ*** whose commands even the gods (obey)

yasya chāyā amṛtam *whose shadow is immortality* ***yasya mṛtyuḥ*** *whose (shadow) is death* ***kasmai devāya haviṣā vidhema*** *let us offer oblations to the divine Ka*

He, who is the giver of soul, the giver of strength
whose commands all beings, even the gods obey
Whose shadow is immortality, whose (shadow) is death
let us offer oblations to the divine Ka

Every philosophy has to explain the world, life and God. Science, materialists, realists, idealists, dualists, monists – all have to explain these three, and be consistent about it. The story of world philosophy is thus the narration of how different people explained these three as real, part-real or non-existent.

In the Veda, God is real, as also the world and its beings. God creates the world and then enters it–*tat sṛṣṭvā tadevānuprāviśat*, after creating it he entered it (*Taittirīya Upaniṣad 2.6.2*). In living beings, he enters as *jīva*, which in reality is nothing but Brahman, however it appears as if identified with the body-mind-ego complex. That same Brahman is the lord and master of everything in the universe; even life and death are like mere shadows before It.

God is being described here as *yaḥ ātmadāḥ*, he who is the giver of Ātman. The living beings are produced from God the way sparks fly out from a blazing fire. These sparks of life are not physical in nature but are pure consciousness, and hence these are one with the universal consciousness, the Brahman. He is also *baladāḥ*, giver of strength that sustains one in life against the vagaries of existence. These two words may also mean that God purifies the soul and gives inner strength so that one may move away from the world towards God.

He is so powerful that *yasya viśve upāsate*, all beings, knowingly or unknowingly worship him, obey his command, and *yasya devāḥ praśiṣam*, whose commands the gods too obey. The gods are the masters of nature, but they pale into insignificance in front of God the way a minor ruler pales before an emperor.

What about life and death, which comprise the world of the living? The sage says *yasya chāyā amṛtam* whose shadow is immortality. The word *amṛtam* may mean life or relative immortality in the heaven. Moreover, *yasya mṛtyuḥ*, even death is its shadow. Yama, the ruler of death and regulator of life in the form of time, is insignificant before God.

It may also mean that freedom and bondage, known as *nirvāṇa* and *saṃsāra* are due to his will. Thus, God alone keeps one in the world, and He alone releases a person from the world. So, *kasmai devāya haviṣā vidhema*, let us offer oblations to Ka.

यः प्राणतो निमिषतो महित्वैक इद्राजा जगतो बभूव ।
य ईशे अस्य द्विपदश्चतुष्पदः कस्मै देवाय हविषा विधेम ॥ 3

yaḥ prāṇato nimiṣato mahitvaika id-rājā jagato babhūva
ya īśe asya dvipadaś-catuṣpadaḥ kasmai devāya haviṣā vidhema

yaḥ *He, who* ***prāṇataḥ*** *that breathes* ***nimiṣataḥ*** *that blinks* ***mahitvā*** *greatness* ***it ekaḥ*** *by whose own* ***rājā jagataḥ babhūva*** *became the ruler of the world*

yaḥ īśe asya *He who rules over this universe* ***dvipadaḥ*** *bipeds* ***catuḥ-padaḥ*** *quadrupeds* ***kasmai devāya haviṣā vidhema*** *let us offer oblation to the divine Ka*

He who has become by his own greatness
the ruler of all beings that move, breathe and blink
He who rules over this universe of bipeds and quadrupeds
let us offer oblation to the divine Ka

Hiraṇyagarbha is being praised as the ruler of all by his power – *yaḥ*, he who *ekaḥ rājā jagataḥ babhūva*, became the sovereign ruler of the universe *mahitvā* by his own greatness *prāṇataḥ nimiṣataḥ*, over those that breathe and blink; *yaḥ īśe asya dvipadaḥ catuṣpadaḥ*, he who rules over the bipeds and quadrupeds; *kasmai devāya haviṣā vidhema*, let us offer oblations to Ka.

The offering can also be done, as Krishna explains to Arjuna in the Gita, through meditation in which one may offer one's mind and soul to become one with Brahman. The Veda, however, recognize the reality that at any given time, there are human beings experiencing life at every possible stage of life. For many, the fulfilment of the bare needs of survival are paramount, and they would ask for nothing more of their god than these. So, there are hymns that seek material riches from the Divine. However, as humans evolve in and across lifetimes, their vision, their understanding deepens and broadens, allowing them to perceive the existence of an underlying Reality that is untouched by the ups and downs of material existence. The Veda recognize these too, and the *Hiraṇyagarbha Sūkta* gently prods the practitioner to wake up to this Reality.

यस्येमे हिमवन्तो महित्वा यस्य समुद्रं रसया सहाहुः ।
यस्येमाः प्रदिशो यस्य बाहू कस्मै देवाय हविषा विधेम ॥ 4

yasyeme himavanto mahitvā yasya samudraṃ rasayā sahāhuḥ
yasyemāḥ pradiśo yasya bāhū kasmai devāya haviṣā vidhema

yasya *whose* ***ime himavantaḥ*** *these snow-clad mountain, Himalayas* ***mahitvā*** *greatness* ***yasya*** *whose* ***samudram*** *oceans* ***rasayā saha*** *with the rivers* ***āhuḥ*** *speak (as majesty of God)*

yasya *whose* ***imāḥ pradiśaḥ*** *these quarters* ***yasya bāhū*** *whose arms are* ***kasmai devāya haviṣā vidhema*** *let us offer oblation to divine Ka*

Whose greatness these snow-clad (mountains) are
whose majesty men call the ocean with the rivers
Whose two arms are the quarters of space
let us offer oblation to the divine Ka

The majesty of God cannot be described by common language, so different examples and imageries are used to communicate a sense of His grandeur. The sacred Gita, for example, says that the universe is like a small speck on the persona of God. And to make this idea clearer, Chapter X of The Gita likens God to the 'best in class' of any species/group of beings.

The Veda were the first to use this kind of examples, as we find in the *Puruṣa* Sūkta where the universe is described as a quarter (figuratively) of Him. The Veda also pick up extraordinary objects from the world and show how these are the testimonies of the greatness of God.

The verse says – *yasya ime himavantaḥ mahitvā* whose greatness these mountains are said to be, and *yasya samudram rasayā saha āhuḥ* whose greatness the ocean along with the rivers are spoken to be, both of course referring to God. The Himalayas are also known as *himavantaḥ* (*hima* means snow). When people look with wonder at the Himalayas, they cannot help but wonder also at the greatness of God who created these and established them.

Similarly, the huge oceans and the mighty rivers reflect the greatness of God. The word *rasa* is used in the sense of fluidity and also of the essence and of joy. Here the word indicates the rivers since these carry *rasa*, the water.

Furthermore, *yasya imāḥ pradiśaḥ yasya bāhū* the quarters (cardinal directions) are like the two arms of God. Why two arms? The commentators narrow the quarters to East and South – East, since these are considered to be noble. The verse concludes with *kasmai devāya haviṣā vidhema* let us offer oblation to divine Ka.

येन द्यौरुग्रा पृथिवी च दृळ्हा येन स्व स्तभितं येन नाकः ।
यो अन्तरिक्षे रजसो विमानः कस्मै देवाय हविषा विधेम ॥ 5

yena dyaurugrā pṛthivī ca dṛḷhā yena sva stabhitaṃ yena nākaḥ
yo antarikṣe rajaso vimānaḥ kasmai devāya haviṣā vidhema

yena dyauḥ ugrā *by whom the sky was made huge* ***pṛthivī ca dṛḷhā*** *and the earth firm* ***yena svaḥ stabhitam*** *by whom heaven was fixed* ***yena nākaḥ*** *(by whom) the stars were fixed*

yaḥ antarikṣe rajasaḥ vimānaḥ *who created the particles in the space* ***kasmai devāya haviṣā vidhema*** *let us offer oblation to the divine Ka*

By whom the sky was made huge and the earth firm
by whom heaven and the solar sphere were fixed
Who created the particles in the space
let us offer oblation to the divine Ka

The glory of God continues to be sung as *yena dyauḥ ugrā*, by whom the huge heavens were made, *pṛthivī ca dṛḷhā*, and the earth was made firm. The idea that the earth is firm because of God's power is universal in India, since every kind of force, including gravitational, is God's power only.

Yena svaḥ stabhitam yena nākaḥ, by whom the space and the stars were fixed; *yaḥ antarikṣe rajasaḥ vimānaḥ*, by whom the particles in space were created; *kasmai devāya haviṣā vidhema*, let us offer oblation to the divine Ka.

In this verse we have three words *dyu, svaḥ* and *antarikṣa* that represent various states of subtleness. Sāyaṇācārya explains *dyu* and *antarikṣa* as space, while *svaḥ* means the highest heaven, *Brahmaloka*. The word *rajas*, used often when talking about creation, usually mean particles. *Vimānaḥ* means to create.

One interesting comment by Sāyaṇācārya on this verse is the mention of the sun being fixed in the sky, when he explains that stars were fixed by God! He thus treats the sun as a star and fixed, implying that the earth moves around it. Thus, he is yet another of the early sages to strike a blow against the geocentric worldview more than seven centuries ago!

यं क्रन्दसी अवसा तस्तभाने अभ्यैक्षेतां मनसा रेजमाने ।
यत्राधि सूर उदितो विभाति कस्मै देवाय हविषा विधेम ॥ 6

yaṃ krandasī avasā tastabhāne abhyaikṣetāṃ manasā rejamāne
yatrādhi sūra udito vibhāti kasmai devāya haviṣā vidhema

yam which (Prajāpati) ***krandasī*** earth and heaven ***avasā*** for protection ***tastabhāne*** to be firm ***abhi aikṣetām*** to see ***manasā*** through mind ***rejamāne*** bright

yatra *where* ***adhi*** *established/held* ***sūraḥ*** *sun* ***uditaḥ*** *to rise* ***vibhāti*** *to shine* ***kasmai devāya haviṣā vidhema*** *let us offer oblation to the divine Ka*

Whom heaven and earth, established by his protection
and shining brightly, regarded with their mind
In whom the risen sun shines forth
let us offer oblation to the divine Ka

Heaven and earth are the shining glory of our existence that create and sustain us. Even these two realized, through their meditative silence, that their creator and protector was God. The sage further says that the sun that rises and shines in the sky does so because of God, *yam krandasī*, whom earth and heaven *rejamāne*, that shine brightly *abhi aikṣetām manasā*, realized in their mind (through contemplation) that *avasā tastabhāne*, these are protected by God.

The word *krandasī* actually means to cry or roar, but here it means the twin deities of earth and heaven, since they realized that they are the protected ones of God. This idea was later taken up in the *Purāṇa* and illustrated beautifully as the earth going to Brahmā (Prajāpati) seeking protection from the rise of evil forces.

The expression *abhi aikṣetām manasā* implies that the gods (earth and heaven) beheld him and realized that all their power and glory are due to him. The idea is that all created things gratefully and reverentially acknowledge their subordination to the Creator.

Also, *yatra adhi sūraḥ uditaḥ vibhāti*, where the sun rises and shines brightly, *kasmai devāya haviṣā vidhema*, let us offer oblation to the divine Ka.

आपो ह यद्बृहतीर्विश्वमायन्गर्भं दधाना जनयन्तीरग्निम् ।
ततो देवानां समवर्ततासुरेकः कस्मै देवाय हविषा विधेम ॥ 7

āpo ha yad-bṛhatīr-viśvamāyan-garbhaṃ dadhānā janayantīr-agnim

tato devānāṃ sam-avartatāsur-ekaḥ kasmai devāya haviṣā vidhema

āpaḥ ha waters ***yat*** when ***bṛhatīḥ*** vast ***viśvam*** all this ***āyan*** to enter ***garbham*** foetus/ seed ***dadhānāḥ*** to give/ put ***janayantīḥ*** to give birth ***agnim*** Agni

tataḥ devānām *then the gods* ***sam avartata*** *were produced* ***asuḥ*** *to become alive* ***ekaḥ*** *the one* ***kasmai devāya haviṣā vidhema*** *let us offer oblation to the divine Ka*

When the vast waters spread over the universe
containing the seed and giving birth to Agni
Then was produced the one breath of the gods
let us offer oblation to the divine Ka

The first mantra said 'Prajāpati was born first.' But 'born or arose from what?' This verse answers that question and says, 'from the waters or from the seed (*garbha*).' Sāyaṇācārya accepts both the possibilities. In the first case, the meaning would be: 'From those waters arose Prajāpati as the one life-breath of all gods.' In the second case, the meaning would be: 'The great waters bore Prajāpati in the form of germ or egg (*garbha*), and from that Prajāpati was born *Vāyu,* the life-breath of gods and other beings.'

According to Vedanta, which is the import of the Veda, Creation takes place by the power of God which is known as Māyā or *Prakṛti*. Prajāpati, the Creator God, comes out of this, and hence this power of God is often termed as Waters or germ, that is, *garbha*.

This is being narrated as *āpaḥ ha yat bṛhatīḥ viśvam āyan garbham dadhānāḥ janayantīḥ agnim*, when the cosmic waters spread over the universe, which contained the seed and gave birth to Agni, *tataḥ devānām sam avartata asuḥ ekaḥ*, then was produced the one breath, *Vāyu* – the life-breath, of the gods.

When the time of Creation came, the power of God, the cosmic waters, spread everywhere. These waters contained the seeds of all the elements, including the fire element, denoted here by *agnim* and referred to as the gods in the Veda. All these elements of Creation were, as if, in the form of womb, or in seed form as potential, known as Prajāpati. It is to this God to whom the worship, in the form of oblations is to be offered, *kasmai devāya haviṣā vidhema*.

यश्चिदापो महिना पर्यपश्यद्दक्षं दधाना जनयन्तीर्यज्ञम् ।
यो देवेष्वधि देव एक आसीत्कस्मै देवाय हविषा विधेम ॥ 8

yaś-cid-āpo mahinā paryapaśyad-dakṣaṃ dadhānā janayantīr-yajñam
yo deveṣv-adhi deva eka āsīt-kasmai devāya haviṣā vidhema

yaḥ *he, who* ***cit*** *indeed* ***āpaḥ*** *waters* ***mahinā*** *great* ***pari-apaśyat*** *beheld* ***dakṣam*** *Prajāpati/ creative power* ***dadhānāḥ*** *to hold* ***janayantīḥ*** *give birth* ***yajñam*** *yajña*

yaḥ *he who* ***deveṣu*** *among the gods* ***adhi devaḥ ekaḥ āsīt*** *was the one supreme god*

kasmai devāya haviṣā vidhema *let us offer oblation to the divine Ka*

He who by his might beheld the waters all around
containing the creative power and giving birth to yajña
He who among the gods was the one supreme god
let us offer oblation to the divine Ka

The verse describes the beginning of Creation when it was all primeval waters from which everything arose. Prajāpati, the Creator, beheld the waters that contained Prajāpati, the personalized form of creator, that is Brahmā, and *yajña* that was to take the Creation forward. This concept of two creators, one impersonal and another personal who enters the Creation and sustains it, is quite common in the Veda, as explained in *Puruṣa Sūkta* too.

Yaḥ cit āpaḥ mahinā pari-apaśyat, He (Prajāpati) who looked at the cosmic waters, *dakṣam dadhānāḥ janayantīḥ yajñam*, that held Prajāpati and the elements of the manifold universe that begins with *yajña*. The word *yajña* here indicates every kind of creation that followed.

Being the first one in the relative world, he was the supreme among the gods, *yaḥ deveṣu adhi devaḥ ekaḥ āsīt.* The sage then says *kasmai devāya haviṣā vidhema*, let us offer oblation to the divine Ka.

मा नो हिंसीज्जनिता यः पृथिव्या यो वा दिवं सत्यधर्मा जजान ।
यश्चापश्चन्द्रा बृहतीर्जजान कस्मै देवाय हविषा विधेम ॥ 9

mā no hiṃsīj-janitā yaḥ pṛthivyā yo vā divaṃ satyadharmā jajāna
yaś-cāpaś-candrā bṛhatīr-jajāna kasmai devāya haviṣā vidhema

mā *not* ***naḥ*** *us* ***hiṃsīt*** *harm* ***janitā yaḥ pṛthivyāḥ yaḥ*** *who procreated the earth* ***vā divam satyadharmā jajāna*** *who holds and begat the heaven by his dharma of truth*

yaḥ ca *and he who* ***apaḥ candrāḥ bṛhatīḥ*** *the shining cosmic waters* ***jajāna*** *gave birth* ***kasmai devāya haviṣā vidhema*** *let us offer oblation to the divine Ka*

May he not harm us, who begat the earth
who holds and begat the heavens by his dharma of truth
He who gave birth to the vast and shining waters
let us offer worship with an oblation to the divine Ka

The hymn is coming to an end, so prayers for favours begin. As mentioned earlier, the Veda contain prayers for one's welfare in this world and the next. Compared to these wants, the exalted philosophy of *mukti* is to be found mostly in the *Upaniṣads* only.

The sage here prays for protection from God *mā naḥ hiṃsīt* may he not harm us, implying may he not stop us from growth, since the grace of God is important for any kind of growth. The prayer is to *yaḥ pṛthivyāḥ janitā* he who gave birth to the earth; *yaḥ satyadharmā vā divam jajāna* he who upholds this universe by being *satyadharmā*, established in truth, and delivered space and the heavens.

The word *satyadharmā* is quite common in the Veda and implies a person whose primary nature is to be established in truth. The word is also interpreted to mean 'unfailing support'. *Satya* means truthfulness in personal conduct, and *dharma* means universal moral order. In early Vedic literature both the meanings were conveyed by the word *ṛta*, the cosmic order, and hence this meaning.

The word can also mean that the person is established in both truth and dharma. The ultimate *satyadharmā* is God, and so anyone who gets established in this quality, is considered godly.

Further, *yaḥ ca apaḥ candrāḥ bṛhatīḥ jajāna* and he delivered the beautiful cosmic waters, which are the cause of all Creation. *Candra* means moon, but here it means beautiful. It is to this God that oblation is to be offered *kasmai devāya haviṣā vidhema.*

प्रजापते न त्वदेतान्यन्यो विश्वा जातानि परि ता बभूव ।
यत्कामास्ते जुहुमस्तन्नो अस्तु वयं स्याम पतयो रयीणाम् ॥ 10

prajāpate na tvad-etāny-anyo viśvā jātāni pari tā babhūva
yatkāmās-te juhumas-tan-no astu vayaṃ syāma patayo rayīṇām

prajāpate *Prajāpati!* ***na tvat etāni anyaḥ*** *no one other than you* ***viśvā jātāni*** *given birth to all this* ***pari tā babhūva*** *that which exists*

yatkāmāḥ *for the want of which* ***te juhumaḥ*** *we offer oblations to you* ***tat naḥ astu*** *may that be ours* ***vayam*** *(and thus) we* ***syāma*** *will become* ***patayaḥ rayīṇām*** *the possessor of riches*

No other than you, Prajāpati
has given existence to all these beings
may that object of our desires

for which we sacrifice to you be ours,
may we be the possessors of riches

After protection, the prayer is now for riches. *Prajāpate na tvat etāni anyaḥ*, no one other than you, Prajāpati, *viśvā jātāni pari tā babhūva*, has given existence to all these beings.

As described in the earlier verse, God alone, in the form of Prajāpati, has given birth to all these beings in the universe. So, it is his responsibility to look after us. *Yatkāmāḥ te juhumaḥ*, the desired objects for which we offer our oblations to you, *tat naḥ astu*, may that be ours, and thus *vayam syāma patayaḥ rayīṇām*, we too will become possessors of riches, instead of being as poor as we are now.

7.
RĀTRĪ SŪKTA
GODDESS
Ṛgveda: X.127

In the Veda, *Rātrī* has been addressed as the goddess of night. She is the daughter of *Divi,* Space, and sister of *Uṣā*, the goddess of dawn, who is often prayed to in the Veda. *Rātrī* means night, but the goddess is not dark, rather she is the bright starlit night, bedecked in all splendour, banishing darkness. At her approach, men, beasts, and birds go to rest. As a dual deity, she is often addressed with *Uṣā* as *Uṣas-Nakta.* She is also credited with bringing the dawn, the goddess *Uṣā.*

Rātrī Sūkta has special importance in *Śakti* worship, where she is invoked as the goddess who drives away all the ills of life, 'she protects her worshippers from the wolf and the thief, guiding them to safety.'

Seen literally, this hymn appears like an ordinary prayer where one wants protection from the fear of night, but it is one of the esoteric prayers of the Veda where the meaning lies at a deeper level, with *Rātrī* being seen as mother *Kālī*, who is worshipped all over India as the mother who protects all from the evil forces of nature.

The hymn is also recited individually to drive away the ills from life, and in the morning by those who have bad/frightening dreams at night.

Devatā: Rātristavaḥ
Ṛṣi: Kuśika Saubhara (Grand-daughter of sage Sobhari) or may be **Rātrī Bhāradvājī** (daughter of Bharadvāja)

रात्री व्यख्यदायती पुरुत्रा देव्यक्षभिः । विश्वा अधि श्रियोऽधित ॥ 1

rātrī vy-akhyad-āyatī purutrā devy-akṣabhiḥ; viśvā adhi śriyo-dhita

rātrī *Rātrī,* ***vi akhyat*** *named* ***āyatī*** *approach* ***purutrā*** *many places* ***devī*** *goddess* ***akṣabhiḥ*** *with her eyes*
viśvāḥ *all* ***adhi*** *on* ***śriyaḥ*** *beauties* ***adhita*** *to hold*

The approaching goddess Rātrī has surveyed all with her eyes (She is) adorned with all beauties

The Divine Mother is the primordial darkness from where all Creation emerges. She is both the source and destination of all. She is effulgent and so she knows all and is present everywhere. She creates bondage and she also grants liberation to the deserving, being the spiritual essence of all, residing within every heart. She is the protector as well as the creator of all our problems, ever impelling us to make choices. These choices, when coloured by our desires, take us deeper into the world of maya. But when we turn towards liberation, our mind, made effulgent by the light of spirituality, leads us to noble thoughts and acts. Mother is the very Consciousness that lights the mind.

Therefore, the sage prays to the Mother to guide us towards doing good and to keep the wolves of desires at bay. *Rātrī vi akhyat āyatī* the goddess named *Rātrī* approaches, implying that spiritual light is dawning upon a person whose heart has been enveloped in complete darkness till then.

Here it is worth noting that though the day under sunlight is infinitely brighter, spiritual light is likened to the gentle luminescence of the starry night, implying the subtleness of inner awakening, and the propensity of the glare of day to mask the beauty of the night.

She is *purutrā devī* the goddess of many places, implying that she is the Goddess and lord of all. As she approaches *akṣabhiḥ viśvāḥ* she looks at all things. This is because the moon and stars at night throw light for her to see all in a special way, by which she can see everyone's true nature.

How is she dressed? It is said *adhi śriyaḥ adhita* she has put on bright raiment. After all, is not the starlit night sky her very garment!

ओर्वप्रा अमर्त्या निवतो देव्युद्वतः । ज्योतिषा बाधते तमः ॥ 2

orvaprā amartyā nivato devyudvataḥ; jyotiṣā bādhate tamaḥ

***ā uru** pervading all **aprāḥ** to fill **amartyā** immortal **nivataḥ** that which lies low **devī** goddess **utvataḥ** that which is high **jyotiṣā** with light **bādhate** dispels **tamaḥ** darkness*

The immortal goddess has pervaded all places, high and low and dispels darkness with her light

Devī Goddess, the universal mother, is described as *amartyā*, that which is beyond life and death, since she has always been and will continue to be, because she is the power of God. When she approaches, whether perceived as the approaching night, or as the spiritual power awakening within a person, she appears to *ā uru aprāḥ* pervade and fill all places – *nivataḥ* low, like creepers, *utvataḥ* or high, like trees. She covers all these with her power, which appears as the darkness of night.

How can darkness be attributed to God? This kind of question actually bogs down the dualists who see God as being only good. India does not have that kind of approach towards God and spirituality; it sees the presence of God everywhere – in good and bad, in life and death, in light and darkness.

She then *bādhate tamaḥ jyotiṣā*, assails, that is, dispels darkness with light of the moon and stars.

The prayer actually is to Mother to dispel all ignorance through her divine effulgence, the light of spirituality.

निरु स्वसारमस्कृतोषसं देव्यायती । अपेदु हासते तमः ॥ 3

niru svasāram-askṛtoṣasaṃ devy-āyatī; aped-u hāsate tamaḥ

niḥ *out* ***u*** *indeed* ***svasāram*** *sister* ***akṛta*** *to clean up* ***uṣasam*** *Uṣā* ***devī*** *goddess* ***āyatī*** *approaching*
apa it u *indeed* ***hāsate*** *removes* ***tamaḥ*** *darkness*

The advancing goddess has prepared the way for her sister Uṣā and then darkness disappears

In spiritual traditions, *Rātrī is* seen as *Cit Śakti*, the power that manifests in the universe as consciousness, while *Uṣā* is seen as *Brahma Vidyāmayī*, the universal consciousness, Brahman. When a spiritual person awakens his *Cit Śakti*, he slowly starts moving towards the knowledge of and oneness with Brahman. This has been described in this verse.

Once *āyatī devī*, the goddess (*Rātrī*) advances, she *niḥ u akṛta*, prepares the way with light for *svasāram uṣasam*, her sister *Uṣā* who represents the ultimate knowledge. It is then that *tamaḥ apet u hāsate* darkness is verily destroyed.

Seen as a physical phenomenon, it is the Night goddess who paves the way for the Dawn goddess. But as anyone can infer, the sages were definitely not just describing something so obvious! Nor did the Brahmins dedicate themselves for ten thousand years or more just to preserve trivia. In truth, neither are these verses mere descriptions of nature, nor are they meant only for *yajña*. The fact is that they contain various layers of spiritual truth, and that is why this hymn is recited during worship and also contemplated in meditation.

सा नो अद्य यस्या वयं नि ते यामन्नविक्ष्महि । वृक्षे न वसतिं वयः ॥ 4

sā no adya yasyā vayaṃ ni te yāmann-avikṣmahi; vṛkṣe na vasatiṃ vayaḥ

sā *may she* ***naḥ*** *towards us* ***adya*** *now* ***yasyāḥ*** *whose* ***vayam*** *we* ***ni*** *back* ***te*** *you* ***yāman*** *to get* ***avikṣmahi*** *to enter* ***vṛkṣe*** *on the tree* ***na*** *as* ***vasatim*** *reside* ***vayaḥ*** *the birds*

May she be favourable to us now
upon whose approach we entered (our dwellings)
as birds (enter) their nest upon the tree

The activities of birds and beasts come to a rest when the goddess *Rātrī* makes her approach. When the same goddess comes to us spiritually, we slow ourselves from the mad rush of the world to find rest in our inner nature from where we may take our spiritual journey forward. This is compared to the birds entering their nests.

The sage prays *adya sā naḥ* may the goddess *Rātrī* be favourable to us *yasyāḥ vayam ni te yāman*, getting whom (the goddess) we found *avikṣmahi*, our rest by entering our homes. What is that like? *Vṛkṣe na vasatim vayaḥ*, the way birds enter their nests at the approach of night.

The prayer is clear in its profound import of the devotee who wishes to find rest within the self. The cycle of birth and death is too tortuous to bear once the understanding of it arises in one's mind. That is when the intense desire to be free starts scorching the soul.

This is yet another example of a seemingly worldly verse praying for a restful night, that reveals hidden treasures of spiritual gems when one digs under the outer layer.

नि ग्रामासो अविक्षत नि पद्वन्तो नि पक्षिणः । नि श्येनासश्चिदर्थिनः ॥ 5

ni grāmāso avikṣata ni padvanto ni pakṣiṇaḥ; ni śyenāsaś-cid-arthinaḥ

ni *indeed* ***grāmāsaḥ*** *the villagers* ***avikṣata*** *entered* ***ni padvantaḥ*** *those with legs* ***ni pakṣiṇaḥ*** *those with wings* ***ni śyenāsaḥ cit*** *indeed even the hawk* ***arthinaḥ*** *the swift*

Men have entered (their dwellings), and beasts and birds
and the swift hawks

Of all the Indian scriptures, Tantras are most famous for being highly esoteric, where their words have multiple meanings. This can be roughly compared to symbolism in poetry, although the comparison is not perfect.

Just like Tantra, some hymns of the Veda are extremely layered. Apparently, these appear to have an obvious superficial meaning but in reality, they convey deeper truths to the spiritually oriented. This verse too is one such. On the face of it, it merely describes all living beings routinely retiring for the night. But the Divine Mother who (also) comes as night, is verily the ultimate place of rest for all beings, beasts and birds. Even their final liberation rests with Her.

This is being conveyed *ni grāmāsaḥ avikṣata* the villagers have entered their homes. The word *grāmāsaḥ* means villagers but here all human beings are implied. Not only men and women but *ni padvantaḥ ni pakṣiṇaḥ* the legged and the winged, meaning animals and birds, have entered their resting place, as also *ni śyenāsaḥ cit arthinaḥ* the swift hawk. The word *arthinaḥ* may mean greedy, but the commentator says that it means swift. After all, every beast and bird, including the hawk, goes out only to fill its belly, while the privilege of being greedy rests only with the humans!

यावया वृक्यं वृकं यवय स्तेनमूर्म्ये । अथा नः सुतरा भव ॥ 6

yāvayā vṛkyaṃ vṛkaṃ yavaya stenam-ūrmye; athā naḥ sutarā bhava

yavaya (yāvayā) *keep away* ***vṛkyam*** *she-wolf* ***vṛkam*** *wolf* ***yavaya*** *keep away* ***stenam*** *the thief* ***ūrmye*** *O Ūrmya* ***atha naḥ*** *now for us* ***sutarā*** *easy to pass* ***bhava*** *be*

Keep off the she-wolf and the wolf, O Ūrmya, keep the thief away be easy for us to pass

It is interesting to note that the Veda uses the word *yāvayā*, while the breakup reads *yavaya*. Actually, both words mean the same, 'to keep away', as used in the mantra later.

Yavaya vṛkyam vṛkam yavaya, keep us away from she-wolf and male wolf, *ūrmye*, o the goddess of Night! The word *yāvayā* and *yavaya* have the same meaning. Moreover, save us from *stenam*, thieves and robbers, and *athā naḥ sutarā bhava*, be you easy for us to pass.

As per some commentators, the she-wolf represents confusion and lust, while the he-wolf represents egotism. The common problems of life like hunger, thirst, grief, old age, death, etc. are the thieves that steal our peace. Only when we get out of the clutches of these distractions, can we aspire to cross the world of duality to reach the boundless ocean of immortality.

उप मा पेपिशत्तमः कृष्णं व्यक्तमस्थित । उष ऋणेव यातय ॥ 7

upa mā pepiśat-tamaḥ kṛṣṇaṃ vyaktam-asthita; uṣa ṛṇeva yātaya

upa *towards* ***mā*** *me* ***pepiśat*** *decorate* ***tamaḥ kṛṣṇam*** *black darkness* ***vyaktam*** *to manifest* ***asthita*** *to stay*
uṣaḥ *Uṣā,* ***ṛṇeva*** *like debt* ***yātaya*** *destroy it*

The all-embracing black darkness has approached me
clear it Uṣā, like a debt

The devotee is pining for the light of immortality, beyond the suffering of the darkness of the world, so he prays to the Divine Mother to save him from the approaching darkness of the world, which is characterized by sense pleasures and fleeting happiness.

In this verse, the prayer is to *Rātrī* to make way for *Uṣā*, implying that spiritual practices have to become fruitful, giving rise to enlightenment.

The sage is worried that *tamaḥ kṛṣṇam* the black darkness of the world is *upa mā pepiśat vyaktam asthita* is approaching to keep him benighted. This has to be destroyed, and hence the prayer to *uṣaḥ* the goddess *Uṣā,* who heralds the dawn to *ṛneva yātaya* clear it like a debt settled.

A man under debt loses his peace and self-respect. The world and its affair are compared here to a huge debt, which cannot be cleared by oneself. This also indicates how prayers are important in spiritual life to get freed of the worldly ways.

उप ते गा इवाकरं वृणीष्व दुहितर्दिवः । रात्रि स्तोमं न जिग्युषे ॥ 8

upa te gā ivākaraṃ vṛṇīṣva duhitar-divaḥ; rātri stomaṃ na jigyuṣe

upa *towards* ***te*** *you* ***gāḥ iva*** *like a cow* ***akaram*** *to come in front* ***vṛṇīṣva*** *to pray* ***duhitaḥ divaḥ*** *daughter of the Sun*
rātri *O Rātrī* ***stomam*** *prayer* ***na*** *like* ***jigyuṣe*** *to overcome*

We approach you as to a milk giving cow! thou daughter of the Sun accept this prayer and grant us victory, O Rātrī

The sage is happy that he has conquered his baser instincts like lust through sacrificial acts, and so he considers himself fit to offer prayers to his *Iṣṭa,* who is the Divine Mother in the form of *Rātrī Devī.*

Duhitaḥ divaḥ, O daughter of the Sun! *Upa te gāḥ iva akaram*, I stand before you as one stands before a milch cow, so *vṛṇīṣva*, accept me as a true devotee. The word *divaḥ* usually means space, but *Rātrī* is described as the daughter of Sun or of the day, since she descends after the day is over.

Rātrī, O *Rātrī!* come to me and *stomam na*, accept my prayers to *jigyuṣe*, help me overpower the enemies of my spiritual life. Here it implies that the way the goddess accepted her oblations and offerings in the past, she should now accept her prayers in the same way.

This verse shows the importance of rituals as the first step to spirituality and then the importance of prayer in enlightenment.

8.
KĀLA SŪKTA
TIME
Atharvaveda: XIX.53.1–4

The human mind has long grappled with the elusive nature of time: what it is, how to record it, how it regulates life, and, even, whether it exists at all as a fundamental building block of the universe.

Western culture accepts a linear conception of time. According to Aristotle, time is 'the calculable measure of motion with respect to before-and-after-ness.' This idea of time as a fixed sequence of events continued till the time of Einstein, who gave us a fresh model of time. In his special theory of relativity, Albert Einstein showed that there can be no 'master clock' for the universe, as Newton had imagined. Instead, measurements of time depend on the motion of each observer. Based on his theories, the British physicist Arthur Eddington came up with 'the arrow of time,' which pointed forward.

In India, Kāla, time, is both a physical entity and a spiritual one. In its physical aspect it is divisible in hundreds of units, with the smallest one equivalent to time taken to blink the eye (around 100-400 milliseconds), and the highest one going to the life span of Brahmā, which is around 311,040,000,000,000 (311.04 trillion) years. Undoubtedly, Indians had a fairly good idea about time! In fact, no other ancient culture came remotely close to even conceiving such truly astronomical numbers, let alone relating to them as units of time!

Also, unlike the linear time of the Western culture, India believes in the cyclic nature of time. On the spiritual side, *Kāla* is God, *Parameśvara*. To distinguish physical time with the spiritual one, Hindus have words like *Kāla, Mahākāla, Kālī* and others.

Philosophically, the trio of Time-Space-Causation creates the dividing line between the Absolute and the relative; Brahman and the empire of mind. Depending on one's orientation, one may see the world as the play of mind, or of time, space or causation. Different philosophers, thinkers and scientists have made their independent choice of the main fulcrum (of mind, time, space, causation) to explain the universe, and, possibly what lies beyond it.

This hymn describes God as *Kāla* who is the creator, sustainer and destroyer of the universe. Further, *Kāla* is eulogized as being the cause of all. Being ever in motion, He is sometimes described as riding a horse and at other times as riding a chariot.

Devatā: Kāla
Ṛṣi: Bhṛgu

कालो अश्वो वहति सप्तरश्मिः सहस्राक्षो अजरो भूरिरेताः ।
तमा रोहन्ति कवयो विपश्चितस्तस्य चक्रा भुवनानि विश्वा ॥1

kālo aśvo vahati sapta-raśmiḥ sahasrākṣo ajaro bhūri-retāḥ
tamā rohanti kavayo vipaścitastasya cakrā bhuvanāni viśvā

kālaḥ aśvaḥ vahati saptaraśmiḥ *Kāla drives a horse with seven reins* ***sahasrākṣaḥ*** *thousand eyed* ***ajaraḥ*** *unaging* ***bhūriretāḥ*** *possessing fertility*

tam ā rohanti kavayaḥ vipaścitaḥ *him the wise sages mount* ***tasya cakrā bhuvanāni viśvā*** *his wheels are all beings*

Kāla drives a horse with seven reins
thousand eyed, unaging, possessing fertility
him the wise sages mount
his wheels are all beings

Kāla, Time, is compared here to a powerful steed who is yoked to seven reins, which represent the seven seasons (six normal, and one season of *adhimāsa*, the two extra months that come in lunar calendar). Unlike other beings, *Kāla* never ages, and has boundless fertility, which results in the birth of beings. Those who mount this horse, reach anywhere they want, since Time is present wherever there is Creation.

The wise sages mount this steed to go beyond the cycle of life and death.

सप्त चक्रान्वहति काल एष सप्तास्य नाभीरमृतं न्वक्षः ।
स इमा विश्वा भुवनान्यञ्जत्कालः स ईयते प्रथमो नु देवः ॥2

sapta cakrān-vahati kāla eṣa saptāsya nābhīr-amṛtaṃ nvakṣaḥ
sa imā viśvā bhuvanāny-añjat-kālaḥ sa īyate prathamo nu devaḥ

sapta cakrān *seven wheels* ***vahati kālaḥ*** *carry Kāla* ***eṣaḥ sapta asya*** *seven are his* ***nābhīḥ*** *naves* ***amṛtam nu akṣaḥ*** *immorality is its axle*

saḥ *he* ***imā viśvā bhuvanāni*** *this world with beings* ***añjat*** *to make manifest* ***kālaḥ*** *Kāla* ***saḥ īyate prathamaḥ nu devaḥ*** *as the first god is he entreated*

Seven wheels carry Kāla, seven are his naves
immorality is its axle
Kāla brings hitherward all worlds
as the first god is he entreated

God, as *Kāla*, is extolled as the first god in the universe. It is in the fitness of things that Time, being the dividing line between the Absolute and the relative, will be regarded as the first god who makes the universe, with all its beings, manifest.

Kāla moves on a chariot (metaphorically) that has seven wheels (the seasons), seven naves (the conjunction point of the seasons), but its axle is immortality. God, the Absolute, never changes during any change like creation, destruction, etc. The wise realizes that and then they try to move on to immortality, leaving the changeable nature.

पूर्णः कुम्भोऽधि काल आहितस्तं वै पश्यामो बहुधा नु सन्तः ।
स इमा विश्वा भुवनानि प्रत्यङ्कालं तमाहुः परमे व्योमन् ॥3

pūrṇaḥ kumbhodhi kāla āhitastaṃ vai paśyāmo bahudhā nu santaḥ
sa imā viśvā bhuvanāni pratyaṅ-kālaṃ tam-āhuḥ parame vyoman

pūrṇaḥ kumbhaḥ *a full vessel* ***adhi kāle āhitaḥ*** *is set upon Kāla* ***tam vai paśyāmaḥ bahudhā nu santaḥ*** *that we see becoming manifold*

saḥ imā viśvā bhuvanāni pratyaṅ *that which is the universe* ***kālam tam āhuḥ*** *they call Kāla* ***parame vyoman*** *which extends up to the heaven*

The universe is a full vessel set upon Kāla
that we see becoming manifold
That which is the universe they call Kāla
which extends up to the heaven

What people know as the universe, is actually *Kāla,* which is like a full vessel unfolding itself variously as months, years, etc. The universe and time are interconnected – a person cannot see one without the other. Note that these insights about the intertwined nature of space and time predate Einstein by several thousand years at the least!

Another interpretation is that God with form, manifesting as the universe, sits on the indivisible consciousness like a full vessel.

स एव सं भुवनान्याभरत्स एव सं भुवनानि पर्यैत्।
पिता सन्नभवत्पुत्र एषां तस्माद्वै नान्यत्परमस्ति तेजः ॥4

sa eva saṃ bhuvanāny-ābharat-sa eva saṃ bhuvanāni paryait
pitā sannabhavat-putra eṣāṃ tasmādvai nānyat-param-asti tejaḥ

saḥ eva sam bhuvanāni ā abharat *He manifests the beings* ***saḥ eva sam bhuvanāni pari ait*** *he only gathered the worlds of living things together*

pitā san *being father* ***abhavat putraḥ eṣām*** *he became son of these* ***tasmāt vai na anyat param asti tejaḥ*** *no other higher power than he exists*

He only made the worlds of life,
he only gathered the worlds of living things together
He, the father, became son of them
No other higher power exists than he

Kāla makes the beings manifest, he sustains them, and gathers them together as a whole to make different *lokās*. More importantly, even though he is the father of all, he is born as their son, since nothing is outside *Kāla*.

This indeed is a very interesting description of God.

The remaining verses (5–10) explain that *Kāla* created things like space, earth, etc., and mind, *Prāṇa* (vital energies), etc. are also in *Kāla* only.

Later spiritual books developed this idea into fully grown philosophies and religious systems.

9.
MĀYĀBHEDA
PIERCING THE VEIL
Ṛgveda: X.177

The hymns of the Veda were used during *yajña* as prayers to various gods and goddesses. That should not make us think that the Veda were only about rituals, these had hymns that often hinted at or talked directly about what lies beyond the realm of mind.

In the simplest presentation of Indian spiritual philosophy, the realm of relative existence characterized by birth and death, subject and object, is identical with mind. To distinguish the perception of the world as real from the reality of its relative existence, the terms often used in Vedanta are mind and *māyā*. The use of 'mind' implies that the world is being perceived as real (by the mind), and the use of '*māyā*' implies the unreality of the absoluteness of the world or mind. For dualists and materialists, the world and mind are real, but that is not so with Vedanta.

What is *māyā*? Speaking simply, it is the divine power of God that makes the absolute appear as relative. It is thus that the all-pervading, indivisible, infinite Brahman appears as manifold. Those under its sway, which includes all who identify themselves with their mind, see the multiplicity, but one who has realized Ātman, remains merged with, and thus sees only the indivisible non-dual, which is beyond *māyā*.

Thus, *māyā* exists only for those who are under its spell due to their identification with mind. But the noble souls who have gone beyond the realm of the mind, realize that *māyā* never had an existence. If *māyā* were to be real, then the possibility of a liberated person to fall under its sway again is also equally real. In that case *mukti* will become a useless term, and all the scriptures too will become useless since there will be no freedom.

This hymn, dedicated to *Māyābheda,* meaning piercing the veil of *māyā,* is aimed at taking one beyond *māyā*. The prayer is addressed to Sun, but as in the *Gāyatrī* mantra, this too is used to pray to God, who is represented here by the Sun.

Devatā: Māyābheda
Ṛṣi: Pataṅgaḥ Prājāpatyaḥ

पतंगमक्तमसुरस्य मायया हृदा पश्यन्ति मनसा विपश्चितः ।
समुद्रे अन्तः कवयो वि चक्षते मरीचीनां पदमिच्छन्ति वेधसः ॥ 1

patamgam-aktam-asurasya māyayā hṛdā paśyanti manasā vipaścitaḥ
samudre antaḥ kavayo vi cakṣate marīcīnāṃ padam-icchanti vedhasaḥ

pataṅgam *Sun* ***aktam*** *manifest* ***asurasya*** *all-consuming* ***māyayā*** *through māyā* ***hṛdā*** *in the heart* ***paśyanti*** *see* ***manasā*** *with the mind* ***vipaḥ citaḥ*** *the sage*
samudre *God* ***antaḥ*** *within* ***kavayaḥ*** *the sages* ***vi cakṣate*** *to watch* ***marīcīnām*** *beam* ***padam icchanti*** *desires for the abode* ***vedhasaḥ*** *the knower*

The sages see with their mind (seated) in their heart
the Sun made manifest by māyā
The wise look into the solar orb for the ordainer
and the knower desire the abode of the rays

This hymn too belongs to the category of esoteric hymns of the Veda where one needs to go deeper to understand the true import of the words. It describes how the sages mediate on the Sun, who is the wonderful manifestation of God in the realm and by the power of *māyā*. Jesus Christ had beautifully said, 'He Who Has Seen Me Has Seen The Father', which when applied here, would mean that one who has realized the manifestation of God in the universe, has realized God. As has been described in the previous sections, there is no single way to see the manifestation of God in this world, implying – as many faiths, so many paths! In this verse, that manifestation is the Sun.

The sage says that *hṛdā paśyanti manasā vipaḥ citaḥ*, the sages see with their controlled mind in their heart. The importance of a complete cessation of *vṛttis* of the mind is a must for the supreme knowledge of God. The *vṛttis* of the mind are the mental activities that arise due to sense inputs, imagination, delusion, memories and dreams. When the wise succeed in silencing the *vṛttis*, they can then behold the spiritual reality. Spiritual realizations do not happen outside of oneself but inside the heart, the seat of meditation. For this reason, *hṛdā paśyanti manasā vipaḥ citaḥ* is quite a common expression, sometimes phrased differently, in the Veda and in the *Upaniṣads*.

What did the sage of this hymn see? *Pataṅgam aktam asurasya māyayā*, the Sun made manifest by *māyā*. The word *pataṅgam* here means the Sun, since it moves (or appears to move), as implied by the word. The characteristic of the Sun is described as the one who *aktam*, has been made manifest *māyayā*, by the power of *māyā* which by its nature is *asura*, all consuming. As one can see, it would be impossible for anyone to understand this line without the help of the commentator, who compares *māyā* with *asura* and explains this term as 'all consuming'.

As with all poetic allegory, the intended meaning can only be grasped by one who is familiar with the social and cultural context in which the verses were composed. This no doubt further vitiated the efforts of various western scholars in the past couple of centuries, who tended to make literal translations of idiomatic expressions.

God manifests variously in this world through its *māyā.* Sun is one of those manifestations. In its orb a sage sees the face of God instead of the sun-rays. This fact has been stated at other places in the Veda too. This idea is elaborated as *kavayaḥ*, the sages *samudre antaḥ vicakṣate*, perceive the reality within the solar orb/ God, once the multiplicity of the world is unified in Him by controlling one's mental activity. The word *samudra* normally means ocean, but it is often used in the Veda to mean God.

The sage wishes to see God by meditating on the solar orb and *padam icchanti*, desirous of attaining His state by being *vedhasaḥ* the knower of the fact that all multiplicity represented by *marīcīnām*, sun rays, become one in the ocean of light. Sun rays here represent multiplicity.

The overall meaning of the verse is that the wise meditate on the solar orb, control their mind, have a direct vision of God in their hearts, and then they become one with the sphere of light known as *Suryaloka*. Or it may mean that the wise control their mind completely to be one with Brahman, and thus efface the distinction between the individual and the universal. This effacement becomes possible only when the multiplicity of the universe is pushed back into the oneness of God, as described by the solar orb and sunlight. A sage sees the Divine within the solar orb only when he goes beyond the sunlight, which is multiplicity. This has also been described in *Īśa Upaniṣad* (mantra 15).

पतंगो वाचं मनसा बिभर्ति तां गन्धर्वोऽवदद्गर्भे अन्तः ।
तां द्योतमानां स्वर्यं मनीषामृतस्य पदे कवयो नि पान्ति ॥ 2

patamgo vācaṃ manasā bibharti tāṃ gandharvo-vadad-garbhe antaḥ
tāṃ dyotamānāṃ svaryaṃ manīṣām-ṛtasya pade kavayo ni pānti

pataṅgaḥ *Sun (God)* ***vācam*** *words (Veda)* ***manasā*** *in the mind* ***bibharti*** *hold* ***tām*** *that* ***gandharvaḥ*** *the vital breath* ***avadat*** *propelled to come out* ***garbhe antaḥ*** *within the womb*

tām *that* ***dyotamānām*** *shine* ***svaryam*** *heavenly* ***manīṣām*** *sages* ***ṛtasya*** *truth* ***pade*** *abode* ***kavayaḥ*** *sages* ***ni pānti*** *protect*

Sun bears the word in his mind
Prāṇa has spoken it, (abiding) within the womb
Sages cherish it in the place of worship
brilliant, heavenly, ruling the mind

The previous mantra taught that the soul (*jīva*) abides within God, which is compared to an ocean. This truth can be known only by contemplating on the words, which are the Veda. This fact is now taken forward in this verse which says that 'words', sum total of ideas, stay with every soul (*jīva*), and so the wise never neglect the 'words'. Neglecting knowledge invariably leads to more and more worldly snares, away from God.

So, the importance of words is being extolled as *pataṅgaḥ vācam manasā bibharti*, God (Sun in the world of *māyā*) had the word in His mind before Creation. Hindus believe that when God wished to create, He had the Veda in His mind, which became the basis of Creation. The Veda is word.

Interestingly, Greeks too had the concept of Creation proceeding from *logos*, words, which was taken up in the Christian tradition as 'In the beginning was the Word, and the Word was with God, and the Word was God.' (John 1.1)

In the next stage of Creation *tām gandharvaḥ avadat garbhe antaḥ*, that word (Veda/ knowledge) is impelled by the vital breaths. The word *gandharva* generally means a kind of demi-gods but here it means 'that which holds the words (one meaning of *gāḥ* is word)', implying *prāṇa*, the vital breath. It may also mean that when Creation took place, the first manifestation of God, *Hiraṇyagarbha* (see *Hiraṇyagarbha Sūkta*), uttered that word, that is, the Veda. In the *Bhāgavata Purāṇa*, this fact has been described beautifully as when the creator God *Brahmā* appeared he was instructed by God as to how to proceed with the difficult work of Creation.

The quality of the word (Veda) is extolled as *dyotamānām svaryam manīṣām*, brilliant, heavenly and ruler of mind, and so *tām*, that *kavayaḥ ni pānti*, is preserved by the sages *ṛtasya pade*, in the abode of Truth, meaning God. This preservation by the sages is carried out through the performance of *yajña* or through other means like worship.

It is envisioned here that the Veda were held in the Mind of God and then uttered by Him, and now preserved by the sages. It is by learning the Veda and contemplating upon their meaning that a person gets to understand the reality about God and himself, and then they get down to realizing their true nature.

अपश्यं गोपामनिपद्यमानमा च परा च पथिभिश्चरन्तम् ।
स सध्रीचीः स विषूचीर्वसान आ वरीवर्ति भुवनेष्वन्तः ॥ 3

apaśyaṃ gopām-anipadyamānam-ā ca parā ca pathibhiś-carantam
sa sadhrīcīḥ sa viṣūcīr-vasāna ā varīvarti bhuvaneṣv-antaḥ

apaśyam gopām *I beheld the protector* ***anipadyamānam*** *never deviating* ***ā ca parā ca pathibhiḥ carantam*** *who moves on his path in various ways*

saḥ *he* ***sadhrīcīḥ*** *with fellow traveller (for Sun the fellow traveller is the night)* ***saḥ viṣūcīḥ vasānaḥ*** *he covers everything* ***ā varīvarti*** *with light* ***bhuvaneṣu antaḥ*** *among the worlds*

I beheld the ever-present God
who moves on his path in various ways
He fills the universe with light
and moves constantly in the midst of the worlds

This mantra (verse) is so important that it comes in RV I.164–31; YV 37.17 and AV IX.10.11 too.

The aim of the Veda is to transport the aspirant to God and have a direct vision of God. Anyone who talks about God or about scriptures should be able to tell boldly that they have seen God. In this mantra, the sage boldly says *apaśyam gopām*, I saw God. This assertion of seeing God is the ultimate test of religion. When Narendranath (later Swami Vivekananda) asked Sri Ramakrishna if he had seen God, the answer was in the affirmative and that he could make Narendranath also realize God, which ultimately came to be true.

The sage boldly asserts *apaśyam gopām*, I beheld the protector. The word *gopām* means protector, which can mean God, Sun, or the soul within a body-mind complex. These three protect their respective kingdoms diligently. The nature of this protector is described as *anipadyamānam*, one who never rests. God, as the lord of the universe, or as Sun, or as the soul, is ever active and watches over its protected ones all the time.

Further he *pathibhiḥ carantam*, moves on the path *ā ca parā ca*, in various ways – the soul moves from one species to another, and the Sun and stars move variously in space giving light to all. Even God is active all the time, as Gita says in III.22. 'I am always engaged in action.'

As light *saḥ sadhrīcīḥ saḥ viṣūcīḥ vasānaḥ*, He (God/ Sun) with Night, who is like his fellow traveller, *ā varīvarti bhuvaneṣu antaḥ*, fills the entire universe with light. God is the divine light whose presence is everywhere, at all times. In the physical world He appears as the light of the sun, moon and the stars, and thus He never rests and never lets anything down.

Thus, God, who is the subject-matter of the Veda, is ever-present and can be directly perceived by anyone who strives to make themselves pure and calm.

10.
SAMJÑĀNA SŪKTA
THE LAST HYMN OF THE ṚGVEDA
Ṛgveda: X.191

This is the last hymn of the Ṛgveda in which the sage prays for unity among the priests/ students so that they can achieve the desired result while performing a *yajña*. For this, they will all need to speak, think, act and aspire in harmony. The problem of discord seems to have ailed India since the ancient times!

Interestingly, this hymn has two different deities for prayer, one of them being Agni and the other one *Saṃjñāna*, unanimity in the assembly.

Devatā: Agni-1, Saṃjñāna (Unanimity in the assembly) **2–4**
Ṛṣi: Saṃvanana

संसमिद्युवसे वृषन्नग्ने विश्वान्यर्य आ ।
इळस्पदे समिध्यसे स नो वसून्या भर ॥ 1

saṃ-sam-id-yuvase vṛṣann-agne viśvāny-arya ā
iḻas-pade sam-idhyase sa no vasūny-ā bhara

sam-sam *together* ***it*** *indeed* ***yuvase*** *to unite* ***vṛṣan*** *showerer of gifts* ***agne*** *Agni!* ***viśvāni*** *of the universe* ***aryaḥ*** *the lord* ***ā*** *towards*

iḷaḥ pade *at the place of worship* ***sam idhyase*** *you are kindled* ***saḥ*** *as such* ***naḥ*** *to us* ***vasūni ā bhara*** *bring the desirable*

Agni! The fulfiller of desires, you are the lord
and you indeed unite with all

You are kindled at the altar of earth
as such bring unto us the desirable

God stays in all beings as existence, intelligence, life, growth, hunger, death, decay, etc. The prayer in this verse shows the thread of unity that runs through all living beings in the form of the fire of hunger, which is one aspect of Agni.

The sage prays *vṛṣan agne*, Agni! You are the fulfiller of all desires by showering gift on the devotees and *aryaḥ* you are the lord of the universe since *samsam* you unite *it yuvase viśvāni ā* all beings in you, by being the fire of hunger within them.

Moreover, *iḷaḥ pade sam idhyase* you are kindled by the priests at the place of worship to honour you. Other gods are not visible to the mortal eye but Agni readily manifests Himself, bright and hot, whenever kindled! Hence, the devotee takes delight in him and prays *saḥ naḥ vasūni ā bhara* bless us with the desirable.

The word *vasu* means something that is beneficent. However, the word is often translated as wealth, which is desired by many, but is not something truly desirable! Sages, saints and monks rarely crave for wealth, and so this prayer will lose its universality if *vasu* is interpreted only as wealth, which is not even its literal meaning.

सं गच्छध्वं सं वदध्वं सं वो मनांसि जानताम् ।
देवा भागं यथा पूर्वे संजानाना उपासते ॥ 2

saṃ gacchadhvaṃ saṃ vadadhvaṃ saṃ vo manāṃsi jānatām
devā bhāgaṃ yathā pūrve saṃjānānā upāsate

sam *together* ***gacchadhvam*** *be* ***sam vadadhvam*** *speak in unison* ***sam*** *alike* ***vaḥ*** *your* ***manāṃsi jānatām*** *understanding by mind*

devāḥ *the gods* ***bhāgam*** *share* ***yathā*** *as* ***pūrve*** *in the past* ***saṃjānānāḥ upāsate*** *accepted the offering*

(O worshippers!) Be you all together and speak in unison
let your understanding be alike
Just as the gods in ancient times accepted
their share of the offerings in harmony

The learned priests are going to perform a *yajña*, so the head priest reminds them all to be focused and to be of one mind all the time. Their words, acts, thoughts and understanding must be one – an essential condition for success in any undertaking. This verse also teaches the importance of unity in any system.

O worshippers! *sam gacchadhvam* you all be together *sam vadadhvam* and speak in unison, let there be no discord of any kind during what you do. And, *vaḥ* let your *sam manāṃsi jānatām* understanding of what you do and speak be alike. Thus, the sage cautions the priests to know what they speak and chant, and in that too they all must have the right understanding. In spirituality, right understanding implies unanimity.

To impress upon the worshippers the importance of non-discord, the sage reminds them how the gods too, in older times, have lived happily because of their unanimity, *devāḥ bhāgam yathā pūrve saṃjānānāḥ upāsate* the way the gods accepted their share of the offering in harmony.

It is in the nature of the self-centred, greedy and the uncultured to fight among themselves for material well-being but the culturally elevated never behave that way. The mention of sharing of offerings by the gods is to exemplify how they act without any discord.

समानो मन्त्रः समितिः समानी समानं मनः सह चित्तमेषाम् ।
समानं मन्त्रमभि मन्त्रये वः समानेन वो हविषा जुहोमि ॥ 3

samāno mantraḥ samitiḥ samānī samānaṃ manaḥ saha cittam-eṣām
samānaṃ mantram-abhi mantraye vaḥ samānena vo haviṣā juhomi

samānaḥ mantraḥ *let your prayers be in unison* ***samitiḥ samānī*** *your coming together be one* ***samānam manaḥ*** *your mind be in harmony* ***saha cittam*** *similar be your thoughts* ***eṣām*** *in this act*

samānam mantram abhi mantraye *I chant a common prayer* ***vaḥ*** *for you* ***samānena vaḥ haviṣā juhomi*** *I offer for you a common oblation*

Let your prayers be in unison, and your acts
let your thoughts and minds be in harmony
I chant for you a common prayer, and
I offer for you a common oblation

The act of *yajña* is extremely important, so the sage cautions that may you all be similar in resolve, thought and act. *Samānaḥ mantraḥ* may the chants and prayers that you utter, be in harmony with your intonations and pronunciations synchronized, and *samitiḥ samānī* may your acts be harmonious. The word *samitiḥ* means group, or the acts of a group. According to some, the word means 'attainment', which implies remuneration. But this interpretation is far-fetched and at odds with the general tone of the prayer.

To avoid discord by word or deed, the sage prays *samānam manaḥ saha cittam eṣām* may your mind and thoughts be united. The words *citta* and *manas* both mean mind but their functions are different. Here *citta* means thoughts, while *manas* means the intellect that has been focused by training from the scriptures and the teachers on what is right.

The sage gives reassurance that he is with those whom he has been instructing, *samānam mantram abhi mantraye vaḥ* I chant prayers for you in unison, and *samānena vaḥ haviṣā juhomi* I offer oblations with you.

For any team, unity has to be at all levels, and it has to be demonstrated in practice by the leader.

समानी व आकूतिः समाना हृदयानि वः ।
समानमस्तु वो मनो यथा वः सुसहासति ॥ 4

samānī va ākūtiḥ samānā hṛdayāni vaḥ
samānam-astu vo mano yathā vaḥ susahāsati

samānī vaḥ ākūtiḥ *may your will be in concord* **samānā hṛdayāni vaḥ** *may your feelings be alike*

samānam astu vaḥ manaḥ *may your thoughts be same* **yathā vaḥ su-saha asati** *thus be there harmony among you*

May your will be in concord
may your feelings be alike

May your thoughts be same
thus be there harmony among you

The sage concludes his instructions and wishes *samānī vaḥ ākūtiḥ*, may your intent be in concord, *samānā hṛdayāni vaḥ*, may your feeling be alike, *samānam astu vaḥ manaḥ*, may your thoughts be the same, and *yathā vaḥ susaha asati*, thus may there be thorough harmony among you.

To complete the *yajña*, or any project, the will, feelings, thoughts, acts – everything – must be in harmony. This is the prayer – the last prayer of the Ṛgveda.

VI

HYMNS TO GOD AS NATURE

It was detailed in Chapter 1, how the Hindus look at existence as being of three layers, known as *sthūla jagat, sūkṣma jagat* and *kāraṇa jagat*, with *mahākāraṇa* being the underpinning state of non-dual existence. Seen closely, the first three spheres of existence are a manifestation of God, while the fourth one is being one with God.

The sages, however, saw the manifestation of God in all three states of *sthūla, sūkṣma* and *kāraṇa jagat*, the way one sees the same water in its various states of ice, vapour and water. They thus deified cosmic entities and events, like Sun, Dawn, Night, etc; they also venerated more tangible manifestations like rivers, mountains and other terrestrial features and phenomena.

The important thing to note in this is that a sacred river or a mountain does not get its sanctity by being itself but because a Hindu sees it as another manifestation of God.

This section offers a glimpse into how the Vedic sages worshipped nature in the form of rivers and clouds.

1.
NADĪ SŪKTA
NADI SUKTA: RIVER
Ṛgveda: X.75

Āpaḥ, the waters, are treated as sacred in the Indian spiritual tradition because of their cleansing and healing powers. It is a common practice in India to pray to all the rivers to come and be present in the water that is to be used for worship. Flowing water is treated as more sacred, since it signifies life, and the end of its journey in the ocean is akin to the individual merging with the universal.

This hymn is dedicated to all the major rivers of India, but particularly to River Sindhu popularly known as Indus, which originates in Western Tibet, flows through the Ladakh and Gilgit-Baltistan regions to present-day Pakistan, and then merges into the Arabian Sea near Karachi, covering a length of more than 3200 km. Compared to it, Ganga is 2500 km long. On its way to the Arabian sea, many tributaries pour their content into Sindhu to make its 'roar sound like that of a bull!'

It is believed that a majority of the hymns in the Veda were composed by sages who lived on or near the banks of the Sindhu. Thus, it had the same appeal to people of those times as Ganga has in present times. This also shows how Hinduism is a living and dynamic religion – moving on to Ganga from praying to Sindhu.

The word Sindhu is mentioned hundreds of times in the Veda, of which a great number of times is in the plural, often used in a generic way, while it is narrowed to refer to Sindhu river in the Ṛgveda.

Devatā: Nadyaḥ (Rivers)
Ṛṣi: Sindhukṣit praiyamedhaḥ

प्र सु व आपो महिमानमुत्तमं कारुर्वोचाति सदने विवस्वतः ।
प्र सप्तसप्त त्रेधा हि चक्रमुः प्र सृत्वरीणामति सिन्धुरोजसा ॥ 1

pra su va āpo mahimānam-uttamaṃ kārur-vocāti sadane vivasvataḥ
pra sapta-sapta tredhā hi cakramuḥ pra sṛtvarīṇām-ati sindhur-ojasā

pra su *to proclaim* ***vaḥ*** *to you* ***āpaḥ*** *O sacred Waters!* ***mahimānam uttamam*** *the grandeur beyond compare* ***kāruḥ vocāti*** *I, the reciter of hymns, will narrate* ***sadane vivasvataḥ*** *at this place of worship*

pra sapta-sapta tredhā hi cakramuḥ pra sṛtvarīṇām *the rivers flow forward triply, seven and seven* ***ati sindhuḥ ojasā*** *Sindhu in might surpasses all*

In this place of worship, I shall narrate your grandeur
O ye Āpaḥ! that is beyond compare
The rivers flow triply, seven and seven
Sindhu surpasses all by its might

The river Sindhu is being extolled by the sage as being superior to all the rivers in the heaven, earth and the mid-regions.

pra su vaḥ āpaḥ mahimānam uttamam kāruḥ vocāti sadane vivasvataḥ – The prayer is being offered by *kāruḥ* the reciter of hymns *Sindhukṣit addressed to Āpaḥ* at *sadane vivasvataḥ* the place of Vivasvān, who might have organized a *yajña* at his place. Or it might be simply at some place of worship. This prayer is about the incomparable grandeur of *Āpaḥ*, the sacred waters, who is flowing as river Sindhu.

pra sapta-sapta tredhā hi cakramuḥ pra sṛtvarīṇām ati sindhuḥ ojasā – Sindhu is superior to all the rivers that flow *tredhā*, in the three spheres of earth, space and heavens, in the group of seven. The seven sacred rivers that have a generic importance in the Indian culture are: *Gaṅgā, Yamunā, Godāvarī, Sarasvatī, Narmadā, Sindhu* and *Kāverī*.

These rivers are believed to have their existence in other spheres of existence too.

प्र तेऽरदद्वरुणो यातवे पथः सिन्धो यद्वाजान् अभ्यद्रवस्त्वम् ।
भूम्या अधि प्रवता यासि सानुना यदेषामग्रं जगतामिरज्यसि ॥ 2

pra te-radad-varuṇo yātave pathaḥ sindho yad-vājān abhya-dravas-tvam
bhūmyā adhi pravatā yāsi sānunā yad-eṣām-agraṃ jagatām-irajyasi

pra te aradat varuṇaḥ yātave pathaḥ *Varuṇa cut the channels for your forward course* **sindho** *O Sindhu!* **yat vājān abhi adravaḥ tvam** *when you ran towards the fertile plains*

bhūmyāḥ adhi pravatā yāsi sānunā *you flow over ridges to the land which lies low* **yat eṣām agram jagatām irajyasi** *since you flow like this you are the lord of all beings*

Varuṇa cut the channels for your forward course
O Sindhu, when you ran towards the fertile plains

You flow over ridges high to the low of earth
since you are like this, you are the lord of all

pra te aradat varuṇaḥ yātave pathaḥ sindho – Varuṇa, the god of waters, made the path for your forward course, O Sindhu! The sage believes that the path for Sindhu has been made by God himself. This idea is repeated in the story of the descent of Ganga in which the sagely king *Bhagīratha* guided it to the plains.

yat vājān abhi adravaḥ tvam – When you ran towards the fertile plains. The origin of Indus being in the Himalayas, it cascades its way through different valleys and finally reaches the plain (now in Pakistan) where it makes the Punjab provinces hugely fertile. This fact is stated in the expression *vājān abhi adravaḥ tvam*, which literally means that 'you ran towards the grain.'

bhūmyāḥ adhi pravatā yāsi sānunā – You flow over high ridges of the mountains to the lower plains of earth.

yat eṣām agram jagatām irajyasi – Since you flow over the high mountain ridges to bless people with water, you are the visible lord of all beings.

दिवि स्वनो यतते भूम्योपर्यनन्तं शुष्ममुदियर्ति भानुना ।
अभ्रादिव प्र स्तनयन्ति वृष्टयः सिन्धुर्यदेति वृषभो न रोरुवत् ॥ 3

divi svano yatate bhūmyopary-anantaṃ śuṣmam-ud-iyarti bhānunā
abhrād-iva pra stanayanti vṛṣṭayaḥ sindhur-yad-eti vṛṣabho na roruvat

divi svanaḥ yatate *his roar is lifted* ***bhūmyā upari*** *up to heaven from the earth* ***anantam śuṣmam ut iyarti bhānunā*** *with shining wave animates his endless speed*

abhrāt iva pra stanayanti vṛṣṭayaḥ *like floods of rain that fall thundering from the cloud*

sindhuḥ yat eti *so Sindhu rushes on* ***vṛṣabhaḥ na roruvat*** *bellowing like a bull*

His roar is lifted up to heaven from the earth
and the shining waves animate his unbridled speed
Like floods of rain that fall thundering from the cloud
so Sindhu rushes on bellowing like a bull

divi svanaḥ yatate bhūmyā upari – Sindhu, although on the earth, the sound of its flow reaches up to the sky, and *anantam śuṣmam ut iyarti bhānunā*, its waves seem to be shining, which move with tremendous speed.

abhrāt iva pra stanayanti vṛṣṭayaḥ sindhuḥ yat eti vṛṣabhaḥ na roruvat – The rushing of the river appears like that of a bellowing bull, and it sounds at that time like rain thundering down from the sky.

अभि त्वा सिन्धो शिशुमिन्न मातरो वाश्रा अर्षन्ति पयसेव धेनवः ।
राजेव युध्वा नयसि त्वमित्सिचौ यदासामग्रं प्रवतामिनक्षसि ॥ 4

abhi tvā sindho śiśum-in-na mātaro vāśrā arṣanti payaseva dhenavaḥ
rājeva yudhvā nayasi tvam-it-sicau yad-āsām-agraṃ pravatām-inakṣasi

abhi tvā *towards you* ***sindho śiśum it na mātaraḥ*** *like mothers to their kids, O Sindhu*

vāśrāḥ *roaring (streams)* ***arṣanti*** *rush* ***payasā iva dhenavaḥ*** *(and) like milk cows*

rājā-iva yudhvā nayasi tvam it *indeed you lead as a king in a war* ***sicau yat āsām agram pravatām inakṣasi*** *when you move between the banks leading these swift streams*

Like mothers to their babies, like cows with their milk
so, Sindhu, unto you the roaring rivers run
You lead as a king in the war when you move
between the banks leading these swift streams

The sages, who lived during the Vedic period, loved the rivers, adored them with prayers and worship, and compared their flow and sound to various objects. In the *Ṛgveda* (III.33.1), the flow and merging of Sutlej and Vyasa has been compared to two mares racing with each other and to cows that rush to lick their calves.

abhi tvā sindho śiśum it na mātaraḥ vāśrāḥ arṣanti payasā- iva dhenavaḥ – Here the merging of various rivers with Sindhu has been compared with a doting mother rushing towards her baby, and a milk cow rushing towards its calf.

sicau yat āsām agram pravatām inakṣasi – When Sindhu flows between its banks in full flow, how does it look? *rājā-iva yudhvā nayasi tvam it* – Indeed, Sindhu then looks like a king leading his army to a war.

The imagery, both as masculine and feminine, is beautiful, depicting both regal majesty and motherly love; but more important is the personalization of the river as distinct from the water that it carries in its course.

इमं मे गङ्गे यमुने सरस्वति शुतुद्रि स्तोमं सचता परुष्ण्या ।
असिक्न्या मरुद्वृधे वितस्तयार्जीकीये शृणुह्या सुषोमया ॥ 5

imaṃ me gaṅge yamune sarasvati śutudri stomaṃ sacatā paruṣṇyā
asiknyā marudvṛdhe vitastayārjīkīye śṛṇuhyā suṣomayā

imam me *this (prayer) of mine* ***gaṅge yamune sarasvati śutudri*** *O Gaṅgā, Yamunā, Sarasvatī Śutudri,* ***stomam*** *this prayer* ***sacatā*** *accept* ***paruṣṇi ā*** *and Paruṣṇi*
asiknyā marutvṛdhe vitastayā ārjīkīye *with Asiknī and Vitastā; O Marudvṛdhā, O Ārjikīya*
śṛṇuhi ā *listen to (this prayer)* ***susomayā*** *Suṣomā*

Accept this prayer of mine, O Gaṅgā,
Yamunā, Śutudrī, Paruṣṇi and Sarasvatī
With Asiknī and Vitastā; O Marudvṛdhā
hear my prayer O Ārjikīya with Suṣomā

To remind, this hymn is actually addressed to *Āpaḥ*, the waters, who appear on the earth as various rivers. After praising Sindhu, the hymn now moves towards other major rivers of India.

This verse lists the names of the major rivers. Some of these names have undergone a change with time: Śutudrī (Śatadru) – Sutlej, Paruṣṇi – Iravati or Ravi, Asiknī – Chenab, Vitastā – Jhelum, Marudvṛdhā – Chenab and Jhelam together, Ārjikīya – Vipās or Vyās, Upper Indus, Suṣomā – Sohan/ Indus (according to Yāska).

तृष्टामया प्रथमं यातवे सजूः सुसर्त्वा रसया श्वेत्या त्या ।
त्वं सिन्धो कुभया गोमतीं क्रुमुं मेहत्न्वा सरथं याभिरीयसे ॥ 6

tṛṣṭāmayā prathamaṃ yātave sajūḥ susartvā rasayā śvetyā tyā
tvaṃ sindho kubhayā gomatīṃ krumuṃ mehatnvā sarathaṃ yābhirīyase

tṛṣṭaamayā prathamam yātave sajūḥ *you first united with* Tṛṣṭāmā ***susartvā rasayā śvetyā tyā*** *and then with* Susartu, Rasā, Śveti, Ti,

tvam sindho *you Sindhu* ***kubhayā mehatnvā*** *(met with) Kubha, and Mehatnu,* ***saratham*** *(as if) mounted on the same chariot* ***yābhiḥ īyase gomatīm*** *when you proceed to meet Gomatī* ***krumum*** *Krumu river/ to move rapidly*

Sindhu! you united with Tṛṣṭāmā
and then with Susartu, Rasā, Śveti, Ti, Kubha, Mehatnu,
With whom you advance
to meet Krumu and Gomatī

The left-bank tributary of Indus in Ladakh is the Zanskar River, and its left-bank tributary in the plains is the Panjnad River, formed by Chenab, Jhelum, Ravi, Beas, and Sutlej. Its principal right-bank tributaries are the Shyok, Gilgit, Kabul, Kurram, and Gomal.

This verse lists the tributaries of Indus as they were known then: Tṛṣṭāmā, Rasā, Susartu, Ti, Mehantu – these are the tributaries whose present names are not known with certainty. Śveti – Gilgit river, Kubha – Kabul river, Gomatī – Gomal flowing through Afghanistan-Pakistan, Krumu – Kurrama, meets Indus in Isa Khel.

Interestingly, Sāyaṇācārya does not mention the river Krumu, probably because he was not aware of that river. Instead, he interprets 'Krumu' as 'fast flowing', to be used as an adjective for Gomatī river. This Gomatī should not be confused with the river flowing in Uttar Pradesh.

ऋजीत्येनी रुशती महित्वा परि ज्रयांसि भरते रजांसि ।
अदब्धा सिन्धुरपसामपस्तमाश्वा न चित्रा वपुषीव दर्शता ॥ 7

ṛjīty-enī ruśatī mahitvā pari jrayāṃsi bharate rajāṃsi
adabdhā sindhur-apasām-apastamāśvā na citrā vapuṣīva darśatā

ṛjītī *straight flowing* ***enī*** *white coloured* ***ruśatī*** *bright* ***mahitvā*** *in her mightiness* ***pari jrayāṃsi*** *to move rapidly* ***bharate*** *full* ***rajāṃsi*** *water*

adabdhā *unimpaired* ***sindhuḥ*** *Sindhu* ***apasām*** *among the flowing waters* ***apaḥ-tamā*** *the best* ***aśvā na citrā*** *like a beautiful mare* ***vapuṣī iva*** *like a handsome lady* ***darśatā*** *appears*

Straight-flowing, white-coloured, bright (Sindhu)
bears along in its might the rapid waters
Most active of the active, Sindhu unrestrained
is speckled like a mare, beautiful as a handsome lady

Sindhu is now praised for its speed and the volumes of water it carries. More importantly, it is compared here to a mare and a lady, making it look feminine, while earlier it was compared to a bull and a king.

स्वश्वा सिन्धुः सुरथा सुवासा हिरण्ययी सुकृता वाजिनीवती ।
ऊर्णावती युवतिः सीलमावत्युताधि वस्ते सुभगा मधुवृधम् ॥ 8

svaśvā sindhuḥ surathā suvāsā hiraṇyayī sukṛtā vājinīvatī
ūrṇāvatī yuvatiḥ sīlamāvaty-utādhi vaste subhagā madhuvṛdham

suaśvā sindhuḥ *rich in horses is Sindhu* ***surathā suvāsāḥ*** *rich in chariots and robes* ***hiraṇyayī sukṛtā vājinīvatī*** *rich in gold, well-fashioned, rich in grains*

ūrṇāvatī *abounding in wool* ***yuvatiḥ*** *ever fresh* ***sīlamāvatī*** *rich in plants* ***uta*** *and* ***adhi vaste*** *decorated with* ***subhagā*** *auspicious (Sindhu)* ***madhu-vṛdham*** *having honey growing flowers*

Rich in horses is Sindhu, rich in chariots and robes
rich in gold, well-fashioned, rich in grains
Abounding in wool, ever fresh, rich in plants
and the auspicious river is flush with flowers

Indus, the great river, is famous for its flora and fauna that produce rich varieties of grains, flowers, wool, horses and other things.

सुखं रथं युयुजे सिन्धुरश्विनं तेन वाजं सनिषदस्मिन्नाजौ ।
महान्ह्यस्य महिमा पनस्यतेऽदब्धस्य स्वयशसो विरप्शिनः ॥ 9

sukhaṃ rathaṃ yuyuje sindhur-aśvinaṃ tena vājaṃ saniṣad-asminn-ājau
mahān-hy-asya mahimā panasyate-dabdhasya svayaśaso virapśinaḥ

sukham *joyful* ***ratham yuyuje sindhuḥ*** *Sindhu has yoked his chariot* ***aśvinam*** *drawn by horses* ***tena*** *with that (chariot)* ***vājam*** *strength* ***saniṣat asmin*** *may he give us* ***ājau*** *in this battle*

mahān hi *great* ***asya*** *its* ***mahimā*** *glory* ***panasyate*** *I recited* ***adabdhasya*** *unimpaired* ***svayaśasaḥ*** *his own glory* ***virapśinaḥ*** *ample*

Sindhu has yoked his car, light-rolling, drawn by steeds
and with that car shall he get us strength in this fight/yajña
So have I praised its power, mighty and unrestrained,
of independent glory, roaring as it runs

The prayer is being recited during a *yajña* in which the sage prays for the glory of Sindhu with the hope that it will bring riches to those who want, and strength to those who aspire for it.

The flow of the river is compared to that of a chariot yoked to powerful steeds, riding which a warrior conquers wars. Here the war is against poverty and weakness. The word *vāja* means grains and also strength. So, the prayer can be interpreted for grains, as also for strength.

2.
PARJANYA SŪKTA
PRAYER TO RAIN GOD
Ṛgveda: V.83

The rains in India are a fascinating spectacle, particularly during the monsoon when dark clouds come rolling like an army bearing down upon its enemy, sometimes silent, at other times thundering, to drive away the eternal enemy of life, the drought. It is then that the parched earth soaks every drop of rain to give life back to the dead or dying creepers, grass, trees, rivers, bipeds, quadrupeds, and humans.

If the rains fail, then God save the land, as has been graphically put by Will Durant in his monumental work *The Story of Civilisations: Our Oriental Heritage*, '... from Delhi to Ceylon, the dominating fact in India is heat: heat that has weakened the physique, shortened the youth and affected the quietest of quietest religion and philosophy of the inhabitants.

The only relief from this heat is to sit still, to do nothing, to desire nothing; or in the summer months the monsoon wind may bring cooling moisture and fertilizing rain from the sea. When the monsoon fails to blow, India starves, and dreams of Nirvana.'

There are many descriptions in scriptures when rains failed to come properly which resulted in death and destruction throughout the land. So, it is natural that the sages would see the rains as the great gift of God to humanity, nay the rains are no less than the visible face of God that comes down to earth to save all.

The Veda have many hymns and verses dedicated to rains. For example, Ṛgveda says:

तिस्रो वाचः प्र वद ज्योतिरग्रा या एतद्दुह्रे मधुदोघमूधः ।
स वत्सं कृण्वन्गर्भमोषधीनां सद्यो जातो वृषभो रोरवीति ॥ RV VII.101.1

tisro vācaḥ pra vada jyotiragrā yā etadduhre madhudoghamūdhaḥ
sa vatsaṃ kṛṇvangarbhamoṣadhīnāṃ sadyo jāto vṛṣabho roravīti

Recite the three texts of Vedas, preceded by light (Oṃ), which milk the water-yielding udder of Parjanya, who becomes quickly manifest, roars loudly, engendering the infant (lightning), and the embryo of the plants.

Sage Vasiṣṭha, having praised *Parjanya*, in order to procure rain, observing the frogs to be delighted by his praises, addresses them in Ṛgveda VII.103, famously known as *Maṇḍūka Sūkta* (hymn of the frog). The first verse reads:

संवत्सरं शशयाना ब्राह्मणा व्रतचारिणः । वाचं पर्जन्यजिन्वितां प्र मण्डूका अवादिषुः ॥
RV VII.103.1

saṃvatsaraṃ śaśayānā brāhmaṇā vratacāriṇaḥ
vācaṃ parjanyajinvitāṃ pra maṇḍūkā avādiṣuḥ

The frogs, like Brahmins observant of their vows, practising penance throughout the year, utter aloud praises agreeable to Parjnaya.

This hymn, dedicated to Parjanya, beautifully expresses the annual onset of rains, the unbearable heat that builds up before the monsoons and the relief of humans and animals when the first rains arrive.

Etymologically, Parjanya means 'one who satisfies; that which is born; that which makes victorious or causes birth; that which helps attain succour', but the general meaning of the word is the rain cloud, which of course fits all the other meaning. The shedding of rain is god Parjanya's most prominent characteristic. He flies around with a watery chariot and loosens the water-skin. In this activity he is associated with thunder and lightning. He is to a special degree the producer and nourisher of vegetation and by implication Earth is his wife.

Devatā: Parjanya
Ṛṣi: Bhauma, son of Atri

अच्छा वद तवसं गीर्भिराभिः स्तुहि पर्जन्यं नमसा विवास ।
कनिक्रदद्वृषभो जीरदानू रेतो दधात्योषधीषु गर्भम् ॥ 1

acchā vada tavasaṃ gīrbhir-ābhiḥ stuhi parjanyaṃ namasā vivāsa
kanikradad-vṛṣabho jīradānū reto dadhāty-oṣadhīṣu garbham

accha vada *having got Parjanya, (O reciters of prayers)* ***tavasam*** *mighty* ***gīḥ bhiḥ ābhiḥ stuhi*** *sing songs of welcome* ***parjanyam namasā*** *worship Parjanya with offerings* ***vivāsa*** *to serve well*

kanikradat *whose sound is like a roar* ***vṛṣabhaḥ*** *who showers rains* ***jīradānuḥ*** *who is bountiful* ***retaḥ dadhāti oṣadhīṣu garbham*** *who gives water to the plants as embryo*

Sing your welcome to the mighty Parjanya
praise him with hymns, worship with offerings
Who sounds like a thunder, gives showers, the bountiful
who lays in plants water as embryo

The sage exhorts those present at the place of worship to pray to *Parjanya*, who is visibly present in the form of the rain bearing clouds, who is mighty and whose roar is the thunder.

He is to be served well and thoroughly since he gives the rains, is bountiful because agriculture depends on him, and he lays rains in the plants as embryo. It is thus that the life of a plant becomes possible only because of the rains sent down by him.

वि वृक्षान्हन्त्युत हन्ति रक्षसो विश्वं बिभाय भुवनं महावधात् ।
उतानागा ईषते वृष्ण्यावतो यत्पर्जन्यः स्तनयन्हन्ति दुष्कृतः ॥ 2

vi vṛkṣān-hanty-uta hanti rakṣaso viśvaṃ bibhāya bhuvanaṃ mahāvadhāt
utānāgā īṣate vṛṣṇyāvato yat-parjanyaḥ stanayan-hanti duṣkṛtaḥ

vi vṛkṣān hanti *he strikes down the trees* ***uta hanti rakṣasaḥ*** *and destroys the evil* ***viśvam bibhāya*** *terrifies all* ***bhuvanam*** *on the earth* ***mahāvadhāt*** *mighty weapon*
uta anāgāḥ *and the innocent* ***īṣate*** *to flee* ***vṛṣṇya-vataḥ*** *one whose function is to pour rain* ***yat parjanyaḥ*** *as Parjanya* ***stanayan*** *thunder* ***hanti*** *kills* ***duṣkṛtaḥ*** *the wicked*

He strikes down the trees, destroys the evil
he terrifies all with his mighty weapon
Even the innocent flees from Parjanya
when he, thundering, slays the wicked

This verse has been explained by Yāska (seventh BCE) in his monumental work *Nirukta*, a work dedicated to etymology of the Veda. According to him, the lightning that accompanies the rain (usual in India) kills the wicked as also the innocent. The sound of thunder terrifies all.

However, the two words *rakṣasa* and *duṣkṛtaḥ* have actually been used for the evil forces that hold back the waters as cloud. Many translators take these words literally, which of course makes no sense.

The idea is that when clouds have formed but are not raining because of the devilish forces that keep the water stuck, then *vṛṣṇya-vataḥ*, which literally means 'one whose function is to pour rain' strikes with thunderous power and the water is released. *Parjanya* is thus the great slayer.

रथीव कशयाश्वाँ अभिक्षिपन्नाविर्दूतान्कृणुते वर्ष्याँ अह ।
दूरात्सिंहस्य स्तनथा उदीरते यत्पर्जन्यः कृणुते वर्ष्यं नभः ॥ 3

rathīva kaśayāśvān abhikṣipann-āvir-dūtān-kṛṇute varṣyān aha
dūrāt-siṃhasya stanathā ud-īrate yat-parjanyaḥ kṛṇute varṣyaṃ nabhaḥ

rathīva kaśayā aśvān abhi-kṣipan āviḥ *as a charioteer whipping on his horses*

dūtān kṛṇute varṣyān aha *brings into view the messenger/soldiers*

dūrāt *afar* ***siṃhasya stanathāḥ*** *roar of a lion* ***ut īrate*** *goes* ***yat*** *when* ***parjanyaḥ*** *Parjanya* ***kṛṇute*** *makes manifest* ***varṣyam nabhaḥ*** *the messengers of the rain*

As a charioteer whipping on his horses
brings into view the messenger
With the roaring of the lion from afar
Parjanya makes manifest the clouds of rain

Just as, during a battle, a charioteer whips his horses and thus makes the soldiers appear, *Parjanya* goads the rain clouds to cover the skies, their roaring thunder heralding the onset of showers.

प्र वाता वान्ति पतयन्ति विद्युत उदोषधीर्जिहते पिन्वते स्वः ।
इरा विश्वस्मै भुवनाय जायते यत्पर्जन्यः पृथिवीं रेतसावति ॥ 4

pra vātā vānti patayanti vidyuta ud-oṣadhīr-jihate pinvate svaḥ
irā viśvasmai bhuvanāya jāyate yat-parjanyaḥ pṛthivīṃ retasāvati

pra vātāḥ vānti *the winds blow strong* ***patayanti vidyutaḥ*** *the lightning flash* ***ut oṣadhīḥ jihate*** *the plants spring up* ***pinvate svaḥ*** *the sky dissolves*

irā *earth* ***viśvasmai bhuvanāya jāyate*** *becomes fit for all creatures* ***yat parjanyaḥ pṛthivīm retasā avati*** *when Parjanya protects the soil with showers*

The winds blow strong, lightning flash
the plants spring up, the sky dissolves
Earth becomes fit for all creatures
when Parjanya protects the soil with showers

The word *retaḥ* is quite common in the Veda, which can mean many things depending on the context. Here it means the water particles that fall during the rains.

यस्य व्रते पृथिवी नन्नमीति यस्य व्रते शफवज्जर्भुरीति ।
यस्य व्रत ओषधीर्विश्वरूपाः स नः पर्जन्य महि शर्म यच्छ ॥ 5

yasya vrate pṛthivī nannamīti yasya vrate śaphavaj-jarbhurīti
yasya vrata oṣadhīr-viśvarūpāḥ sa naḥ parjanya mahi śarma yaccha

yasya vrate *through whose functions* ***pṛthivī nannamīti*** *the earth is bowed down*

yasya vrate *through whose functions* ***śaphavat*** *the hoofed* ***jarbhurīti*** *thrive/ move*

yasya vrate oṣadhīḥ viśvarūpāḥ *through whose function plants assume all kinds of forms*

saḥ *may that* ***naḥ*** *us* ***parjanya*** Parjanya ***mahi*** *great* ***śarma yaccha*** *give happiness*

Through whose functions the earth is bowed down
through whose functions hoofed cattle thrive
Through whose function plants assume all kinds of forms
may that great Parjanya give us happiness

It has been beautifully described how the rains provide life in India. The interesting expression in the verse is *yasya vrate*, by whose *vrata*. The word means a sacred vow resulting in a commendable religious act. Here it simply means the act, which can be interpreted as sacred duty performed by Parjanya.

दिवो नो वृष्टिं मरुतो ररीध्वं प्र पिन्वत वृष्णो अश्वस्य धाराः ।
अर्वाङेतेन स्तनयित्नुनेह्यपो निषिञ्चन्नसुरः पिता नः ॥ 6

divo no vṛṣṭiṃ maruto rarīdhvaṃ pra pinvata vṛṣṇo aśvasya dhārāḥ
arvāṅ-etena stanayitnunehy-apo niṣiñcann-asuraḥ pitā naḥ

***divaḥ** from the sky **naḥ** for us **vṛṣṭim** rains **marutaḥ** O maruta!*
rarīdhvam** give **pra pinvata vṛṣṇaḥ** flow of the rains **aśvasya
*widely spread **dhārāḥ** stream*

***arvāṅ** before us **etena** with **stanayitnunā** thundering clouds **ā ihi** here **apaḥ ni-siñcan** raining columns of water **asuraḥ** sender of rain **pitā** father **nāḥ** our*

Send down for us, Maruta, the rain from the sky
the stream of rains from sky full of clouds
Come before us, Parjanya, pouring water by this thundering (cloud)
thou who are the sender of rain, our protector

The content of this verse is simple, but the words used in it are quite uncommon which made many translators come up with strange interpretations.

Vṛṣṇo, the rains, *aśvasya dhārāḥ*, widely spread. The word *aśva* usually means a horse, but here it implies 'widely spread', and *vṛṣṇo* means rains. *Stanayitnunā* means rains accompanied by thunder.

Asura is a common term for demons. But according to grammar, it may also mean water or cloud, and gods are those who make water flow, *udakānām nirasitāpi san*. So, at times, the word *asura* has been used in the Veda to mean gods and also sages.

अभि क्रन्द स्तनय गर्भमा धा उदन्वता परि दीया रथेन ।
दृतिं सु कर्ष विषितं न्यञ्चं समा भवन्तूद्वतो निपादाः ॥ 7

abhi kranda stanaya garbham-ā dhā udanvatā pari dīyā rathena
dṛtiṃ su karṣa viṣitaṃ nyañcaṃ samā bhavantūdvato nipādāḥ

abhi kranda *make sound facing the earth* ***stanaya*** *roar aloud* ***garbham ā dhāḥ*** *impregnate (the plants with life)* ***udanvatā*** *full of water* ***pari dīya*** *move all around* ***rathena*** *with the chariot*

dṛtim *water bag* ***su karṣa*** *pull well* ***viṣitam*** *open* ***nyañcam*** *facing downward* ***samāḥ bhavantu*** *to become equal* ***utvataḥ*** *high places* ***nipādāḥ*** *low lying*

Roar aloud over the earth, nourish the plants
traverse (the sky) with your water-laden chariot
Draw open the tight-fastened, downward-turned water-skin
and may the high and low places be made level (water level)

Parjanya is being entreated to make a thunderous sound facing the earth and pour water as falls from *dṛtim*, the water-skin. It is an ancient word which meant a large leather water-skin whose mouth opened downward.

The prayer is for so much of rain that the high and low places look alike because of the water level.

महान्तं कोशमुदचा नि षिञ्च स्यन्दन्तां कुल्या विषिताः पुरस्तात् ।
घृतेन द्यावापृथिवी व्युन्धि सुप्रपाणं भवत्वघ्न्याभ्यः ॥ 8

mahāntaṃ kośam-ud-acā ni ṣiñca syandantāṃ kulyā viṣitāḥ purastāt
ghṛtena dyāvāpṛthivī vy-undhi suprapāṇaṃ bhavatv-aghnyābhyaḥ

mahāntam *voluminous* ***kośam*** *container* ***ut aca*** *raise* ***ni siñca*** *pour down* ***syandantām*** *flow* ***kulyāḥ*** *rivers* ***visitāḥ*** *let loose* ***purastāt*** *forward*

ghṛtena *with water* ***dyāvāpṛthivī*** *earth and heaven* ***vi undhi*** *make it wet sufficiently* ***suprapānam bhavatu*** *be easy to drink* ***aghnyābhyaḥ*** *for the cows*

Raise and pour down the voluminous sheath (of water)
let the rivers flow forward unimpeded
Saturate with water both heaven and earth
and let there be abundant water for the cows

The sage prays to *Parjanya* to rain as if pouring water from the sky, so that the rivers may flow forward unimpeded. The word *purastāt* may also mean 'eastward flowing rivers', instead of 'forward going'.

The interesting word here is *aghna*, which is used for cow, which usually means 'unkillable', implying how the killing of cow was prohibited in the Vedic period.

यत्पर्जन्य कनिक्रदत्स्तनयन्हंसि दुष्कृतः ।
प्रतीदं विश्वं मोदते यत्किं च पृथिव्यामधि ॥ 9

yat-parjanya kanikradat-stanayan haṃsi duṣkṛtaḥ
pratīdaṃ viśvaṃ-modate yat-kiṃ-ca pṛthivyāmadhi

yat *when* ***parjanya*** *ye Parjanya* ***kanikradat*** *roar* ***stanayan*** *thunder* ***haṃsi*** *destroy* ***duṣkṛtaḥ*** *the wicked (clouds)*

prati idam viśvam modate *this universe rejoices* ***yat kim ca pṛthivyām adhi*** *and all that is upon the earth*

When you, with thunder and roar, ye Parjanya, destroy the wicked (clouds)
This universe rejoices and all that is upon the earth

Rains being the life blood, everyone feels relieved, nay becomes full of delight, when rains come thundering down from the sky to the earth.

अवर्षीर्वर्षमुदु षू गृभायाकर्धन्वान्यत्येतवा उ ।
अजीजन ओषधीर्भोजनाय कमुत प्रजाभ्योऽविदो मनीषाम् ॥ 10

avarṣīr-varṣam-ud-u ṣū gṛbhāyākar-dhanvāny-atyetavā u
ajījana oṣadhīr-bhojanāya kam-uta prajābhyo-vido manīṣām

avarṣīḥ *you have rained* ***varṣam ut u*** *the rains* ***ṣū gṛbhāya*** *(now) withhold well* ***akaḥ*** *water* ***dhanvāni*** *desert* ***ati-etavai u*** *fit for travel*

ajījanaḥ *(you have) given life* ***oṣadhīḥ*** *to plants* ***bhojanāya*** *as food of* ***kam uta prajābhyaḥ*** *from people* ***avidaḥ*** *to receive* ***manīṣām*** *hymns of praise*

You have rained; now withhold it
you have made the deserts fit for travel
you have given life to plants for food (to men)
verily you have obtained adulations from the people

This verse is meant for stopping the rains when there has been too much of it, causing floods everywhere.

Parjanya is being praised and thanked for making it possible to cross the desert, as also for giving a new life to the plants for the sustenance of men.

No wonder, *Parjanya* is praised with hymns by all!

VII

LIFE, WORLD, SOCIETY

In the sacred Gita, we come across the verse (VII.16), 'Four types of people worship me: the distressed, the seeker of Self-knowledge, the seeker of wealth, and the enlightened one who has experienced the Supreme Being,' implying that people approach God with various intentions.

The Veda have prayers that fulfil the need of all these four types. In this part, some hymns and mantras have been selected to show the nature and outlook of the ancient Hindu way of life, adopting which, individuals may grow to fulfil their aspirations. Many of the prayers here are from Atharvaveda, which specializes in these kinds of prayers, which at times, border on sounding like magic charms. Here it should be remembered that desire for worldly prosperity and enjoyment is a perfectly natural aspiration, and not tabooed in Hindu religion.

The first chapter is devoted to self-growth.

1.
SELF-GROWTH
THE IMPORTANCE OF GUIDANCE: VIŚVEDEVĀ

The Veda have individual gods, dual divinities and also groups of gods. To make sure that none of them was left out during prayers, the sacred books used the term Viśvedevā to denote all of them. In this mantra, God, as Viśvedevā, is prayed to as the guide in life and spirituality.

अक्षेत्रवित्क्षेत्रविदं ह्यप्राट् स प्रैति क्षेत्रविदानुशिष्टः ।
एतद्वै भद्रमनुशासनस्योत स्रुतिं विन्दत्यञ्जसीनाम् ॥ RV X.32.7

akṣetravit-kṣetravidaṃ hy-aprāṭ sa praiti kṣetravidānuśiṣṭaḥ
etad-vai bhadram-anuśāsanasyota srutiṃ vindaty-añjasīnām

akṣetravit *one who knows not* ***kṣetravidam*** *the (field) way* ***hi aprāṭ saḥ*** *indeed he asks* ***pra eti*** *proceeds* ***kṣetravidā anuśiṣṭaḥ*** *instructed by knower of the way*

etat vai bhadram anuśāsanasya uta *such verily is the noble utility of instruction* ***srutim*** *path/ stream* ***vindati*** *one knows* ***añjasīnām*** *the right (path)*

The stranger asks the way of him who knows it
and directed by the knower he proceeds
This, verily, is the blessing of instruction
he finds the path that leads directly forward

To grow in life, it is important to receive right instructions at the right time. In the matters of personality growth and also for spiritual growth, one needs the guidance from the right teacher, who instructs the learner what he had learnt from the scriptures.

The example taken here is of a thirsty person who is looking for a stream to drink water, who asks for direction. Guided correctly, he heads straight towards it.

Path to spiritual growth

व्रतेन दीक्षामाप्नोति दीक्षयाप्नोति दक्षिणाम् ।
दक्षिणा श्रद्धामाप्नोति श्रद्धया सत्यमाप्यते ॥ YV XIX.30

vratena dīkṣām-āpnoti dīkṣayāpnoti dakṣiṇām
dakṣiṇā śraddhāmāpnoti śraddhayā satyamāpyate

vratena dīkṣām āpnoti *through vrata one gets dīkṣā* ***dīkṣayā āpnoti dakṣiṇām*** *through dīkṣā one gets dakṣiṇā*

dakṣiṇā śraddhām āpnoti *grace brings śraddhā* ***śraddhayā satyam āpyate*** *śraddhā leads to truth*

Through vrata (vows) one gets dīkṣā (fitness)
through dīkṣā one gets dakṣiṇā (grace)
Dakṣiṇā brings śraddhā
śraddhā leads to truth

The way to Truth is described in steps. The first is *vrata* – self-control. One has to be established in some values before one can aspire to grow in spiritual life. *Vrata* usually signifies some particular vow to be kept by the aspirant. This kind of self-control creates psychic energy that makes one fit for higher thoughts.

The next is *dīkṣā* – fitness. It is like the ready field where one can plant anything. Then comes *dakṣiṇā* – grace. Once the first steps are covered, one gets the grace of God, Guru or scriptures. Only when one gets the grace of these three, one gets *śraddhā* – the mental capability to attain Truth.

Prayer for success

It was mentioned in the first chapter how the Atharvaveda deals with many mundane topics that make this Veda sound like a book of voodoo. But that is not the case. The remedies for thousands of problems, including how to woo a woman and other such, are there for people who have failed in all their efforts to succeed.

This mantra on success is from the hymn that prays to various gods for the success of the householder.

इन्द्रेमं प्रतरं कृधि सजातानामसद्वशी । रायस्पोषेण सं सृज जीवातवे जरसे नय ॥ AV VI.5.2

indremaṃ prataraṃ kṛdhi sajātānām-asadvaśī; rāyaspoṣeṇa saṃ sṛja jīvātave jarase naya

indra *Indra* ***imam prataram kṛdhi*** *put this man far forward*
sajātānām *among his fellows* ***asat vaśī*** *may he be controller*
rāyaḥ poṣeṇa sam sṛja *unite him with abundance of wealth*
jīvātave jarase naya *conduct his life to old age*

Put this man far forward, O Indra, may he be controller of his fellows
unite him with abundance of wealth, conduct him to old age

All that a person may want in life, and all that are parameters of success, are covered here.

Uprooting one's jealousy

Jealousy, ah! That viper roosting in the heart of a person and pouring its venom in the vital organs at the very moments of one's success, joy and misery! One who has been scorched by its flames knows what it means to be jealous. So, the sages gave us a beautiful prayer to banish jealousy:

ईर्ष्याया ध्राजिं प्रथमां प्रथमस्या उतापराम् ।
अग्निं हृदय्यं शोकं तं ते निर्वापयामसि ॥ AV VI.18.1

īrṣyāyā dhrājiṃ prathamāṃ prathamasyā utāparām
agniṃ hṛdayyaṃ śokaṃ taṃ te nirvāpayāmasi

īrṣyāyāḥ dhrājim prathamām *the first blast of jealousy* ***prathamasyāḥ utāparām*** *and the one after the first*

agnim hṛdayyam śokam tam te *the fire that burns within your heart* ***niḥ vāpayāmasi*** *this we quench and drive away*

The first blast of jealousy
and the one after the first
the fire that burns within your heart
this we quench and drive away

As can be seen, it sounds like black magic, nevertheless, this is a highly potent mantra. Its next verse prays:

यथा भूमिर्मृतमना मृतान् मृतमनस्तरा । यथोत मम्रुषो मन एवेर्ष्योर्मृतं मनः ॥ 2

yathā bhūmir-mṛtamanā mṛtān mṛtamanas-tarā; yathota mamruṣo mana everṣyor-mṛtaṃ manaḥ

Even as the earth is dead-minded, more dead-minded than the dead and as the mind of one who is dead, so be dead the jealous mind of this jealous man

Individuals burning in the fire of jealousy and resentment are well advised to memorize and chant these mantras, as willing surrender of wickedness to the Lord is the first step to transformation and regeneration.

Be a master of the world

सत्यं बृहदृतमुग्रं दीक्षा तपो ब्रह्म यज्ञः पृथिवीं धारयन्ति ।
सा नो भूतस्य भव्यस्य पत्न्युरुं लोकं पृथिवी नः कृणोतु ॥ AV XII.1.1

satyaṃ bṛhad-ṛtam-ugraṃ dīkṣā tapo brahma yajñaḥ pṛthivīṃ dhārayanti
sā no bhūtasya bhavyasya patny-uruṃ lokaṃ pṛthivī naḥ kṛṇotu

satyam bṛhat *the great Truth* ***ṛtam ugram*** *formidable Law* ***dīkṣā*** *consecration* ***tapaḥ*** *austerity* ***brahma yajñaḥ*** *prayer and sacrifice* ***pṛthivīm dhārayanti*** *uphold the earth*

sā naḥ bhūtasya bhavyasya patnī *may that earth, the mistress of our past and future*

urum lokam pṛthivī naḥ kṛṇotu *make a wide world for us*

Great Truth, formidable Law, consecration, austerity,
prayer and sacrifice – these uphold the earth

May that earth, the mistress of our past and future
make a wide world for us

Brahma here means Vedic learning or self-control, since these lead to the knowledge of Brahman.

The essential traits like *satya, ṛtam, dīkṣā, tapaḥ, yajñaḥ* and *brahma*, which are universal in nature, have been pointed out to be the qualities that uphold the earth, implying that these are the values to be practised by all. Success in the world comes only to those who practise these. All of these denote immense reverence for both Creator and Creation, and stand at the very foundation of the Veda.

The importance of *śraddhā* for getting success

Hindu scriptures stress a lot on cultivating *śraddhā,* and declare that the personality, orientation, and attitude of a person is governed by the *śraddhā* that he has cultivated. The word *śraddhā* cannot be translated perfectly in English, although it is a normal practice to use the word 'faith' for it.

Śraddhā is the disposition of a person born of an affirmative faith, conviction and reverential attitude towards Spiritual Reality. It is born of the words learnt and values imbibed from the scriptures, teachers and parents. When *śraddhā* is practised for a long time, it gives rise to humility, sincerity, attentiveness, perseverance and concentration, which lead one to success. To highlight this, Ṛgveda has one whole hymn dedicated to *śraddhā*, according to which, every noble thought is performed because of it.

श्रद्धयाग्निः समिध्यते श्रद्धया हूयते हविः ।
श्रद्धां भगस्य मूर्धनि वचसा वेदयामसि ॥ RV X.151.1

śraddhayāgniḥ samidhyate śraddhayā hūyate haviḥ
śraddhāṃ bhagasya mūrdhani vacasā vedayāmasi

śraddhayā *by śraddhā* ***agniḥ sam idhyate*** *Agni is kindled* ***śraddhayā hūyate haviḥ*** *by sraddhā is oblation offered*
śraddhām bhagasya mūrdhani *who sits upon the head of wealth* ***vacasā vedayāmasi*** *we glorify śraddhā with prayer*

Agni is kindled by śraddhā, by śraddhā is oblation offered
we glorify śraddhā with prayer, who sits upon the head of wealth

The deity of this hymn is *Śraddhā,* and the sage is *Śraddhā Kāmāyanī.* Another beautiful hymn by a female sage! The *ṛṣikā* here reminds all that every noble act is performed due to *śraddhā,* and the results ensuing out of these acts come from *Śraddhā,* the goddess.

The idea is further continued in a later verse:

श्रद्धां देवा यजमाना वायुगोपा उपासते । श्रद्धां हृदय्यया आकूत्या श्रद्धया विन्दते वसु ॥
RV X.151.4

śraddhāṃ devā yajamānā vāyugopā upāsate
śraddhāṃ hṛdayyayā ākūtyā śraddhayā vindate vasu

The gods, worshippers and those protected by Vāyu, solicit Śraddhā (the goddess); they cherish śraddhā with heartfelt desire, through śraddhā one acquires wealth.

Fitness through brahmacharya

ब्रह्मचर्येण तपसा राजा राष्ट्रं वि रक्षति । आचार्यो ब्रह्मचर्येण ब्रह्मचारिणमिच्छते ॥
ब्रह्मचर्येण कन्या युवानं विन्दते पतिम् । अनड्वान् ब्रह्मचर्येणाश्वो घासं जिगीर्षति ॥
AV XI 5.17–18

brahmacaryeṇa tapasā rājā rāṣṭraṃ vi rakṣati; ācāryo brahmacaryeṇa brahmacāriṇam-icchate
brahmacaryeṇa kanyā yuvānaṃ vindate patim; anaḍvān brahmacaryeṇāśvo ghāsaṃ jigīrṣati

brahmacaryeṇa *through brahmacarya* ***tapasā*** *self-control* ***rājā rāṣṭram vi rakṣati*** *the king protects his kingdom* ***ācāryaḥ*** *the teacher* ***brahmacaryeṇa*** *through brahmacarya* ***brahmacāriṇam icchate*** *desires his pupil*

brahmacaryeṇa kanyā yuvānam vindate patim *through brahmacarya the maiden gets a youthful husband* ***anaḍvān*** *an ox* ***brahmacaryeṇa*** *through brahmacarya* ***aśvaḥ*** *horse* ***ghāsam jigīrṣati*** *strives to gain food*

Through brahmacarya and self-control the king protects his kingdom
Through brahmacarya the teacher desires his pupil
Through brahmacarya the maiden gets a youthful husband
Through brahmacarya a bull, a horse strives to gain grass

The hymn of *Atharvaveda* from which these two mantras have been taken, is dedicated to *brahmacarya*, in which a detailed discussion has been done on how a person takes to the life of celibacy at the Guru's ashram, and then grows to spiritual greatness. The term *brahmacarya* involves many qualities, all related to self-control, which leads to success in Vedic studies, as also in celibacy. Here *brahmacarya* does not mean only celibacy.

Continuing the discussion, the hymn explains that self-control, *brahmacarya,* is not only essential in spirituality but in every walk of life for success. Even the success of a bull and a horse depends on his self-control. This example is intended to show the importance of self-control even among animals.

Brahmacāriṇam icchate – (the teacher) desires students. To get talented students who will sacrifice all to devote themselves to a subject, is difficult. So, the teacher who gets good students is being praised as one who has self-control.

Speech and silence

This mantra explains the formation of words from the depths of silence.

चत्वारि वाक्परिमिता पदानि तानि विदुर्ब्राह्मणा ये मनीषिणः ।
गुहा त्रीणि निहिता नेङ्गयन्ति तुरीयं वाचो मनुष्या वदन्ति ॥ RV I.164.45

catvāri vākparimitā padāni tāni vidur-brāhmaṇā ye manīṣiṇaḥ
guhā trīṇi nihitā neṅgayanti turīyaṃ vāco manuṣyā vadanti

catvāri vāk *speech of four types* ***parimitā padāni*** *are there (measured, known)* ***tāni viduḥ*** *know them* ***brāhmaṇāḥ ye manīṣiṇaḥ*** *the sages who are wise*

guhā trīṇi nihitā *three of them, hidden in the cave* ***na iṅgayanti*** *are unutterable* ***turīyam vācaḥ manuṣyāḥ vadanti*** *men speak the fourth*

Of Speech there are four types
the sages who are wise know them
Three of them, hidden in the heart (are mystical), are unutterable
men speak the fourth

This mantra is so special that only a meditative sage can understand it. According to the Indian tradition, speech comes in four types, known as – *parā, paśyantī, madhyamā, vaikharī*. The spoken words are known as *vaikharī*. In this state, the words become indicators of objects and ideas to all.

When a person utters words silently, it is known as *madhyamā*. Those who read very fast know how words are formed neatly in the mind without finding any audible expression.

The third stage is *paśyantī*, when the vocal cords too get silent. In this state the words become generalized, that is, ideas alone remain, without taking the form of a particular word. This state is achieved easily by those who practise spirituality intensely. Once this stage is reached during silent *mantra jāpam*, the speed of *jāpam* becomes very high, and meditation becomes very deep, focused on the idea that is represented by the mantra. Those who reach this state can read very fast. Swami Vivekananda could read a page by merely glancing at it.

The fourth state is *parā*, which is characterized by one single undulated sound, often known as *Nāda* or divine sound. Spiritual practitioners from every religion have reported this state. The unified sound heard is like the last prolonged sound of Oṃ, or that of a gong sounding at a distance.

A yogi can attain God only after transcending this last stage of sound. Sri Ramakrishna described this as, 'One attains the Absolute by going beyond the universe and its created beings conjured up by maya. By passing beyond the Nāda one goes into samadhi. By repeating "Oṃ" one goes beyond the Nāda and attains samadhi.'

Thus are the pearls of Eternal Existence, Awareness and Bliss strewn with joyous abandon, to sparkle and scintillate across the Veda.

2.
MEDHĀJANANA SŪKTA
PRAYER FOR A BRIGHT INTELLECT
Atharvaveda: I.1

This hymn, which is the first one of the Atharvaveda, is a prayer for the enhancement of one's intellect. *Medhājanana* means to acquire the power to gain and retain knowledge that one has obtained by studying scriptures like the Veda. The word *janana* means to give birth. The implication is that one can give birth to *medhā* by hard work and the grace of God. One good way to do it is to pray to Brahmā, who is the god of the Veda, since it is he who breathes the Veda, knowledge in entirety, at the time of Creation. *Vācaspati* is the god of speech, which is indicative of Brahmā himself.

Devatā: Vācaspati
Ṛṣi: Atharvā

ये त्रिषप्ताः परियन्ति विश्वा रूपाणि बिभ्रतः ।
वाचस्पतिर्बला तेषां तन्वो अद्य दधातु मे ॥ 1

ye trisaptāḥ pariyanti viśvā rūpāṇi bibhrataḥ
vācaspatir-balā teṣāṃ tanvo adya dadhātu me

ye triṣaptāḥ *the thrice seven* ***pariyanti viśvā*** *that are there in the universe* ***rūpāṇi*** *various forms* ***bibhrataḥ*** *taking up*
vācaḥ-patiḥ *Vācaspati* ***balā*** *strength* ***teṣām*** *their* ***tanvaḥ*** *of their body* ***adya*** *today* ***dadhātu me*** *may assign to me*

The thrice seven that go about, bearing many forms
May Vācaspati give me today their powers

The intellect, as we know, is the highest level of application of language. Thus, this prayer is dedicated to *Vācaspati*, the god of speech. To remind, all such prayers are to God only, but depending on one's orientation and the context, the names of appropriate deities are invoked.

The sage here prays to God, who is the creator and sustainer of all the universes, to grace him with the spiritual knowledge contained in the Veda. This knowledge is distributed in the various beings and gods who are the guardians of the universe.

The word *triṣaptāḥ*, triple seven, has been explained variously by scholars, which in general may mean that the universe is a combination of three and seven, like three *guṇas* (*sattva, rajas, tamas*), three loka (*sthūla, sūkṣma* and *kāraṇa jagat*), three gods (Brahmā, Viṣṇu, Śiva), etc., and seven *lokas* (*bhūḥ, bhuvaḥ, svaḥ, jana, mahaḥ, tapaḥ, satya)*, seven Vedic fires, seven sages, seven Vedic metres, etc. The manifestation of God in the universe is best described by this combination of three and seven. The prayer is to be granted that knowledge through which one can know this entire manifestation.

The Veda, being the sum total of all knowledge in the universe, need to be studied, and more importantly, retained well for that purpose. That is possible only by the grace of God, and hence this prayer.

पुनरेहि वाचस्पते देवेन मनसा सह ।
वसोष्पते नि रमय मय्येवास्तु मयि श्रुतम् ॥ 2

punarehi vācaspate devena manasā saha
vasoṣpate ni-ramaya mayyevāstu mayi śrutam

punaḥ ā ihi vācaḥ-pate *come again, Vācaspati,* ***devena*** *divine* ***manasā saha*** *with mind*
vasoḥ-pate *O Vasoṣpati* ***ni ramaya*** *make it stay* ***mayi eva*** *in me* ***astu mayi*** *in myself be* ***śrutam*** *what is heard/ studied*

Come again, Vācaspati, with divine intelligence
Vasoṣpati, make it stay, in me, in myself be what is heard

Intelligence is defined as *grahaṇa-dhāraṇa sāmarthyam,* the capability to grasp and retain what is learnt. This prayer to Brahmā, the lord of minds, addressed here as Vācaspati, is for getting divine intelligence with the help of which a person can grasp and retain what they hear and learn.

Vedic learning was practiced entirely through the faculty of hearing, hence the word *śrutam*.

The prayer in the second line is to *Vasoṣpati*, the preserver of noble qualities. The implied meaning remains the same.

इहैवाभि वि तनूभे आर्त्नी इव ज्यया ।
वाचस्पतिर्नि यच्छतु मय्येवास्तु मयि श्रुतम् ॥ 3

ihaivābhi vi tanūbhe ārtnī iva jyayā
vācaspatir-ni yacchatu mayyevāstu mayi śrutam

iha eva *here (on me)* ***abhi*** *fully* ***vi tanu*** *to spread* ***ubhe*** *both* ***ārtnī*** *the bow ends* ***iva*** *like* ***jyayā*** *the cord*

vācaḥ-patiḥ *Vācaspati* ***ni yacchatu*** *to give* ***mayi eva astu*** *knowledge be in me* ***mayi śrutam*** *what I have learnt*

Just here stretch your twin grace
like the two bow-ends strained with cord
May Vācaspati make fast
in me be knowledge, in myself be what I learnt

The seeker prays that God may stretch His grace like a cord stretched on the two ends of a bow, and thus what they hear and learn, may that stay with them.

The word *ubhe* has been interpreted variously as 'knowledge and knowledge-based action,' as also 'knowledge and prosperity'.

उपहूतो वाचस्पतिरुपास्मान् वाचस्पतिर्ह्वयताम् ।
सं श्रुतेन गमेमहि मा श्रुतेन वि राधिषि ॥ 4

upahūto vācaspatir-upāsmān vācaspatir-hvayatām
saṃ śrutena gamemahi mā śrutena vi rādhiṣi

upahūtaḥ vācaḥ-patiḥ *Vācaspati has been invoked* ***upa asmān vācaḥ-patiḥ hvayatām*** *may he give us inspiration (as a result of our prayer)*

sam śrutena gamemahi *may we adhere to sacred knowledge* ***mā śrutena vi rādhiṣi*** *never may we go away from it*

Vācaspati has been invoked
may he give us inspiration
May we adhere to sacred knowledge
never may we go away from it

Thus ends this beautiful hymn on how to generate intellect and then preserve it.

3.
ABHAYA SŪKTA
FREEDOM FROM FEAR
Atharvaveda: XIX.15

Devatā: Indra
Ṛṣi: Atharvā

Fear, imagined or real, is considered to be the most powerful emotion, which in extreme cases can incapacitate the mind and the limbs, while in its lighter mode it can sap away the tranquillity and the sense of well-being of a person.

The problem of fear is faced by every created being, including the gods, which includes fear of annihilation, loss of respect, insecurity, vulnerability and other such situations of potential loss in life.

The sages realized the problem, and so gave us this beautiful prayer, which is considered to be extremely potent in getting rid of the negativity born of fear.

यत इन्द्र भयामहे ततो नो अभयं कृधि ।
मघवञ्छग्धि तव त्वं न ऊतिभिर्वि द्विषो वि मृधो जहि ॥ 1

yata indra bhayāmahe tato no abhayaṃ kṛdhi
maghavañ-chagdhi tava tvaṃ na ūtibhir-vi dviṣo vi mṛdho jahi

yataḥ *from what* ***indra*** *Indra* ***bhayāmahe*** *afraid of* ***tataḥ*** *from that* ***naḥ*** *us* ***abhayam*** *fearless* ***kṛdhi*** *you please make*

maghavan *Indra* ***śagdhi*** *capability* ***tava*** *your* ***tvam*** *you* ***naḥ*** *us* ***ūtibhiḥ*** *protect* ***vi dviṣaḥ vi mṛdhaḥ jahi*** *turn away the hater and the enemy*

Free us Indra, from the fear
of all that we are afraid of
May you, Maghvan, with your saving power
turn away the hater and the enemy

The prayer is addressed to Indra, the relatable face of God during the Vedic period. The interesting thing to note in this verse is *vi dviṣaḥ vi mṛdhaḥ jahi* – turn away (or destroy) the hater and the enemy. These two kinds of people are capable of causing fear in the future, and hence this expression.

इन्द्रं वयमनूराधं हवामहेऽनु राध्यास्म द्विपदा चतुष्पदा।
मा नः सेना अररुषीरुप गुर्विषूचीरिन्द्र द्रुहो वि नाशय ॥ 2

indraṃ vayam-an-ūrādhaṃ havāmahenu rādhyāsma dvipadā catuṣpadā
mā naḥ senā araruṣī-rupa gur-viṣūcīr-indra druho vi nāśaya

indram vayam anūrādham havāmahe *we invoke Indra, the worthy of worship* **anu rādhyāsma dvipadā catuḥ-padā** *may we be prosperous with progeny and cattle through this worship* **mā naḥ senāḥ araruṣīḥ upa guḥ viṣūcīḥ** *let no army of evil ever come near us* **indra druhaḥ vi nāśaya** *Indra, make the hostile disperse and disappear*

We invoke Indra, the bounteous giver
may we be prosperous with progeny and cattle
Let no army of evil ever come near us
make the hostile disperse and disappear

The prayer here is for prosperity, as also for staying away from adversity.

The word *rādham* means adorable, which has been used twice in this mantra. The expression *dvipadā* and *catuḥ-padā*, which literally mean bipeds and quadrupeds, is used for humans in the form of children and grandchildren, and cattle. The wish is that the devotee may be free from the fear of not having a full family and enough wealth.

The 'army of evil' is used for detractors and evil forces, who have to be dispersed and then made to disappear so that they do not cause any problem in the future too.

इन्द्रस्त्रातोत वृत्रहा परस्फानो वरेण्यः।
स रक्षिता चरमतः स मध्यतः स पश्चात्स पुरस्तान्नो अस्तु ॥ 3

indra-strātota vṛtrahā parasphāno vareṇyaḥ
sa rakṣitā caramataḥ sa madhyataḥ sa paścāt-sa purastānno astu

indraḥ trātā *Indra is the saviour* ***uta*** *and* ***vṛtrahā*** *slayer of Vṛtra,* ***parasphānaḥ*** *protector from others* ***vareṇyaḥ*** *adorable* ***saḥ rakṣitā caramataḥ*** *may he be our ultimate protector* ***saḥ madhyataḥ*** *(may) he (protect) from the middle* ***saḥ paścāt*** *(may) he (protect) from the back* ***saḥ purastāt*** *(may) he (protect) from the front* ***naḥ astu*** *(may he) protect us*

Adorable Indra, our saviour
the slayer of Vṛtra, protector from others
May he be our ultimate protector
from the middle, behind and the front

The word *Vṛtra* may mean *Vṛtra,* the demon or the clouds. Indra is often praised as the slayer of *Vṛtra.*

उरुं नो लोकमनु नेषि विद्वान्त्स्वर्यज्ज्योतिरभयं स्वस्ति।
उग्रा त इन्द्र स्थविरस्य बाहू उप क्षयेम शरणा बृहन्ता ॥ 4

uruṃ no lokam-anu neṣi vidvāntsvaryajjyotir-abhayaṃ svasti
ugrā ta indra sthavirasya bāhū upa kṣayema śaraṇā bṛhantā

urum *wide* ***naḥ*** *us* ***lokam*** *the lokas* ***anu neṣi*** *make us get* ***vidvān*** *O wise one!* ***svaḥ yat*** *where brightness* ***jyotiḥ*** *light* ***abhayam*** *fearlessness* ***svasti*** *there is*

ugrā te indra *valiant are your* ***sthavirasya*** *great* ***bāhū*** *arms* ***upa kṣayema*** *may we get* ***śaraṇā*** *refuge* ***bṛhantā*** *huge*

Lead us to the free world, Wise One!
where lie the divine lustre, light and fearlessness
Valiant are your huge arms, O Indra!
may we get refuge in those

The prayer here is to get shelter in the powerful arms of Indra, the God, so that one may stay safe in their embrace and attain the highest heaven after death, where exists not fear of any kind.

In the *Kaṭhopaniṣad*, belonging to Atharvaveda, we come across a similar prayer where Nachiketā asks Yama (K. Up I.1.12) the way to reach the immortal heaven where there is no fear.

अभयं नः करत्यन्तरिक्षमभयं द्यावापृथिवी उभे इमे ।
अभयं पश्चादभयं पुरस्तादुत्तरादधरादभयं नो अस्तु ॥ 5

abhayaṃ naḥ karaty-antarikṣam-abhayaṃ dyāvāpṛthivī ubhe ime
abhayaṃ paścād-abhayaṃ purastād-uttarād-adharād-abhayaṃ no astu

abhayam naḥ karati antarikṣam *may Space free us from all fear* ***abhayam dyāvā-pṛthivī ubhe ime*** *these heaven and earth make us secure*

abhayam paścāt *may there no fear for us from the west* ***abhayam purastāt*** *no fear from the east/ front* ***uttarāt adharāt*** *no fear from below* ***abhayam naḥ astu***

May Space free us from all fear
and these heaven and earth make us secure.
May there be no fear for us from back
no fear from front, nor from below

The verse may also mean that protection is sought from all directions like east, west, etc.

अभयं मित्रादभयममित्रादभयं ज्ञातादभयं पुरो यः ।
अभयं नक्तमभयं दिवा नः सर्वा आशा मम मित्रं भवन्तु ॥ 6

abhayaṃ mitrād-abhayam-amitrād-abhayaṃ jñātād-abhayaṃ puro yaḥ
abhayaṃ naktam-abhayaṃ divā naḥ sarvā āśā mama mitraṃ bhavantu

abhayam mitrāt *fearlessness from friend* ***abhayam amitrāt*** *fearlessness from enemies* ***abhayam jñātāt*** *fearlessness from the known* ***abhayam puraḥ yaḥ*** *fearlessness (from) that is away*

abhayam naktam abhayam divā naḥ *fearlessness by night and day for us* ***sarvāḥ āśāḥ mama mitram bhavantu*** *may all directions be our friend*

May there be no fear from friend, no fear from foe
no fear from the known, no fear from the unknown.
May there be no fear for us from night, nor day
may all the directions be our friend

Thus ends this hymn on freedom from fear.

4.
JÑĀNA SŪKTA
PURSUIT OF KNOWLEDGE
Ṛgveda: X.71.1–5

The chief pursuit of the noble people of Bharat was knowledge, *jñāna*, towards which they had dedicated one whole class of their society, now known as the Brahmins. This hymn describes what knowledge is, how it is acquired, and how one becomes superior by having it.

The hymn begins with the sage telling all this to himself. This style of narration has been quite common in India. Saint Kabir is famous for immortalizing this style.

Devatā: Jñānam
Ṛṣi: Bṛhaspati, son of Aṅgirasa

बृहस्पते प्रथमं वाचो अग्रं यत्प्रैरत नामधेयं दधानाः ।
यदेषां श्रेष्ठं यदरिप्रमासीत्प्रेणा तदेषां निहितं गुहाविः ॥ 1

bṛhaspate prathamaṃ vāco agraṃ yat-prairata nāmadheyaṃ dadhānāḥ
yad-eṣāṃ śreṣṭhaṃ yad-aripram-āsīt-preṇā tad-eṣāṃ nihitaṃ guhāviḥ

bṛhaspate *O Brihaspati!* ***prathamam vācaḥ agram*** *the first beginning of speech was* ***yat prairata nāma-dheyam dadhānāḥ*** *when one gave names to objects*

yat eṣām śreṣṭham *the superior knowledge* ***yat aripram*** *that sinless Vedic knowledge* ***āsīt*** *was* ***preṇā*** *love* ***tat eṣām nihitam guhā āviḥ*** *becomes manifest through (their love)*

O Brihaspati! the beginning of speech was
when one gave names to objects.
The superior knowledge hidden within the words
becomes manifest through their love

Sage Bṛhaspati is looking at his companions during a *yajña* (described towards the end of the hymn) and musing at the fact that these learned Brahmins, who are chanting the Veda from their memory, had taken their first step into knowledge when they started addressing their parents as 'Papa' and 'Mama'. How far they have come since then!

The sage then adds that the knowledge of the sinless Veda that they have acquired was all along hidden in their hearts, which got manifested by their love for it through the grace of Goddess Sarasvatī. The word *preṇā* should be *premṇā,* but 'm' is silent to maintain the metre.

In the Hindu tradition, all knowledge comes from within, information is only the outward spark that ignites it. Add to that the grace of God, and thus is a scholar born.

सक्तुमिव तितउना पुनन्तो यत्र धीरा मनसा वाचमक्रत ।
अत्रा सखायः सख्यानि जानते भद्रैषां लक्ष्मीर्निहिताधि वाचि ॥ 2

saktumiva tita-unā punanto yatra dhīrā manasā vācam-akrata
atrā sakhāyaḥ sakhyāni jānate bhadraiṣāṃ lakṣmīr-nihitādhi vāci

saktum *sattu* ***iva*** *like* ***tita-unā*** *winnow fan* ***punantaḥ*** *to cleanse* ***yatra*** *where* ***dhīrāḥ*** *the wise* ***manasā vācam akrata*** *the wise create language (by giving words to thoughts)*

atrā (atra) sakhāyaḥ sakhyāni jānate *friends then recognize friendship* **bhadrā eṣām lakṣmīḥ nihitā adhi vāci** *good fortune is then showered upon their words*

Like men cleansing sattu in a winnow
the wise use language through wisdom.
Friends then realize friendship
good fortune is then showered upon their words

Sattu is prepared by grounding gram seeds in a particular way. Just like flour is cleansed with a winnow, *sattu* chaff is also removed with the help of a winnow. In the same way, the wise cleanse their language from the use of uncultured words. The word *Saṃskṛta* means well-crafted, cultured, which is applicable to the language as also to one's character. The verse here explains how the learned become cultured.

Atra sakhāyaḥ sakhyāni jānate, friends then realize friendship. According to Sāyaṇācārya, the learned, as opposed to the ignorant, become friendly with knowledge (or, *Vāk*) by knowing the meaning of the words that they utter. This brings them success, and the goddess of fortune smiles on such people.

यज्ञेन वाचः पदवीयमायन्तामन्वविन्दन्नृषिषु प्रविष्टाम् ।
तामाभृत्या व्यदधुः पुरुत्रा तां सप्त रेभा अभि सं नवन्ते ॥ 3

yajñena vācaḥ padavīyam-āyantām-anvavindann-ṛṣiṣu praviṣṭām
tām-ābhṛtyā vyadadhuḥ purutrā tāṃ sapta rebhā abhi saṃ navante

yajñena *through yajña* ***vācaḥ*** *vāk* ***padavīyam āyan*** *to achieve* ***tām*** *that* ***anu avindan*** *realized* ***ṛṣiṣu praviṣṭām*** *centred in the ancient sages*

tām ābhṛtya *having acquired that* ***vi adadhuḥ purutrā*** *they spread it far and wide* ***tām sapta*** *those seven* ***rebhāḥ*** *eulogist* ***abhi sam navante*** *meet together(unite in vāk)*

The wise attained vāk through yajña
they found it centred in the ancient sages.
Having acquired it they spread it far and wide
the seven bird-like (metres like Gāyatrī) meet together (in vāk)

The Veda being eternal and discovered by the sages through meditation, this knowledge has to be acquired by the learner afresh by first making oneself fit through certain disciplines like performance of yajña. These learners then spread this knowledge far and wide, implying that mere book learning can be of no use when it comes to the Veda (in fact, this is true of all knowledge).

Once spread, this wisdom is available for anyone to hear through the seven metres in which it is sung. The metaphor used here is of the seven metres compared to birds that sing aloud the Veda, implying it is not the priests that sing the Veda but the seven metres. (In fact, this metaphor applies to the name of this work as well, *Veda Vihangam*, the Winged Veda.)

उत त्वः पश्यन्न ददर्श वाचमुत त्वः शृण्वन्न शृणोत्येनाम् ।
उतो त्वस्मै तन्वं वि सस्रे जायेव पत्य उशती सुवासाः ॥ 4

uta tvaḥ paśyanna dadarśa vācamuta tvaḥ śṛṇvanna śṛṇotyenām
uto tvasmai tanvaṃ vi sasre jāyeva patya uśatī suvāsāḥ

uta tvaḥ paśyan *some even though see (her)* ***na dadarśa*** *fail to see* ***vācam uta tvaḥ śṛṇvan*** *some even though hear vāk* ***na śṛṇoti enām*** *fail to hear (her)*

uto tvasmai tanvam vi sasre *to some others, vāk reveals herself* ***jāyā-iva patye*** *the way a spouse (reveals) to her husband* ***uśatī suvāsāḥ*** *like a well decked desirous spouse*

Some fail to see vāk even after seeing
some fail to hear her even after hearing.
To some others, vāk reveals herself
like a well attired, desirous spouse to her husband

Can one attain knowledge by their effort? The Veda say, no. Only when knowledge reveals itself to the fit seeker that one can acquire it. The example given is that of a well-attired wife revealing herself to her husband when she wants to be with him.

उत त्वं सख्ये स्थिरपीतमाहुर्नैनं हिन्वन्त्यपि वाजिनेषु ।
अधेन्वा चरति माययैष वाचं शुश्रुवाँ अफलामपुष्पाम् ॥ 5

uta tvaṃ sakhye sthirapītam-āhur-nainaṃ hinvanty-api vājineṣu
adhenvā carati māyayaiṣa vācaṃ śuśruvān aphalām-apuṣpām

uta tvam sakhye sthirapītam āhuḥ *they invite those who are friends with vāk* ***na enam hinvanti api vājineṣu*** *their words never get ignored by the learned*

***adhenvā carati māyayā** another wanders with an illusion that is barren **eṣaḥ vācam śuśruvān aphalām apuṣpām** bearing speech that is without fruit, without flowers*

They invite one who is a friend of vāk
his words never get ignored by the learned.
Another wanders with an illusion that is barren
bearing speech that is fruitless, flowerless

A wise person knows the meaning of the words (of the Veda) that they utter, and so they gain respect, while those who chant the Vedas without understanding the meaning, remain barren of result.

The word *sthirapītam* is of importance here. It means 'in whom the meaning becomes clear.' This idea has been repeated in the Veda many times, indicating how the sages laid importance on understanding the meaning of what one studies. This is the way to success.

5.
KĀMA SŪKTA
FULFILMENT OF DESIRE
Atharvaveda XIX.52

Devatā: Kāma
Ṛṣi: Brahmā

Man has innumerable desires with which they are tied to the state of being immobile and in wild motion simultaneously.

Recognizing this fact of life, the Hindu system developed four goals of life, one of which is *kāma*, desire for enjoyment. But how to fulfil desires, which at times seem too far away?

This prayer is meant to fulfil desires. It is based on the premise that when God created the universe, its seed was His desire. So, desire in the individual mind is born at the time of Creation itself. The sage here prays that the desires of the devotee be fulfilled by the same power of desire that originally was with God!

कामस्तदग्रे समवर्तत मनसो रेतः प्रथमं यदासीत्।
स काम कामेन बृहता सयोनी रायस्पोषं यजमानाय धेहि ॥ 1

kāmas-tad-agre sam-avartata manaso retaḥ prathamaṃ yad-āsīt
sa kāma kāmena bṛhatā sayonī rāyas-poṣaṃ yajamānāya dhehi

kāmaḥ tat agre sam avartata *in the beginning, there was Kāma* ***manasaḥ*** *born of the divine mind* ***retaḥ*** *seed* ***prathamam yat āsīt*** *was the first to be*

saḥ kāma kāmena bṛhatā *O Kāma, dwelling with the desire great* ***sayonīḥ rāyaḥ poṣam yajamānāya dhehi*** *bless the yajamāna with abundance of wealth*

In the beginning, there was Kāma, born of the (divine) mind
and that was the first seed (of the world of existence)
O Kāma, dwelling with desire great
bless the yajamāna with abundance of wealth

Kāma, desire for enjoyment, is the first seed of the cosmic mind as also of the individual one. Here the sage prays that since the desire to have wealth by the householder (*yajamāna*, lit. one who is getting the *yajña* performed) was born with the cosmic mind, so may it be fulfilled.

त्वं काम सहसासि प्रतिष्ठितो विभुर्विभावा सख आ सखीयते।
त्वमुग्रः पृतनासु सासहिः सह ओजो यजमानाय धेहि ॥ 2

tvaṃ kāma sahasāsi pratiṣṭhito vibhur-vibhāvā sakha ā sakhīyate
tvam-ugraḥ pṛtanāsu sāsahiḥ saha ojo yajamānāya dhehi

tvam kāma *you, Kāma* ***sahasā asi*** *(you) are the victorious* ***pratiṣṭhitaḥ*** *famous* ***vibhuḥ*** *all pervasive* ***vibhāvā*** *shining/ glorious* ***sakhe ā sakhīyate*** *a friend of one seeking friendship*

tvam *you (are)* ***ugraḥ pṛtanāsu sāsahiḥ sahaḥ*** *mighty, overpowering in battle* ***ojaḥ yajamānāya dhehi*** *give strength and vigour to the yajamāna*

You, Kāma, are the victorious, famous, potent, glorious,
a friend to him who seeks your friendship.
Mighty and overpowering in battle you
give strength and vigour to the sacrificer

Kāma, the god, is mighty, overpowering, unassailable in the battle, friendly to those who seek him, and glorious. So, he is being invoked to fulfil the wish of the devotee.

दूराच्चकमानाय प्रतिपाणायाक्षये।
आस्मा अशृण्वन्नाशाः कामेनाजनयन्त्स्वः ॥ 3

dūrāc-cakamānāya pratipāṇāy-ākṣaye
āsmā aśṛṇvann-āśāḥ kāmenājanayant-svaḥ

dūrāt cakamānāya *to him, who desired from afar* ***pratipāṇāya*** *to fulfil* ***akṣaye*** *inexhaustible*

ā asmai aśṛṇvan āśāḥ *the quarters listen to that* ***kāmena ajanayan svaḥ*** *due to desire created joy*

To him, who desired from afar (since birth)
that bordered on the inexhaustible
The quarters listen to him
and create joy for him

The sage explains that a person becomes desirous to achieve the seemingly unachievable because of the latent impressions that he carries from previous births. Goaded by these impressions, one desires, and *āśā*, the quarters (ten directions), fulfil them.

It is interesting to note here how the quarters are believed to fulfil the desires. This idea continues in later literature too.

कामेन मा काम आगन्हृदयाद्धृदयं परि।
यदमीषामदो मनस्तदैतूप मामिह ॥ 4

kāmena mā kāma āgan-hṛdayādd-hṛdayaṃ pari
yad-amīṣām-ado manas-tadait-ūpa mām-iha

kāmena mā kāmaḥ ā agan *by Kāma is desire fulfilled,* ***hṛdayāt hṛdayam pari*** *out of heart to heart*

yat amīṣām adaḥ manaḥ *the mind that is theirs in the past* ***tat ā etu upa mām iha*** *may that come to me here and bless*

By Kāma is desire fulfilled, out of heart to heart
The mind that is theirs in the past, may that come to me here and bless

This refers to the beginning of Creation when Brahmā, the creator God, created the first beings from his mind to populate the world. The sage prays that he too may get that mind so that his desires may get fulfilled! After all, desires are referred to as coming from the heart, but get fulfilled by the mind. So, one needs a very powerful mind to fulfil those desires that seem difficult to achieve.

यत्काम कामयमाना इदं कृण्मसि ते हविः ।
तन्नः सर्वं समृध्यतामथैतस्य हविषो वीहि स्वाहा ॥ 5

yat-kāma kāmayamānā idaṃ kṛṇmasi te haviḥ
tannaḥ sarvaṃ sam-ṛdhyatām-ath-aitasya haviṣo vīhi svāhā

yat kāma kāmayamānāḥ *O Kāma, desiring whatever* **idam kṛṇmasi te haviḥ** *we offer this havi (oblation)*

tat naḥ sarvam sam ṛdhyatām *and we pray you accept this homage* **atha etasya haviṣaḥ vīhi** *and be pleased to bless* **svāhā** *Svāhā*

O Kāma, desiring whatever we offer this havi
may all that be fulfilled.
We pray you accept this homage
and be pleased to bless. Svāhā

The sage concludes with the prayer that his *havi* (oblations) offered in the sacrificial fire, that is being offered with the concluding term *svāhā,* be accepted by the deity. *Svāhā* is the common way to end a prayer while offering oblations.

6.
LIFE DURING THE VEDIC PERIOD
Select mantras

This short selection draws a brief sketch of life during the Vedic period. The mantras are quite interesting and also beautiful to read.

Move ahead, O widowed woman

This mantra has been taken from a hymn of Ṛgveda that has quite a few gods named as deities. Essentially, the hymn is a prayer to have a life free of the shadow of death that assails society every now and then. One of these mantras (RV X.18.3) reads, 'May those who are living, remain separate from the dead; may our invocation of the gods today be successful; let us go forward to dancing and laughter, assuming a longer and better life.'

Continuing the flow, the request is made in this verse to a lady who has just lost her husband in a battle. She is requested to come back to life from the gloom of death.

उदीर्ष्व नार्यभि जीवलोकं गतासुमेतमुप शेष एहि ।
हस्तग्राभस्य दिधिषोस्तवेदं पत्युर्जनित्वमभि सं बभूथ ॥ RV X.18.8

ud-īrṣva nāry-abhi jīvalokaṃ gatāsum-etam-upa śeṣa ehi
hastagrābhasya didhiṣos-tavedaṃ patyur-janitvam-abhi saṃ babhūtha

ut īrṣva *rise* ***nāri*** *lady* ***abhi jīvalokam*** *come unto the world of life* ***gata-asum etam*** *he is lifeless* ***upa śeṣe ā ihi*** *come, by whose side you lie*

hastagrābhasya didhiṣoḥ *wifehood with intimacy* ***tava idam*** *was yours* ***patyuḥ janitvam abhi sam babhūtha*** *who took your hand and wooed you as a lover*

Rise, come unto the world of life, O lady
come, he is lifeless, by whose side you lie.
Wifehood with this, your husband, was yours
who took your hand and wooed you as a lover

The background is that a warrior has died in the battlefield. His wife is crying piteously holding on to the dead body. The widowed lady is then addressed by someone from the family, probably the warrior's younger brother, to come back to the world of living, and that he would continue with the unfinished battle with the enemies.

The pain and shock of losing one's husband is devastating. There are innumerable cases when a lady went into permanent depression, or even committed suicide due to such a loss. This mantra clearly shows how the Veda valued life more than death, and the custom of *satī* was not approved during the Vedic period.

Blessing a daughter: Indra

The tenth book of the Ṛgveda has a large number of assorted hymns that deal with innumerable topics. Of these, RV X.85

is a large hymn, dealing with more than one subject. The latter half of the hymn is dedicated to marriage.

In these two beautiful mantras, the father of a newlywed bride invokes Indra to bless her to be the centre of the new household and to have ample number of children.

इमां त्वमिन्द्र मीढ्वः सुपुत्रां सुभगां कृणु ।
दशास्यां पुत्राना धेहि पतिमेकादशं कृधि ॥
सम्राज्ञी श्वशुरे भव सम्राज्ञी श्वश्र्वां भव ।
ननान्दरि सम्राज्ञी भव सम्राज्ञी अधि देवृषु ॥ RV X.85.45–46

imāṃ tvam-indra mīḍhvaḥ suputrāṃ subhagāṃ kṛṇu
daśāsyāṃ putrānā dhehi patim-ekādaśaṃ kṛdhi
samrājñī śvaśure bhava samrājñī śvaśrvāṃ bhava
nanāndari samrājñī bhava samrājñī adhi devṛṣu

imām *this bride* ***tvam indra mīḍhvaḥ*** *O bounteous Indra* ***suputrām subhagām kṛṇu*** *make blessed in her sons and good fortune* ***daśa asyām putrān ā dhehi*** *bless her with ten sons* ***patim ekādaśam kṛdhi*** *and make her husband the eleventh*

samrājñī śvaśure bhava *may you be the empress over her father-in-law* ***samrājñī śvaśrvām bhava*** *be the empress over your mother-in-law* ***nanāndari samrājñī bhava*** *and over the sister of your husband* ***samrājñī adhi devṛṣu*** *and brothers of your husband*

O Bounteous Indra, make this bride blessed in her sons and fortune
bless her with ten sons, and make her husband the eleventh
Over your husband's father and mother may you be the queen
and over the sister and brothers of your husband, rule supreme

A father stays worried for his daughter when she is given away in marriage, particularly in India. In this prayer a father prays that his daughter may have good fortune in matters of children and wealth, and also may have a say in the affairs of her new home. This has been going on in India for tens of thousands of years!

Note that the first two lines invoke Indra to bless the girl, while the remaining two are direct blessings from the father to the apple of his eye!

Caste and duties: Soma

This verse, from the ninth book shows how people, desirous of earning wealth, engaged in various works, even though belonging to the same family. This beautiful verse bears witness that, wherever the hereditary 'caste' system came from, it certainly wasn't from the Veda, which describe a wonderful freedom to choose one's calling according to one's nature.

कारुरहं ततो भिषगुपलप्रक्षिणी नना ।
नानाधियो वसूयवोऽनु गाइव तस्थिमेन्द्रायेन्दो परि स्रव ॥ RV IX.112.3

kāruraham tato bhiṣag-upalapraksiṇī nanā
nānādhiyo vasūyavonu gā-iva tasthimendrāyendo pari srava

kāruḥ aham *I am a reciter of hymns* ***tataḥ bhiṣak*** *my father is a healer* ***upalaprakṣiṇī nanā*** *my mother a grinder of corn*

nānādhiyaḥ *having various occupations* ***vasū yavaḥ anu gāḥ iva*** *desiring riches we remain like cattle* ***tasthima indrāya indo pari srava*** *flow, Soma, for Indra*

I am a reciter of hymns, my father is a healer, mother a grinder of corn
having various occupations, desiring wealth.
We remain in the world like cattle in a shed
flow, Soma, for Indra (so that we may get favours of him)

This mantra gives us a glimpse of life during Vedic times when individuals pursued occupations according to their talent (or inclination), and were not forced by birth into any family trade.

Importance of charity in life: Dāna Stuti

The poor Brahmin (or some beggar) goes about in the hope that he will get some money as *dāna*, in charity. But his hopes are dashed, since no one is interested in obliging him. Ṛgveda has a beautiful hymn that portrays the plight of such a person, and also praises charity by extolling the virtue of gift making.

न वा उ देवाः क्षुधमिद्वधं ददुरुताशितमुप गच्छन्ति मृत्यवः ।
उतो रयिः पृणतो नोप दस्यत्युतापृणन्मर्डितारं न विन्दते ॥ RV X.117.1

na vā u devāḥ kṣudham-id-vadhaṃ dadur-utāśitam-upa gacchanti mṛtyavaḥ
uto rayiḥ pṛṇato nopa dasyaty-utāpṛṇan-marḍitāraṃ na vindate

na vai u devāḥ *the gods have not* ***kṣudham*** *hunger* ***it vadham daduḥ*** *ordained as death*

uta āśitam upa *even to the well-fed man* ***gacchanti mṛtyavaḥ*** *goes death*

uto rayiḥ pṛṇataḥ *the riches of the charitable* ***na upa dasyati*** *never diminish* ***uta apṛṇan marḍitāram na vindate*** *while he who will not give finds none to comfort him*

The gods have not ordained hunger as death
even to the well-fed man goes death.
The riches of the charitable never diminish
while he who will not give finds no consoler

The seeker of gifts reminds all that hunger is not the gift of god but death is. So, one must be generous, otherwise they will not find anyone who can console them. The miserly are never happy in life, says the mendicant.

The narration goes on to proclaim:

मोघमन्नं विन्दते अप्रचेताः सत्यं ब्रवीमि वध इत्स तस्य ।
नार्यमणं पुष्यति नो सखायं केवलाघो भवति केवलादी ॥ RV X.117.6

mogham-annaṃ vindate apracetāḥ satyaṃ bravīmi vadha itsa tasya
nāryamaṇaṃ puṣyati no sakhāyaṃ kevalāgho bhavati kevalādī

mogham annam vindate *acquires wealth (grains) in vain* ***apracetāḥ*** *man with unclear wisdom* ***satyam bravīmi*** *I (the sage) speak the truth* ***vadhaḥ it saḥ tasya*** *since it is death for him*

na aryamaṇam puṣyati *he serves neither god* ***no sakhāyam*** *nor friend* ***kevala-aghaḥ bhavati kevalādī*** *he who eats alone is a mere sinner*

I speak the truth: the man with unclear wisdom
acquires wealth in vain, since it is death for him.
He serves neither god, nor friend
he who eats alone is a mere sinner

A person who does not make gifts, is described as *apracetāḥ*, a person with muddled wisdom. Established in self-centredness, he loses friends, peace and even a better after-life.

The idea of charity for one's growth has played a very important role in Hindu religious life, giving birth to innumerable stories and narrations on the importance of gift-making.

Getting rid of poverty: Alakṣmīghna

One hymn in the Veda is dedicated to Alakṣmīghna – the destroyer of Alakṣmī, that is, poverty. Lakṣmī being the goddess of wealth and grandeur, Alakṣmī stands for all that is its opposite.

Poverty has been the bane of most nations in the ancient times, and India, though the most prosperous nation through much of human history, was not immune to poverty either. Thus, the Vedic sages had a goddess for this too, whom they wanted to stay away. In many places in India, it is customary to worship *Alakṣmī* on the Lakṣmī puja day by lighting up lamps and asking her to leave the house.

अरायि काणे विकटे गिरिं गच्छ सदान्वे ।
शिरिम्बिठस्य सत्वभिस्तेभिष्ट्वा चातयामसि ॥ RV X.155.1

arāyi kāṇe vikaṭe giriṃ gaccha sadānve
śirimbiṭhasya satvabhis-tebhiṣ-ṭvā cātayāmasi

arāyi *miserly* ***kāṇe*** *evil looking* ***vikaṭe*** *deformed* ***girim gaccha sadānve*** *go to the barren land that is your home*

śirimbiṭhasya *of śirimbiṭha* ***satvabhiḥ*** *noble acts* ***tebhiḥ*** *by this* ***tvā*** *you* ***cātayāmasi*** *will destroy*

O Miserly, evil looking, deformed, ever-screeching
go to the hill that is your home
I, Śirimbiṭha, will destroy you
by sacred acts

Arāyi is the goddess of famine and poverty. She belongs to barren lands, so she is being sternly asked by the sage Śirimbiṭha to go and live there. She is being threatened that if she does not go then the sage will perform sacred acts, *satvabhiḥ*, which may also mean rain waters, to drive her away.

This mantra is recited to get rid of bad times born of poverty. Later, the sage suggests:

अदो यद्दारु प्लवते सिन्धोः पारे अपूरुषम् ।
तदा रभस्व दुर्हणो तेन गच्छ परस्तरम् ॥ RV X.155.3

ado yaddāru plavate sindhoḥ pāre apūruṣam
tadā rabhasva durhaṇo tena gaccha parastaram

adaḥ yat dāru plavate *the wood that is floating yonder* ***sindhoḥ pāre*** *off seashore* ***apuruṣam*** *(which has) no owner*

tat ā *take that (plank)* ***rabhasva*** *go* ***duḥ-hano*** *(you, who are) difficult to destroy* ***tena gaccha paraḥ-taram*** *take that and go to a distant shore*

The wood that has no owner, floating by the far off shore
Take that and go to a distant shore, O difficult to be destroyed

Alakṣmī is then requested to take that owner-less plank that is floating by the other shore, and then go away to some distant land, or to the abode of God, since she is impossible to be destroyed.

Bad dreams: Duḥsvapnaghnam

One hymn in the Veda is dedicated to getting rid of bad dreams, since these are a great hindrance in life. The name of the deity for it is *Duḥsvapnaghnam* – the destroyer of bad dreams. Those suffering from bad dreams recite this for peace, and those who get bad dreams once in a while, recite this to get rid of the sin that might have caused it.

अपेहि मनसस्पतेऽप क्राम परश्चर । परो निर्ऋत्या आ चक्ष्व बहुधा जीवतो मनः ॥
RV X.164.1

apehi manasas-patepa krāma paraś-cara; paro nirṛtyā ā cakṣva bahudhā jīvato manaḥ

apa ihi manasaḥ-pate *Manasaspate, lord of the mind! go* **apa krāma paraḥ-cara** *move away to a distant land*
paraḥ niḥ-ṛtyai ā cakṣva *go and look at Nirṛti who stays far away* **bahudhā jīvataḥ manaḥ** *a living mind has many desires*

Manasaspate! go away, move away to a distant land
go and look at Nirṛti who stays far away
(tell her that) a living mind has many desires

A living mind has many desires! The sage knows that such a mind must not go waste because of bad dreams, so the lord of the mind, who is also responsible for the bad dream, is requested to go to the distant land of *Nirṛti*, the goddess of sorrow.

It is interesting to see how the Veda had gods and goddesses for bad dreams and sorrow too, since nothing is outside the purview of God. Good is the face of God, and bad too is the face of God. Those who are not yet ready to accept bad as the face of God, like to pray to see only the noble face of God. This prayer belongs to that category.

यदाशसा निःशसाभिशसोपारिम जाग्रतो यत्स्वपन्तः ।
अग्निर्विश्वान्यप दुष्कृतान्यजुष्टान्यारे अस्मद्दधातु ॥ RV X.164.3

yad-āśasā niḥśasābhiśasopārima jāgrato yat-svapantaḥ
agnir-viśvāny-apa duṣkṛtāny-ajuṣṭāny-āre asmad-dadhātu

yat *whatever* ***āśasā*** *in anticipation* ***niḥśasā*** *without expectation* ***abhiśasā*** *being in expectation* ***upa-ārima*** *(sin we may have) committed* ***jāgrataḥ yat svapantaḥ*** *whether during waking or sleeping*

agniḥ *may Agni* ***viśvāni apa*** *remove all such* ***duṣkṛtāni*** *vile* ***ajuṣṭāni*** *shameful* ***āre asmat dadhātu*** *establish them in a far land*

Whatever sin we may have committed in anticipation
with or without expectation, whether waking or sleeping
may Agni remove all such hateful sins from us

The words *āśasā, niḥśasā, abhiśasā* are explained variously, but the chief meaning is the acts – verbal, mental or physical –

that are performed in anticipation, which may or may not be born of expectation. This includes speaking to others, speaking against others, and speaking evil about others, indicating the sum total of acts whose impelling force may be manifested or may yet be in seed form, and which result in bad dreams, be removed.

In the meeting: Sabhā

The people of Vedic times were fond of meetings which they called *Sabhā* and *Samiti*, which were often used interchangeably. These two were referred to as the daughters of Prajāpati, thus giving them a religious sanctity. These assemblies discussed various issues, including spiritual discussions. With time these terms acquired different meanings, with *Sabhā* being a larger body and *Samiti* the smaller.

सभा च मा समितिश्चावतां प्रजापतेर्दुहितरौ संविदाने।
येना संगच्छा उप मा स शिक्षाच्चारु वदानि पितरः संगतेषु ॥ (AV VII.12.1)

sabhā ca mā samitiś-cāvatāṃ prajāpater-duhitarau saṃvidāne
yenā saṃgacchā upa mā sa śikṣāccāru vadāni pitaraḥ saṃgateṣu

sabhā ca mā samitiḥ cā *may the assembly and the council* **avatām** *protect* **prajāpateḥ duhitarau** *the two daughters of Prajāpati* **saṃvidāne** *be in concord*

yena saṃgaccha *may everyone I meet* **upa mā saḥ śikṣāt** *guide me* **cāru vadāni pitaraḥ saṃgateṣu** *dear ancestors, may I speak well in the meetings*

May the assembly and the council
the two daughters of Prajāpati, be in concord and protect me.
May everyone I meet, guide me
dear ancestors! may I speak well in the meetings

The hymn is addressed to *Sabhā*, but the prayer is to the *Pitṛs*, who are ancestors residing in the higher worlds. The sage prays for concord and for beauty in his speech.

Later, the prayer reads:

यद्वो मनः परागतं यद् बद्धमिह वेह वा । तद्व आ वर्तयामसि मयि वो रमतां मनः (AV VII.12.4)

yadvo manaḥ parāgataṃ yad baddhamiha veha vā; tadva ā vartayāmasi mayi vo ramatām manaḥ

Whether your thoughts are turned away, or are bound fast here and there,
I turn those thoughts of yours around, in me may your thoughts delight

The speaker thus wishes that the collective mind of all those present in the assembly get tuned with his own thoughts and that his view may get accepted.

Prayer for the departed soul: Bhāva Vṛtta

Hindus are the only civilization that continues to stay connected with their ancestors who might have lived thousands of years ago. We believe that our noble ancestors attained the realm of the gods or at least that of the *Pitṛs*, forefathers, which is also a higher world.

This prayer in Ṛgveda (X.154) is for the departed soul to go the highest of the heavens which can normally be attained only by the greats, as expressed in these mantras.

सोम एकेभ्यः पवते घृतमेक उपासते । येभ्यो मधु प्रधावति ताँश्चिदेवापि गच्छतात् ॥
RV X.154.1

soma ekebhyaḥ pavate ghṛtameka upāsate
yebhyo madhu pradhāvati tāñś-cidevāpi gacchatāt

somaḥ ekebhyaḥ pavate *Soma flows for some* ***ghṛtam eke upa āsate*** *ghee for others*
yebhyaḥ madhu pradhāvati *honey for yet others* ***tān cit eva api gacchatāt*** *may you attain those lokas*

Soma flows for some (Sāmavedin)
Ghee for others (Yajurvedin)
Honey for yet others (Atharvavedin)
may you, O departed one! attain those lokas

It was held during the Vedic period that those who perform *yajña*, go to the appropriate heavens, which have corresponding kinds of enjoyment. Here, the prayer for the departed one is to attain one of those where the best of Brahmins who practice the different Veda, go.

The hymn then continues: 'May you go to those who engaged in valorous battles, who gave up their love for life in the battle... who became blessed by their meritorious acts, who increased *ṛta* (contributed to divine order), and who performed intense tapasya.'

We thus see how caring people were for the departed soul, whom they wanted to see in the highest heavens.

This short selection gives a fairly good idea of how our ancestors looked at life, led it, and what they wanted from it, and beyond from the hereafter.

7.
AKṢA SŪKTA
THE GAMBLER'S LAMENT
Ṛgveda: X.34 (select verses)

Devatā: Akṣa

Ṛṣi: Kavaṣa Ailūṣa

Board games played variously, with or without a bet, has been in vogue in India since the most ancient times. The number of squares in these boards varies according to the game, as also the die and the pieces.

In Vedic times, there used to be the board known as *iriṇa* in which about one hundred and fifty nuts of a large tree called *vibhītaka* or *baheḍā* were used. The gamblers used to go crazy about these games, and even losing everything at times, as happened with King Nala and King Yudhiṣṭhira who both lost their kingdoms due to their addiction to these games.

The mention of these games comes in the Upaniṣads, Mahābhārata and Gita too, apart from the Veda. One can conclude from this that gambling was quite common during the Vedic period, as also a pastime for many.

In this long hymn of fourteen verses (only a few are given here), gambling has been condemned. It is believed that the prayer can detoxify anyone who has this addiction.

प्रावेपा मा बृहतो मादयन्ति प्रवातेजा इरिणे वर्वृतानाः ।
सोमस्येव मौजवतस्य भक्षो विभीदको जागृविर्मह्यमच्छान् ॥ 1

prāvepā mā bṛhato mādayanti pravātejā iriṇe varvṛtānāḥ
somasyeva maujavatasya bhakṣo vibhīdako jāgṛ-virmahyam-acchān

prāvepāḥ *the rattling (dice)* ***mā*** *me* ***bṛhataḥ*** *hugely* ***mādayanti*** *exhilarate* ***pravātejāḥ*** *born on hilly slopes* ***iriṇe*** *flowing* ***varvṛtānāḥ*** *rollling (on the ground)*

somasya iva mauja-vatasya bhakṣaḥ *as drinking of Soma of Mujavān (delights the gods)*

vibhīdakaḥ jāgṛviḥ mahyam acchān *the exciting dice animates me*

The rattling dice exhilarates me hugely
born on the slopes, when they roll on the ground
The exciting dice animates me
as drinking of Soma of Mujavān (delights the gods)

The *vibhītaka* fruit was often used during gambling. The tree of this fruit was usually found on hilly slopes. When these fruits roll on the ground as pieces of the board, they exhilarate the gambler, with the anticipation of loss or gain, in the same way as the drinking of Soma gave joy to the gods. Mujavān is the place where the herbs for the Soma were found. At present, it is difficult to say where exactly this place was. It was probably somewhere in present day Afghanistan.

न मा मिमेथ न जिहीळ एषा शिवा सखिभ्य उत मह्यमासीत् ।
अक्षस्याहमेकपरस्य हेतोरनुव्रतामप जायामरोधम् ॥ 2

na mā mimetha na jihīḻa eṣā śivā sakhibhya uta mahyam-āsīt
akṣasyāham-ekaparasya hetor-anuvratām-apa jāyām-arodham

na mā mimetha *never has been angry with me* ***na jihīḷe eṣā*** *this (my wife)* ***śivā*** *kind/ auspicious* ***sakhibhyaḥ*** *to my friends* ***uta mahyam āsīt*** *and to me*

akṣasya *because of die* ***aham*** *I* ***ekaparasya hetoḥ*** *for one fault* ***anuvratām apa jāyām*** *affectionate wife* ***arodham*** *abandoned*

This (my wife) has never been angry with me
kind was she to me and to my friends
Yet, for the sake of the only fault of die
have I deserted my affectionate wife

The gambler and his wife led a happy life, but because of his addiction, he deserted his affectionate wife.

द्वेष्टि श्वश्रूरप जाया रुणद्धि न नाथितो विन्दते मर्डितारम् ।
अश्वस्येव जरतो वस्न्यस्य नाहं विन्दामि कितवस्य भोगम् ॥ 3

dveṣṭi śvaśrūr-apa jāyā ruṇaddhi na nāthito vindate marḍitāram
aśvasyeva jarato vasnyasya nāhaṃ vindāmi kitavasya bhogam

dveṣṭi śvaśrūḥ *my mother-in-law reviles me* ***apa jāyā ruṇaddhi*** *my wife stays away (from me)* ***na nāthitaḥ vindate marḍitāram*** *the borrower (me) meets no benefactor (who will lend money)*

aśvasy-iva *like a horse* ***jarataḥ*** *grown old* ***vasnyasya*** *(who was) valuable* ***na aham*** *I do not* ***vindāmi*** *know* ***kitavasya*** *of the gambler* ***bhogam*** *enjoyment*

My mother-in-law reviles me, my wife has left me
the borrower (me) meets no benefactor
I no more get the enjoyment of a gambler
than that of a valuable horse grown old

The poor gambler, having seen his pathctic plight in which he has been abandoned by all, now wants to get out of the addiction of gambling, since his enjoyment of the game is worn out like that of an old horse, which was valuable in the past.

अन्ये जायां परि मृशन्त्यस्य यस्यागृधद्वेदने वाज्यक्षः ।
पिता माता भ्रातर एनमाहुर्न जानीमो नयता बद्धमेतम् ॥ 4

anye jāyāṃ pari mṛśanty-asya yasyāgṛdhad-vedane vājy-akṣaḥ
pitā mātā bhrātara enam-āhur-na jānīmo nayatā baddham-etam

anye jāyām pari mṛśanti *others touch (hair, cloth, etc.) the wife* ***asya*** *of him* ***yasya*** *whose* ***agṛdhat*** *covet* ***vedane*** *wealth* ***vājī*** *potent* ***akṣaḥ*** *die*

pitā mātā bhrātaraḥ enam āhuḥ *his mother, father, brothers say* ***na jānīmaḥ nayata baddham etam*** *we know him not, take him away bound (wherever you will)*

Others touch (hair, cloth, etc.) the wife of him
whose wealth the potent die covet
His mother, father, brothers say,
'we know him not, take him away bound'

The pathetic plight of the gambler is starkly described in the above verse. He, who wishes to earn wealth through gambling, actually fails, nay, refuses to see that his wealth is in reality coveted by the powerful die! He then takes money from anywhere that he can manage, on ruinous terms, and then loses that too. Verily, even his own flesh and blood ultimately disowns him in disgust and desperation, not wishing to be dragged into the living hell he has created for himself. His own spouse however is not so fortunate, and becomes the helpless object of hateful attention, as is briefly but ominously hinted here. The famous, fateful scene with Draupadi in the Mahabharata bears testimony to this, where Yudhishthira and his 'flesh and blood' stood watching mutely while she was dragged by her hair and dishonoured in front of the entire royal court, in the vilest manner.

But the gambler himself continues to be utterly incorrigible, as can be seen the next verse.

यदादीध्ये न दविषाण्येभिः परायद्भ्योऽव हीये सखिभ्यः ।
न्युप्ताश्च बभ्रवो वाचमक्रतँ एमीदेषां निष्कृतं जारिणीव ॥ 5

yadādīdhye na daviṣāṇy-ebhiḥ parāyadbhyova hīye sakhibhyaḥ nyuptāś-ca babhravo vācam-akrataṃ emīd-eṣāṃ niṣkṛtaṃ jāriṇīva

***yat ādīdhye** whenever I reflect **na daviṣāṇi ebhiḥ parāyadbhyaḥ** that I will play no more **ava hīye sakhibhyaḥ** I become the contemplator of my gambler friends*

***ni-uptāḥ ca babhravaḥ vācam akrata** and when the brown dice rattle as they are thrown*

***emi it eṣām niṣkṛtam** I hasten to their accustomed place **jāriṇī iva** as a harlot (to a customer)*

When I reflect to say that I will play no more
I become the contemplator of my gambler friends
And when the brown dice rattle as they are thrown
I hasten to their accustomed place as a harlot to a customer

Poor gambler! He regularly vows to stay away from the game. But that is when he starts thinking more of the die and his gambler friends, and then rushes to where the game is on. Such is the insanity of addiction!

The description of the games, his loss and then the lamentations continue. In one of the mantras, the gambler says how he lost because of one extra piece on the board, which gives some idea about how the game was played.

He then advises others to give up gambling and take up some noble profession like farming, and concludes with:

मित्रं कृणुध्वं खलु मृळता नो मा नो घोरेण चरताभि धृष्णु ।
नि वो नु मन्युर्विशतामरातिरन्यो बभ्रूणां प्रसितौ न्वस्तु ॥ 14

mitraṃ kṛṇudhvaṃ khalu mṛḻatā no mā no ghoreṇa caratābhi dhṛṣṇu
ni vo nu manyurviśatāmarātiranyo babhrūṇāṃ prasitau nvastu

mitram kṛṇudhvam *be friend with us (O dice!)* ***khalu mṛḷata naḥ*** *bestow upon us happiness* ***mā naḥ ghoreṇa carata abhi dhṛṣṇu*** *approach us not in terrible wrath*

ni vaḥ nu manyuḥ viśatām *let your anger light upon* ***arātiḥ*** *our enemies* ***anyaḥ*** *let others (my enemies)* ***babhrūṇām prasitau nu astu*** *fall under the bondage of tawny dice*

Be friend with us (O dice!), bestow upon us happiness
approach us not in terrible wrath.
Let your anger light upon our enemies
let our enemy fall under the bondage of tawny dice

The prayer to the dice is to spare him and take its wrath out to those who are the enemies of this gambler! See, even now he is unwilling to stop, and is praying for 'good luck' instead! So many emotions, so many aspects of life are presented here. This gambler's lament is a living testimony that human nature has remained unchanged since most ancient times.

VIII

THE ESSENCE OF THE VEDA

This last section presents the essence of the Veda in two chapters. The first one is a selection of how to worship God, and the second one presents the complete view of life.

1.
LOVING GOD IN DAILY LIFE
Select mantras

The Veda provides succour at all levels – physical, mental and spiritual, which includes life after death and *mukti.* This chapter is a selection of mantras from various hymns on how the sages prayed to God for His love.

May God come to me: Savitā

The devotees want that they may get the affection of God as also His blessings. In this mantra, the intensity of love is shown through various examples.

गाव इव ग्रामं यूयुधिरिवाश्वान्वाश्रेव वत्सं सुमना दुहाना ।
पतिरिव जायामभि नो न्येतु धर्ता दिवः सविता विश्ववारः ॥ RV X.149.4

gāva iva grāmaṃ yūyudhir-ivāśvān-vāśreva vatsaṃ sumanā duhānā
patiriva jāyāmabhi no nyetu dhartā divaḥ savitā viśvavāraḥ

gāvaḥ iva grāmam yūyudhiḥ iva *as cattle hasten to the village* ***aśvān vāśrā iva*** *as the warrior to his horse* ***vatsam sumanāḥ duhānā*** *as affectionate milk-giving cows to the calf*
patiḥ iva jāyām abhi *as a husband to his wife* ***naḥ ni*** *hasten to us* ***etu dhartā divaḥ savitā***
so may Savitā, the upholder of the sky ***viśvavāraḥ*** *the desired of all*

As warriors to their steeds, cattle to their village
as mother cows hasten to their calves.
As man goes to his wife, so may Savitā come to us
heaven's bearer, adored by all

God is the bearer of the heavens but He is also the Inmost Being. The prayer wishes that one may have the realization of God, who is loving, caring and majestic.

Had I been thou: Agni

यदग्ने स्यामहं त्वं त्वं वा घा स्या अहम् । स्युष्टे सत्या इहाशिषः ॥ RV VIII.44.23

yad-agne syām-ahaṃ tvaṃ tvaṃ vā ghā syā aham; syuṣṭe satyā ihā-śiṣaḥ

yat agne syām aham tvam *if, Agni! I were you* ***tvam vā ghā syāḥ aham*** *and you were I*

syuḥ te satyāḥ iha āśiṣaḥ *your prayers here would have come true*

If Agni! I were you and you were I
Your prayers here would have come true

This prayer is addressed to Agni, in which the poor devotee prays, 'Had I been as rich as you are and if you were as poor as I am, then all your wants would have been met by me.' The prayer has the wistfulness of a child asking his mother for something. In such endearing manner does the sage entreat God Agni – 'Just as I would have given you, now please take care of me!'

I will not sell you: Indra

महे चन त्वामद्रिवः परा शुल्काय देयाम् ।
न सहस्राय नायुताय वज्रिवो न शताय शतामघ ॥ RV VIII.1.5

mahe cana tvām-adrivaḥ parā śulkāya deyām
na sahasrāya nāyutāya vajrivo na śatāya śatām-agha

mahe *huge* ***cana*** *not even* ***tvām*** *you* ***adrivaḥ parā*** *mighty one* ***śulkāya deyām*** *I would not sell you for a large sum*

na sahasrāya *not for a thousand* ***na ayutāya*** *nor for ten thousand* ***vajrivaḥ*** *won't give up* ***na śatāya*** *not for countless hundred* ***śatāmagha*** *O mighty rich one!*

I will not sell you for the highest price
not for a thousand, nor for ten thousand
O Mighty One, nor for an infinite amount
O Lord of countless wealth!

This prayer to Indra highlights the fact that one has to sacrifice everything for God, but God must not be sacrificed for anything. The stories of countless sages and saints are a living testimony of this fact.

Prayer to God in pain: Viśvedevā

It is wrong to think that a man of God does not suffer. In fact, being an honest person, their sufferings may be far worse than that of a common man. In this mantra, the sage prays to God to relieve him of pain and suffering the way a father takes care of his child.

मूषो न शिश्ना व्यदन्ति माध्य स्तोतारं ते शतक्रतो ।
सकृत्सु नो मघवन्निन्द्र मृळयाधा पितेव नो भव ॥ RV X.33.3

mūṣo na śiśnā vyadanti mādhya stotāraṃ te śatakrato
sakṛtsu no maghavann-indra mṛḻayādhā piteva no bhava

mūṣaḥ na śiśnā *as mice eat threads* ***vi adanti mā ādhyaḥ*** *causing severe pain in the heart* ***stotāram te śatakrato*** *to your devotee, O Indra*

sakṛt su naḥ maghavan indra mṛḻaya adha *show thy mercy on us as one, O Gracious Lord!* ***pita iva naḥ bhava*** *be to us as a father*

As mice eat threads, pain consumes me
your devotee, O Shatakratu (Indra)!
Favour us right away, O Gracious Lord!
and be like a father to us

Gita mentions how four kinds of people worship God, one of whom is *ārta,* a man in distress. When one surrenders oneself completely to God to take care of him, it is known as *śaraṇāgati* – complete self-abnegation. This prayer belongs to this category.

This prayer is efficacious in removing suffering from life. No scripture promises removal of hardships, but always offers assured relief from the mental agony that is the cause of our suffering, that indeed blocks us from taking the steps required to relieve ourselves of the hardships to the extent possible.

God, the saviour: Indra

त्रातारमिन्द्रमवितारमिन्द्रं हवेहवे सुहवं शूरमिन्द्रम् ।
ह्वयामि शक्रं पुरुहूतमिन्द्रं स्वस्ति नो मघवा धात्विन्द्रः ॥ RV VI.47.11

trātāram-indram-avitāram-indraṃ have-have suhavaṃ śūram-indram
hvayāmi śakraṃ puruhūtam-indraṃ svasti no maghavā dhātv-indraḥ

trātāram indram *God (Indra) the rescuer* ***avitāram indram*** *God the saviour*

have-have suhavam *happily invoked at each invocation* ***śūram indram*** *mighty Indra*

hvayāmi *I invoke* ***śakram*** *powerful* ***puruhūtam indram*** *Indra, invoked by many*

svasti naḥ *confer on us well-being* ***maghavā*** *the bounteous* ***dhātu indraḥ*** *may Indra grant (us favour)*

God (Indra) the rescuer, God the saviour
mighty God, happily invoked at each invocation
God, powerful, invoked of many, I invoke
may Indra, the bounteous, confer on us well-being

God, the mighty, is seen in this mantra as the saviour of those who are in some kind of trouble.

Prayer for divine vision: Surya

चक्षुर्नो धेहि चक्षुषे चक्षुर्विख्यै तनूभ्यः । सं चेदं वि च पश्येम ॥ RV X.158.4

cakṣur-no dhehi cakṣuṣe cakṣur-vikhyai tanūbhyaḥ; saṃ cedaṃ vi ca paśyema

cakṣuḥ naḥ dhehi cakṣuṣe *give sight to our eyes* ***cakṣuḥ vikhyai tanūbhyaḥ*** *give sight to see our bodies*

sam ca idam vi ca paśyema *may we see the world as complete and in detail*

Give sight to our eyes (to see the world)
sight to see our bodies
May we see the world as complete and also in detail

This prayer is for the power to know the world in detail and in totality, as also to know ourselves, our nature. The Vedic sages were clear that while it is important to care for life after death, it is more important to take care of this world.

The forgiver of sins: Indra

मा न एकस्मिन्नागसि मा द्वयोरुत त्रिषु । वधीर्मा शूर भूरिषु ॥ RV VIII.45.34

mā na ekasminn-āgasi mā dvayor-uta triṣu; vadhīr-mā śūra bhūriṣu

mā *not* ***naḥ*** *us (the weak ones)* ***ekasmin na*** *not for one* ***āgasi*** *sin* ***mā dvayoḥ uta triṣu*** *nor for two, nor three*
vadhīḥ *destroy* ***mā*** *not* ***śūra*** *O Lord!* ***bhūriṣu*** *yet for many sins*

Not for one sin nor for two, nor three
Destroy me not, O Lord! for my many sins

Men commit mistakes, sometimes knowingly and at other times unknowingly. The sage here asks to be forgiven for any number of *āgasi*, sin, the transgression that he may be committing. Sin, as is commonly understood in English, means to act against the command of God. This concept is common to Abrahamic religions but is alien to the Hindus. In Hindu religion, any act that takes one away from God is a sort of detour from the path, and can be corrected anytime. This in turn arises from a comprehension of one's own innate divinity, and the necessary journey through *māyā*-born ignorance to reawaken to one's true self.

Nevertheless, such prayers are a reminder to oneself not to indulge in unholy acts, which will only prolong the *māyā*-world journey. Walking the path of *dharma* minimizes the journey. Anything else results is a detour.

Worship with a joyous heart: Agni

अग्निं मन्द्रं पुरुप्रियं शीरं पावकशोचिषम् । हृद्भिर्मन्द्रेभिरीमहे ॥ RV VIII.43.31

agniṃ mandraṃ purupriyaṃ śīraṃ pāvaka-śociṣam; hṛdbhir-mandrebhir-īmahe

agnim mandram *loving Agni* ***purupriyam*** *dear to many* ***śīram*** *holy* ***pāvakaśociṣam*** *purifying brilliance*
hṛtbhiḥ mandrebhiḥ *with loving heart* ***īmahe*** *we pray*

We pray with joyous heart the loving God
Dear to all, abiding with purifying brilliance

Here Agni is being worshipped with a heart full of joy. The real devotion begins only when the worshipper is full of love for God. Worship performed out of fear or expectation arises from attachment to the world of *māyā*, and is thus an outcome of delusion. While this may be the only way out while in the clutches of *māyā*, sooner the seeker rises to loving worship, the better for them!

We are thine: Indra

वयं घा ते त्वे इद्विन्द्र विप्रा अपि ष्मसि ।
नहि त्वदन्यः पुरुहूत कश्चन मघवन्नस्ति मर्डिता ॥ RV VIII.66.13

vayaṃ ghā te tve idv-indra viprā api ṣmasi
nahi tvad-anyaḥ puruhūta kaścana maghavann-asti marḍitā

vayam gha te *we are your* ***tve it u indra viprāḥ api smasi***
therefore we, your worshippers, depend on you, Indra

nahi tvat anyaḥ *none other than you* ***puruhūta*** *worshipped by many* ***kaḥ cana maghavan asti marḍitā*** *there is any giver of happiness, Indra*

Truly God! We are thine, we worshippers depend on you
except you, O much-invoked, there is none
O Mighty One, to show us grace

A man of spirituality slowly moves away from the world and learns to depend only on God. This is known as *śaraṇāgati*. The real journey in spiritual life begins only after one has surrendered themselves completely to God.

The word *puruhūta*, meaning much invoked, is often used for various gods in the Veda to imply that these gods have been worshipped in the past by many sages, as also in the present by many.

Prayer offered at all times: Indra

मम त्वा सूर उदिते मम मध्यंदिने दिवः ।
मम प्रपित्वे अपिशर्वरे वसवा स्तोमासो अवृत्सत ॥ RV VIII.1.29

mama tvā sūra udite mama madhyaṃdine divaḥ
mama prapitve apiśarvare vasavā stomāso avṛtsata

mama tvā sūre ut-ite *my prayers when the Sun has risen* ***mama madhyandine divaḥ*** *my prayers at the time of noon*

mama prapitve apiśarvare *my prayers at the coming of the darkness of night* ***vaso ā stomāsaḥ avṛtsata*** *O Vasu, have gone forth to thee*

My prayers when the Sun has risen
my prayers praises at the time of noon.
My prayers at the coming of the darkness of night
O Indra, have gone forth to you

Spirituality is a full time offering of oneself to God, with no break and no holiday in it. This prayer shows how the sage prays at all the times of the day to offer himself to God.

God, the lover of songs: Indra

परि त्वा गिर्वणो गिर इमा भवन्तु विश्वतः ।
वृद्धायुमनु वृद्धयो जुष्टा भवन्तु जुष्टयः ॥ RV I.10.12

pari tvā girvaṇo gira imā bhavantu viśvataḥ
vṛddhāyum-anu vṛddhayo juṣṭā bhavantu juṣṭayaḥ

pari *encomapss* ***tvā*** *you* ***girvaṇaḥ*** *O Lover of songs* ***giraḥ*** *prayers* ***imāḥ*** *these* ***bhavantu*** *may these be* ***viśvataḥ*** *in this world/ fully*

vṛddhāyum anu *may they augment your power* ***vṛddhayaḥ*** *who are long-lived* ***juṣṭāḥ bhavantu juṣṭayaḥ*** *and (being agreeable to you), may they bring delight to us*

Lover of song, may these our songs
on every side encompass you
Strengthening you of lengthened life
may they be dear delights to us

The sage expects that his prayers, *giraḥ,* will be accepted and liked by Indra, who is *girvaṇ,* one who loves to hear the prayers, that is, God. This, in turn will bring delight to the sage, *bhavantu juṣṭayaḥ*.

God looks after all: Pūṣan

Pūṣan is the great god who provides for all. Here he is being worshipped as one who looks after all.

यो विश्वाभि विपश्यति भुवना सं च पश्यति ।
स नः पूषाविता भुवत् ॥ RV III.62.9

yo viśvābhi vipaśyati bhuvanā saṃ ca paśyati; sa naḥ pūṣāvitā bhuvat

yaḥ viśvā abhi vipaśyati bhuvanā *He who looks after the entire universe* ***sam ca paśyati*** *(and) who knows them all*
saḥ naḥ pūṣā avitā bhuvat *may he be our protector*

He who looks upon all the worlds
who knows them all
May He, Pūṣan, be our protector

This mantra for protection is especially effective for those who are in some kind of fear or want, since God is the ultimate provider and protector.

2.
THE IDEAL HINDU LIFE
Yajurveda: XL (select verses)

This, last chapter of this work presents the complete Hindu view of life, which has been taken from the fortieth, the last chapter of the Yajurveda, known famously as the *Īśa Upaniṣad*.

Yajurveda mantras are used during a *yajña* while pouring oblations in the fire, but this chapter is not used in any *yajña*. The chief reason for this is that it talks about the reality of Ātman, which by its very nature is beyond the duality of action and result, which is the chief characteristic of a *yajña*.

More than its presentation of Ātman as the ultimate reality, it presents a complete view of the Hindu way of life in a mere eighteen verses, which by itself is a marvel! Thus, this last chapter of the Yajurveda sums up the essence of all the Vedas – it is the end of the Veda in both senses!

We have taken this collection from *Īśa Upaniṣad*, belonging to *Kāṇva* tradition, on which Shankaracharya wrote his commentary. So the order of the mantras is slightly different from what one usually gets in the Yajurveda.

The first two verses of this hymn are so important that if all the scriptures of the world were to get destroyed, and only these two mantras survived, then all the religions of the world, including Hindu religion, can spring back to life again. When it comes to practicing religion in life, these two verses are the ultimate essence for anyone.

The two ways of life

A person desirous of leading a higher way of life has two options before him. The first one is to look at everything as the manifestation of God, and then give up every kind of craving. The second one is to lead the life of enjoyment in the world, but without being attached to it.

ईशा वास्यमिदँ सर्वं यत्किञ्च जगत्यां जगत्।
तेन त्यक्तेन भुञ्जीथा मा गृधः कस्य स्विद्धनम् ॥ 1

īśā vāsyam-idaṃ sarvaṃ yatkiñca jagatyāṃ jagat
tena tyaktena bhuñjīthā mā gṛdhaḥ kasya svid-dhanam

īśā vāsyam idam sarvam *should be enveloped by the Lord* ***yat kim ca jagatyām jagat*** *all this that moves in this universe*

tena tyaktena bhuñjīthāḥ *protect the Self by giving up (all)* ***mā gṛdhaḥ kasya svit dhanam*** *covet not anybody's (or your own) wealth*

All this that moves in this universe
should be enveloped by the Lord.
Protect the Self by giving up
covet not anybody's wealth

The path to God is through giving up. Give up all, covet nothing in this world, see everything as a manifestation of God, and that will make you free from the bondage of the world.

The path shown in this verse is practiced by monks, but can be practiced by anyone.

कुर्वन्नेवेह कर्माणि जिजीविषेच्छतँ समाः ।
एवं त्वयि नान्यथेतोऽस्ति न कर्म लिप्यते नरे ॥ 2

kurvanneveha karmāṇi jijīviṣecchataṃ samāḥ
evaṃ tvayi nānyathetosti na karma lipyate nare

kurvan eva iha karmāṇi *perform karma (and enjoying its fruits) here (in the world)* ***jijīviṣet śatam samāḥ*** *if you wish to live for a hundred years (and enjoy the fruits)*

evam tvayi *for a man such as you (who wants to live thus)* ***na anyathā itaḥ*** *there is no other way than this* ***asti na karma lipyate nare*** *whereby karma may not cling to you*

If you wish to live for a hundred years
do so by performing karma (duties).
For such a person, there is no way than
staying unselfish in all that they do

Not everyone can give up all attachment of this world. For them it is advised that they should perform all their duties unselfishly. That is the way to a long and fulfilled life.

Karma has many meanings in Hindu tradition. Here it means one's duties that include performing religious acts, household chores, service to the society, and others, known as *svadharma.* To grow in spirituality, one must perform one's acts unselfishly, which means, not to focus on the results of the acts. When one applies his mind and emotions to the results of the acts, then they get involved in it, which saps away the quality of work, and also produces new desires in the mind, to fulfill which one gets into the vicious cycle of desire-acts-results-desires. Such a person cannot hope to get out of the cycle of birth and death.

As mentioned, the previous mantra and this one contain the seed of entire religious life, not only of the Hindus, but of others too.

The consequence of not realizing one's Self

असुर्य्या नाम ते लोका अन्धेन तमसावृताः ।
ताँस्ते प्रेत्याभि गच्छन्ति ये के चात्महनो जनाः ॥ 3

asuryyā nāma te lokā andhena tamasāvṛtāḥ
tāṃste pretyābhi gacchanti ye ke cātmahano janāḥ

asuryyāḥ nāma te lokāḥ *those, named as worlds of the asura*
andhena tamasā āvṛtāḥ *are covered by blinding darkness*
tān te pretya abhi gacchanti *there they go after death*
ye ke ca ātmahanaḥ janāḥ *those persons who kill the Self in themselves*

The worlds of asura are covered by blinding darkness
The slayers of the Self within themselves go there after death

The goal of life is self-realization, Self – the infinite, timeless, beyond matter. Till one realizes one's true nature as one with this Self, one has to go through the unbreakable cycle of birth and death. Thus, they become slayers of their own self!

Even the gods do not have the knowledge of Self, and hence they too are *asura*. To remind, *asura* has been used quite a few times for the gods in the Veda. The *loka* of *asura* is characterized by the blinding darkness of lack of self-knowledge.

The *Upaniṣad* asserts that, until a person realizes his identity with Ātman, they will have to face the grind of *saṃasāra* indefinitely.

The benefit of being spiritual

यस्मिन् सर्वाणि भूतान्यात्मैवाभूद्विजानतः ।
तत्र को मोहः कः शोक एकत्वमनुपश्यतः ॥ 7

yasmin sarvāṇi bhūtāny-ātmaivā-bhūd-vijānataḥ
tatra ko mohaḥ kaḥ śoka ekatvam-anupaśyataḥ

yasmin *to whom* ***sarvāṇi bhūtāni*** *all beings* ***ātmā eva*** *atman alone* ***abhūt*** *has become* ***vijānataḥ*** *knows*
tatra kaḥ mohaḥ *What delusion there,* ***kaḥ śokaḥ*** *what sorrow (can be there)* ***ekatvam anupaśyataḥ*** *for him who sees oneness*

To the knower of ātman, all things have verily become the Self
What delusion, what sorrow can be there for him who beholds that oneness

Consciousness alone exists, which appears as various beings and objects. If a person can reach that state where they behold only the oneness of Consciousness, how can then they experience any delusion, feel any sorrow? Or how indeed can they have any expectation, where they already know themselves to be both subject and object of every expectation!

A self-realized person has already gone beyond wants, fears, expectations and sorrow.

The next mantra describes the nature of Ātman, knowing which one becomes free of all bondages, forever.

The nature of Ātman

स पर्यगाच्छुक्रमकायमव्रणमस्नाविरँ शुद्धमपापविद्धम् ।
कविर्मनीषी परिभूः स्वयम्भूर्याथातथ्यतोऽर्थान् व्यदधाच्छाश्वतीभ्यः समाभ्यः ॥ 8

sa paryagācchukram-akāyam-avraṇam-asnāviraṃ śuddham-apāpaviddham
kavir-manīṣī paribhūḥ svayambhūr-yāthātathyatorthān vyadadhācchāśvatībhyaḥ samābhyaḥ

saḥ pari agāt *He is all pervasive* ***śukram*** *bright/pure* ***akāyam*** *bodiless* ***avraṇam*** *without wounds* ***asnāviram*** *without sinews* ***śuddham*** *taintless* ***apāpaviddham*** *untouched by evil*

kaviḥ *seer* ***manīṣī*** *ruler of mind* ***paribhūḥ*** *transcendent* ***svayambhūḥ*** *uncreated* ***yāthātathyataḥ*** *their respective* ***arthān*** *duites* ***vi adadhāt*** *allotted* ***śāśvatībhyaḥ*** *eternal* ***samābhyaḥ*** *the world creators (Prajāpati) known as years*

He is all pervasive, bright, bodiless, without scars and sinews
pure, untouched by evil
Seer of all, ruler of mind, transcendent, uncreated
He has duly allotted to the eternal World Creators
their respective duties

The Upaniṣads talk in detail about the nature of Ātman. This verse is one of those.

Ātman is infinite – this is the only thing that can be said about It. Every other characteristic, described variously in the scriptures, is mere elaboration of this fact. Ātman is Consciousness, and hence It is beyond the ken of mind or matter.

However, not everyone can take the path of renunciation to become a knower of the Ātman as instructed in the first verse. The humanity has to remain content with the second path, which is the path of action. One has to perform their duty without any attachment or aversion. This too awakens spirituality in a person, who then goes to the highest heaven after death. The next verses detail the prayer of such a person on the deathbed.

Prayer at the deathbed

हिरण्मयेन पात्रेण सत्यस्यापिहितं मुखम् । तत्त्वं पूषन्नपावृणु सत्यधर्माय दृष्टये ॥ 15

hiraṇmayena pātreṇa satyasyā-pihitaṃ mukham
tattvaṃ pūṣann-apāvṛṇu satya-dharmāya dṛṣṭaye

hiraṇmayena pātreṇa by a golden disc ***satyasya apihitam mukham*** the face of Truth (Brahman behind the Solar orb) is covered

tat tvam pūṣan apāvṛṇu Open it, O Pūṣan! ***satyadharmāya*** established in the dharma of Truth ***dṛṣṭaye*** *I may* behold it

The face of Truth is covered by a golden disc
Open it, O Pūṣan! So that I, established in the dharma of Truth, may behold it

The householder, who had lived the life of a Karmayogī, performing his duties unselfishly, now wishes to see the face of his *Iṣṭa*, God to whom he had been praying through *yajña* and mantras (like Gāyatrī) all his life. The sincere aspirants, who have been true to their responsibilities, get to see their chosen God at least at the time of their death.

The interesting part of the prayer is the expression *satyadharmāya dṛṣṭaye* – I wish to see the face of God as my right, and not as a favour. The devotee has led the life of righteousness all along, so he asserts his right towards God to see His face which is hidden behind bright sunlight. Such power of conviction in one's righteousness!

वायुरनिलममृतमथेदं भस्मान्तं शरीरम् । ॐ क्रतो स्मर कृतं स्मर क्रतो स्मर कृतं स्मर ॥ 17

vāyur-anilam-amṛtam-athedaṃ bhasmāntaṃ śarīram
Oṃ krato smara kṛtaṃ smara krato smara kṛtaṃ smara

vāyuḥ *my breath* **anilam amṛtam** *the all-pervading, immortal Prāṇa* **atha idam** *now may* **bhasmāntam** *be burnt to ashes* **śarīram** *may this body*

Oṃ *Oṃ* **krato smara kṛtam smara krato smara kṛtam smara** *O mind, remember, remember all the noble things that I have done*

Now may my breath return to the all-pervading, immortal Prāṇa!
May this body be burnt to ashes!
Oṃ. O mind, remember, remember all the noble things
that I have done

This second last prayer by the noble householder is to bring to his mind all the noble religious acts that he has done throughout his life. It is the firm belief of the Hindus, starting from the Vedic times, that the continuation of the next life depends entirely on the last thoughts that one has before his vital energies leave his body for the future.

The last prayer of the dying

अग्ने नय सुपथा राये अस्मान् विश्वानि देव वयुनानि विद्वान् ।
युयोध्यस्मज्जुहुराणमेनो भूयिष्ठां ते नम उक्तिं विधेम ॥ 18

agne naya supathā rāye asmān viśvāni deva vayunāni vidvān
yuyodhy-asmajjuhurāṇa-meno bhūyiṣṭhāṃ te nama-uktiṃ vidhema

agne naya supathā *Agni, lead us by the noble path* ***rāye asmān*** *for the enjoyment of the fruit of our action* ***viśvāni deva vayunāni*** *god, all noble deeds* ***vidvān*** *knowing*

yuyodhi *remove* ***asmat*** *from us* ***juhurāṇam enaḥ*** *our sin of misdeeds* ***bhūyiṣṭhām te namaḥ uktim vidhema*** *we offer, by words, our salutations to you*

Agni, lead us by the noble path
for the enjoyment of the fruit of our action.
You know, O God, all our deeds, destroy our sin of misdeeds
we offer, by words, our salutations to you

This highly touching last prayer of the person who lived all his life religiously, is no more able to get up from the bed, and consequently is not able to perform the rituals that he is to perform to worship Agni, the family god. So, he mentally offers his last prayer that he may be taken up by the noble path to the highest heaven, which he rightly deserves because of all the noble deeds he has done in this life.

He also requests Agni to burn down the sins that he might have committed, unknowingly, while leading his life.

This short selection defines and describes the ideal Hindu Way.

With this ends this work on the Veda – *Veda Vihangam*, which presents the essential Veda in the simplest possible way.

Oṃ Tat Sat. Oṃ

ॐ

SELECT BIBLIOGRAPHY

Arya, Ravi Prakash. *Atharvaveda Saṃhitā*. Parimal Publications.

——. *Ṛgveda Saṃhitā*. Parimal Publications.

——. *Sāmavedā*. Parimal Publications.

Bose, A.C. *The Call of the Vedas*. Bharatiya Vidya Bhavan.

Durant, Will. *The Story of Civilisations: Our Oriental Heritage*.

Gambhirananda, Swami. *Eight Upaniṣads*. Kolkata: Swami Gambhirananda Advaita Ashrama.

Gour, Ramswaroop Sharma. *Atharvaveda Saṃhitā with Sayanacharya's commentary*. Varanasi: Chowkhamba Vidyabhavan.

——. *Sāmaveda Saṃhitā with Sayana's commentary*. Varanasi: Chowkhamba Vidyabhavan.

Griffith, Ralph T.H. *Ṛgveda*.

Macdonell, Arthur Anthony. *A Vedic Reader*.

——. *Vedic Selections*. University of Calcutta.

Nikhilananda, Swami. *The Upanishads*. 4 vols. New York: Ramakrishna-Vivekananda Centre.

——. *The Gospel of Sri Ramakrishna*.

Renou, Louis. *Vedic India*. Kolkata: Susil Gupta (India) Ltd.

Samarpan. *The Hindu Way*. New Delhi: Pan Macmillan India.

——. *Life of Swami Vivekananda by His Eastern and Western Disciples*.

——. *Living Hinduism*. New Delhi: Niyogi Books.

——. *The World of Religions*. New Delhi: Niyogi Books.

Sharma, Dr Bhishmadutta. *Ṛgveda Saṃhitā with Sayanacharya's commentary*. 1–5 vols. Chowkhambah Krishnadas Academy.

Shastri, Dr Ramakrishna. *Śukla Yajurveda Saṃhitā with the commenatry of Mahidhara*. Varanasi: Chowkhamba Vidyabhavan.

Sri Aurobindo. *The Secret of the Veda*.

Swami Vivekananda. *Complete Works of Swami Vivekananda*. Kolkata: Advaita Ashrama.

Whitney, W.D. *Atharvaveda Saṃhitā*. 2 vols. Delhi: Motilal Banarasidass Publishers Private Limited.

Wilson, H.H. *Ṛgveda*.

YOUTUBE LINKS

https://youtu.be/id_IO0D25qg
https://youtu.be/iMbSd5e_sNI
https://youtu.be/PpUZZVEX-Lg
https://youtu.be/iCBHypwiajI
https://youtu.be/HvUAtQmaFb4
https://youtu.be/id_IO0D25qg
https://youtu.be/iMbSd5e_sNI
https://youtu.be/PpUZZVEX-Lg
https://youtu.be/iCBHypwiajI
https://youtu.be/HvUAtQmaFb4
https://youtu.be/nd-FileO_hc

ACKNOWLEDGEMENTS

This huge work, in which the entire corpus of the Veda has been presented as a handbook, would have been impossible without the grace of God. It would be an absolute lie on my part to claim even the slightest credit for the work, so I prostrate before the Lord who is everywhere, who has become everything, and who gave me the resolve and patience to work on this project, lasting fifteen years.

My deepest and most sincere gratefulness to Sri Sri K. Gopalakrishnan, Bangalore and Mrs Moumita Kundu, London, who have been with me on this work from day one of the final leg of the project that was taken up nearly a year ago. The credit for thorough cross-checking, editing and correcting every word and sentence that I wrote, goes to them. It is entirely due to this duo that the manuscript acquired its freedom from errors and left my table to fly across the globe. They also kept making important suggestions at every stage of the work. Honestly, no words of thanks can be enough for what they have done for this work.

Two Sanskrit scholars, Shubhadip Maharaj and Sri Santanu Nayek, have gone through the manuscript thoroughly to check for its correctness. The work owes hugely to them for its correct presentation.

My heartfelt thanks to my great friends whose love and care for me can never be repaid! They are the strength of my staying power in the service of my mother religion, Hinduism. Some of them prefer not to be named. My thanks to them.

My grateful thanks to Sri Ajay Nayak, IAS (retd.), who has been with me during my turbulent times, encouraging me all the way to doing this kind of work. His words of appreciation and admiration have been a great power source for me even during my darkest days. Thank you, sir!

My excellent friends Dr Hema, Sri Dibyajyoti, and Sri Rajshekhar have been pillars of support in my life. In spite of their busy schedule, they have always been with me whenever I needed them. Grateful thanks to them.

Ms Shiwangi has been with me like a doting mother through my good and bad days. Thank you, Shiwangi for being there when no one seemed around. Her husband Sri Devmurty ji, a great friend of mine, too has always been around me to lend a supporting hand. Now their child, Kartikeya, too has started lending his words of admiration for me. Thanks to this beautiful family.

Sri D.N. Gautam, former Director General of Police, Bihar, has been a great well-wisher of mine and has helped me hugely in honing my skills at writing since my Tiya days. My grateful thanks to him for his unconditional support from the day that we first met.

Thanks to Dr Alok Bajpayee, M.D., Kanpur, who has been with me like a brother and who always reads the manuscript before it goes to the publishers.

Mrs Payal Garg has been a great fan of my work and has been untiring in her efforts to make my works popular. Thanks to her, my good friend.

Sri Ajey Ranade, IPS, has been associated with me and my work for a long time. A great admirer of my books, it is to his credit that our work on YouTube could materialize.

Mr Shyam Anand Jha from Muzaffarpur, who is associated with management teaching, has taken a lot of responsibilities that I was supposed to carry. Without his active support, even my monastic life would not have been possible. Thank you, sir.

My every work demands special thanks to Sri Abhayananda ji, formerly Director General of Police, Bihar, and his scholarly wife. They have been great support for me for more than three decades now. Soft spoken, the couple has inspired me by their saintliness and silent encouragement. Thank you.

I would like to thank my good friends Sri Avinash Singh, Mrs Adrija Sen, Ms Abhinanda Dhar, Sri Amit Ray Chowdhury, Sri Biswanath Bose, Dr Gurmeet S. Narang, Sri Arpan Chakraborty, Mrs Piyali Datta, Ms Indrani Ghosh, Mrs Sumana Ghosh (Scotland), Sri G. Sreenivas, Sri Siddharth Baskhor and Sri Buddhadev Das, and Mrs Arpana have been supporting me unflinchingly for years. Thanks to you all.

No great work can be completed without the constant support of the staff at the work place. I take this opportunity to offer my heartfelt thanks to Sri Bikramjit Chowdhury, Sri Bikram Bahadur Thapa, Sri Chandan Das, Sri Ganesh Mallick, Sri Gobinda Chandra Shil, Sri Gour Chand Mondal, Sri Jagadish Thakur, Sri Surya Biswakarma, Sri Dinesh Mallick, Sri Khem Bahadur (Mangal), Sri Ramesh Rana, Sri Samir Roy, Sri Shantimoy Roy, Sri Soumyadeep Roy Chowdhury, Sri Top Bahadur Rana, Sri Vivek Kumar Singh and Sri Partha Tanti. They have been always there whenever I needed them. Thank you, my dear friends!

My good friends, Sri Rajdeep Mukherjee of Pan Macmillan India and Ms Teesta Guha Sarkar, publisher of the book, have been very kind to bear with me patiently during the formative stage of the book, as also during its production. Thank you so much!